# MUHAMMAD

# 11 LEADERSHIP QUALITIES THAT CHANGED THE WORLD

# MUHAMMAD ﷺ
# 11 LEADERSHIP QUALITIES THAT CHANGED THE WORLD

## Nabeel Al-Azami

FOREWORD
by John Adair

REVISED AND EDITED
by Sharif H. Banna

**CLARITAS**
BOOKS

1 2 3 4 5 6 7 8 9 10

CLARITAS BOOKS

Bernard Street, Swansea, United Kingdom
Milpitas, California, United States

**CLARITAS**
BOOKS

First Published in June 2019

Typeset in Helvetica 14/10

MUHAMMAD☺: 11 Leadership Qualities
That Changed The World
by Nabeel Al-Azami
Edited by Sharif H. Banna

A CIP catalogue record for this book is available from the British Library

ISBN: 978-1-905837-59-5

## DEDICATION

*To Ammu, Dada, and Nana, your love and inspiration still carries me through every day.*

*To Amma, for loving me like her own son and*

*To Boro Khalu and Samia, you are always in our hearts.*

## AUTHOR PROFILE

**Nabeel Al-Azami** is an award-winning HR and leadership specialist. He is the Founder and Managing Partner at Murabbi Consulting which specialises in values-based HR, ethical leadership development and people-centred strategy. His career spanned areas such as leadership development, talent management, performance, strategy, values and culture, conflict resolution, and employment law. He has been listed as a leading global leadership trainer by the OIC's Islamic Development Bank (IDB).

He is a trustee of Citizens UK, former Head of Global HR at IR Worldwide, as well as former HR Business Partner and Analyst at Ford Motor Company (UK & Europe Division). He went on to professionally qualify from the Chartered Institute of Personnel and Development (CIPD). Nabeel Al-Azami completed his Bachelor's degree in Management and his Masters in Human Resource Management from the University of Manchester (including Manchester Business School). This is the author's first major leadership publication, drawing on his research and professional experience over the past twenty years. He resides in London with his wife and three children.

# ACKNOWLEDGEMENTS

*I would like to acknowledge the following people without whom this book would not have been possible.*

Thank you to Professor John Adair for honouring me with his wonderful and generous foreword!

To Abbu, Dadu, Nanu, Ma and Abba – for their wisdom and love. To Nasreen – without whose support I simply could not have achieved this book. And my children – Sulaiman, Safiyya and Samir – for inspiring me to be the best father I can be. And to my brother Sameer – you live on, in honour of both our mothers, through my son Samir. To my siblings Nazeel, Usaama, Lubaaba and Nusaiba – for making me a proud Boro Bhaiya. To Boro Khalamma, Choto Khalamma, Boro Mama and Choto Mama and family – you keep Ammu's memory and spirit alive. To my uncles, Boro Chachu, Mejo Chachu, Shejo Chachu, Choto Chachu, and Shudu Chachu and family, including my beloved cousin brothers and sisters – thank you for your support and affection. To my in-laws and Nasreen's brothers and sisters – what an amazing family and what a privilege to be a part of them!

To my mentors – Dr.Bari, Andy, Sh.Hasan, and Sh.Fahim – you have shaped my personal and professional life more than you know. God bless you! To Junaid, my dear friend and *amir*, thank you for our voyage of discovery for a good decade and the amazing memories. Unforgettable. To the whole of my Murabbi team, especially Tanim, who I've adopted as my own younger brother, and who stuck with me through thick and thin in recent years. Thank you! To Nadim and Sh.Hasan of the IIDR team who first gave me and Murabbi a platform in 2008 to deliver my first ever leadership course and have supported me numerous times since, thank you for your incredible support.

And to my publishers for accepting my book, and giving everything to make it a success. Thank you Wali bhai, Marian, Sh.Faruq, Michael and the entire Claritas Books team. And thanks most of all to my friend, mentor and editor - 'Baizan' – who I caused sleepless nights to get my book to a point we could all be proud of. Allah knows how much your gift means to me.

All praise is ultimately due to God who made this dream possible. Everyone and everything else were His divine means.

# CONTENTS

# FOREWORD

BY JOHN ADAIR,

WORLD'S FIRST LEADERSHIP PROFESSOR

First, may I say what a privilege and pleasure it is for me to be writing this Foreword. That statement is grounded not simply in the fact Nabeel happens to be a valued associate and long-standing friend of mine, but because the world needs this book.

In the following pages, Nabeel gives us an unforgettable portrait of the Prophet Muhammad as, in my words, a 'good leader and a leader for good'. The light of that leadership that still shines today, is herein refracted into a spectrum of 11 colours or qualities. From my perspective as the world's first Professor of Leadership, I can assure you that these are the very qualities of leadership that the world cries out for today.

To change the metaphor, Nabeel opens up for us the book of leadership which is to be read in the life of the Prophet. Each of its 11 chapters has within it a personal message for you and me. And in the closing section, which Nabeel calls 'Standing Up', he challenges us to become the kind of leader that we see reflected in these pages. All Muslims, especially those young enough to be still on the threshold of life – the leaders of tomorrow – will find nourishment and inspiration in these pages.

If I may, I should like to end on a personal note. As Nabeel knows, I do have a personal name for him – *Ibn Sweillim*, 'Son of Sweillim'. Just to make this intelligible, I should explain that this name arises from the time that I spent when I was 20 years old as a National Service officer in the *Jaish al-Arabi*, the Arab Army, known outside Jordan as the Arab Legion. The 900 Bedouin from all over Arabia who comprised the Ninth Regiment spoke no English, so on the day of my arrival they gave me one of their own names, *Sweillim*. It stayed with me throughout my service, and indeed has been a symbol of my semi-Bedouin identity ever since.

About three centuries ago, there was a celebrated Bedouin poet called Sweillim Ibn Tweim al-Dawnam. I mention him because he happened to belong to the Bani Huananzi tribe, the very same tribe, you may recall, in whose desert tents Muhammad spent the first four or five years of his life. My own book, *The Leadership of Muhammad* (2010), rested on my belief that in the black tents of the Huananzi, the child Muhammad imbibed with his foster mother's milk not only the pure Arabic language of the desert but also the ways of the Bedouin. Nabeel builds on my work but gives us a much wider picture.

It is no sin for a 'father' to be proud of his 'son's' achievements, as I am of this remarkable and timely book. For me it, falls within the compass of Milton's famous definition:

> *A good book is the precious life-blood of a master spirit, embalmed and treasured up on purpose to a life beyond life.*

## PROLOGUE

BY SHARIF H. BANNA,

AUTHOR OF *THE SIRAH OF THE FINAL PROPHET*

'Anyone can hold the helm when the seas are calm', said Publilius Syrus over 2,000 years ago. Today, there are few calm seas, few periods without crisis and turmoil. A good captain has the capacity to apply his or her refined judgement in uncertain situations and to encourage others to follow, and then to learn from the experience and be ready for the next storm. Leadership matters, and individuals and organisations must find and develop that quality to outlast and overcome those stormy seas.

Very few intelligent people would dispute the global leadership crisis in the world today, but where do we look for direction and inspiration? For Muslims, the obvious answer is their final prophet, Muhammad who has been described not only as a role model (Quran 33:21) but also as someone who embodied ethical integrity and was known as *al-Amin* (a person of integrity/trustworthy). The Quran testifies *'And indeed you embody exemplary character and ethics'* (68:4). Such was the importance of ethical integrity that it was only through this paradigm that Khadija, the Prophet's wife, and a business leader in her own right, reasoned with the claim of Prophet Muhammad. When he encountered the angel Gabriel for the first time, and related this to her, she responded: *'Truly I swear by God who has my soul in His Hands that you will be the nation's Prophet. God will surely not desert you, for you are kind to your family, you help the helpless, you make guests welcome, you support the weak and the oppressed.'*

Leadership is about *power* and *authority.* Syed Naquib al-Attas, one of the foremost contemporary Muslim philosophers highlights the ethical crisis of leadership and the need to restore *adab* at the centre of power and authority. And it is this *adab*, or ethical integrity, which Prophet Muhammad personified through his exemplary leadership and ethical exercise of power and influence. As the British historian Lord Acton (d. 1902) noted, *'power tends to corrupt and absolute power corrupts absolutely'*. However, Prophet Muhammad was able to tame the excess of power through principled and values-driven engagement. His was a vision penetrating the deeper reaches of the souls of his followers, and his character was a reflection of that vision: ethical, just and compassionate.

Harvard University Professor Joseph Nye, in his thought-provoking work *The Powers to Lead* speaks about soft power and hard power. Leadership, according to Nye, is a relation between leaders and followers, and requires a mix of hard power – coercion – and soft power – persuasion and inspiration. Nye argues that the most effective leaders are actually those who combine hard and soft power skills in proportions that vary with different situations. He calls this 'smart power'. Prophet Muhammad mastered smart power to the extent that his followers were not only inspired by him, but they followed him because they *loved* him.

Leadership is about *justice.* John Rawls's *justice as fairness* paradigm, applying not just to individuals but also to organisations, is relevant to the prophetic paradigm despite some reservations. Rawls makes the goal of leadership follower-centric. Using this theory of ethical leadership compels leaders to work collaboratively with followers so that the principles of justice that are developed provide the most comprehensive set of basic liberties to all. Prophet Muhammad's drafting and negotiation of the *Sahifa*/Charter of Medina provides an insight into the centrality of *justice as fairness* principle. Different tribes and religions had to coexist with mutually equal rights and responsibilities, such that the *umma* (community) referred to in this earliest of political documents in Islamic history included the minority Jewish community of Medina.

Leadership is about *transformation of people and societies.* Under the leadership of Muhammad, he transformed his people and community and laid down the foundations of a new civilization. Karen Armstrong in her book *Muhammad: A Prophet for Our Time* notes that: '*Mecca had achieved astonishing success. The city was now an international trading centre and its merchants and financiers had become rich beyond their wildest dreams. Only a few generations earlier, their ancestors had been living a desperate, penurious life in the intractable deserts of northern Arabia. Their triumph was extraordinary, since most Arabs were not city dwellers but nomads.*'

Starting from the early biographers of Muhammad, Ibn Ishaq (d. 768) and Ibn Hisham (d. 833), the recording of the Sirah, the prophetic biography, has been focused on a chronological documentation of his life from birth to death. A refreshing approach is to explore the life of the greatest human being to walk this earth through a thematic lens. Hence, we find the classical works of *Shamail* (description of the appearance and character of the Prophet) or *Maghazi* (battles of the Prophet) as early precedents of that thematic approach to the Sirah.

Prophet Muhammad had a multidimensional and multilayered personality. The great Maliki jurist Shihab al-Din al-Qarafi (d. 1285), in his work *Al-Furuq*, proposes examining the Prophet's life based on his different capacities and roles, and classified his legacy as legislator, judge and leader. The Tunisian scholar Tahir Ibn Ashur (d. 1973) developed these categories, and added to it the Prophet's role in guidance, counselling, mediating, advising and aspiring for high ideals.

In developing that Qarafian methodology of a thematic approach to the multidimensional legacy of Prophet Muhammad, further research and work is needed in articulating Prophet Muhammad's diverse exemplary roles as a parent, husband, teacher, friend, mentor, counsellor, entrepreneur, mediator and leader, and as a human.

There are few contemporary works on the intersection of Prophet Muhammad's life and leadership studies, and noteworthy amongst them are Professors Rafik Beekun and Jamal Badawi's co-authored work on *Leadership: An Islamic Perspective;* Yawar Baig's *Leadership Lessons from the Life of Rasoolullah* and The *Leadership of Muhammad* by John Adair, the world's first leadership professor, who has also contributed a foreword to this book.

Two distinct approaches to the intersection of Leadership and

Sirah can be identified: one which takes leadership research and then integrates the Sirah as case studies without being critical of the theories that the Prophet's life is being subjected to. The second approach focuses on the Sirah and simply draws basic leadership lessons. What is required in fact is a methodology of critical engagement with leadership theories and paradigms and exploring ways in which the Sirah actually enhances and contributes uniquely to understanding leadership itself. It should be a methodology that is underpinned by the *specificity* of our sources and the *universality* of its relevance and application.

*Muhammad ☪: 11 Leadership Qualities That Changed the World* by Nabeel al-Azami is a pioneering contribution to the field of both Leadership and Sirah studies. Drawing from the rich legacy of the leadership of Muhammad, 11 traits are outlined and explained. The unique feature of this book is that it is authored by someone who not only brings cutting edge research in leadership studies and valuable leadership insights from the life of Prophet Muhammad in constructing a paradigm for prophetic leadership, but also draws on his twenty years of senior management and leadership experience working for multinationals in the private sector and global award-wining NGOs. For over a decade, he has also been delivering leadership training programmes for leaders and organisations across diverse sectors and industries through his own leadership consulting firm, Murabbi Consulting (whose clients/partners include Ernest & Young, CIMB Islamic Bank in Malaysia, BT and Transport for London). So, this unique blend of academic research, practitioner experience and entrepreneurial insights, affords the author a distinct perspective which should be considered seriously.

The methodology of searching for good leadership paradigms from different sources, cultures and traditions – secular or religious – is also much needed. Expanding our sources to include *aql*/reason and *naql*/scriptures and *urf*/lived human experiences allows us to identify both the specificities and universals in theories of leadership. Wisdom has no race, religion or geography, and is neither Western nor Eastern. Prophet Muhammad taught his followers that wisdom is actually the lost property of the believer and wherever it is found, it should be claimed and adopted.

One of the critical qualities mentioned in this book, which will be the subject of much discussion and contention, is the author's interesting formulation of Spiritual Intelligence (SQ). He considers it the new intelligence to be featured alongside IQ and EQ as an integral leadership quality. Building on the work of MIT and Harvard educated Danah Zohar (who is also a globally recognized management thought leader, and author of SQ *Spiritual Intelligence: The Ultimate Intelligence*), the author not only integrates the Sirah with SQ but also proposes a reconciliation of the spiritual, spirituality and religious frameworks by addressing the multidimensional sources of meaning, values and purpose.

Working closely with the author, my dear brother and friend Nabeel, on this book, and helping him write and edit his book whilst witnessing him first-hand fighting a potentially life-threatening illness was an experience which I found quite challenging. Nabeel was determined to finish writing the book from his hospital bed and his wheelchair, and worked daily between pain, treatment and therapy in order to share his ideas on leadership with the world. It was both inspiring and daunting at the same time. I wasn't just helping him to work on a book discussing theories of ambition, resilience and courage, but was actually witnessing these values in action. May God ease his pain and cure him and lighten the burden on all his loved ones.

Islam is more than just a way of life; it is a way of *being*. And aspiring for great leadership from an Islamic perspective commences with learning how the Prophet *was* – to believe in him, to love him, to emulate him, and to share his transformational legacy with the rest of humanity. The world needs prophetic leadership, and this book helps you to reflect deeply on that paradigm.

## INTRODUCTION

What kind of leadership do we want to see in the world today? And why are so many leaders falling short of our expectations?

As we suffer the consequences of poor leadership worldwide, questions are increasingly being asked about those in power. Abraham Lincoln famously said:

> *'Nearly all men can stand adversity, but if you want to test a man's character, give him power.'*

There is something about power that affects the human condition unlike anything else. It has an uncanny ability to change people, their behaviour and their actions, which in turn says something about their character. Power placed upon a weak character corrupts absolutely. And there seems to be no shortage of weak characters seeking and acquiring leadership and power.

Power can take many forms and can come about through many means. Power is not just political or organisational, but can also be economic/financial, social and even religious. Each can test our character (if you think religious power doesn't test one's character, you are mistaken!)

A person once described a leader as an honest man, only for his friend to ask, 'honest up to how much?' One is hence left to wonder whether everyone's character has a price tag.

We clearly live in a time when the world is demanding better leadership, whether one looks in the 'East' or the 'West'. Widespread dissatisfaction with corrupt leadership and the breakdown of trust in many leaders and institutions is clearly visible through the media, and in society generally.

In the West, we have seen many cases over the years raising concerns over the integrity and credibility of leaders and role models, such as the multifaceted Trump saga, corruption of the big banks (who collectively have been fined over $300bn since the recession of 2008), the VW emissions scandal, the Berlusconi scandals, Blatter's FIFA and past classics such as the Clinton–Lewinsky affair and Enron. In the UK alone, recent examples of scandals include Tesco fiddling its accounts, the notorious MPs' expenses crisis, bank rate fixing, phone hacking by Murdoch's *News of the World*, horsemeat deception, the Jimmy Savile scandal, and the poor behaviour of business leaders from Philip Green[1] (who hung BHS staff out to dry) and Mike Ashley (known for inhumane treatment of Sports Direct staff).

In the East, corrupt dictatorial leadership is sadly the norm in many countries which find themselves on the bottom rung of Transparency International's 'Corruption Perception Index' (CPI), among other measures. The Arab Spring attempted to shed its corrupt leaders (albeit with very limited success), and where a few long-running dictators were moved on, societies were still left with a vacuum and a chronic shortage of good and able leaders who could offer a real alternative, bring unity or command widespread respect.

The words of Martin Luther King Jr ring true, when he famously lamented how our scientific (and technological) advances have outstripped our human and spiritual advancement, hence 'we have guided missiles and misguided men'.

However, this anathema faced by voters, employees and people the world over, is not due to the non-existence of knowledge about what makes a good leader. When the world's first leadership professor – John Adair asked former British Prime Minister Jim Callaghan if he had studied leadership, the response was, *'I haven't, and perhaps if I had, I might have been a better leader'*.

There is hence an urgent need for education, cultivation and coaching of current and emerging leaders at all levels, from socio-political to organisational leaders, on how to be a good leader, if we are to build better organisations, societies and a better world. And of the many leadership qualities one might be educated on, of foremost importance is integrity, which involves the imbedding of ethics into one's character.

Our opening quotation revealed how notable leaders such as Lincoln understood the importance of character and integrity when one steps into the arena of leadership. There are too few leaders today who have managed to embody this. But among those who were marked by greatness due to their integrity in recent history include the likes of Mandela, Gandhi, Luther King Jr and Malcolm X.

But when considering the greatest leader of all time, the name of Muhammad must come to the fore, not just in the eyes of Muslims worldwide, but even to noted non-Muslim researchers and historians such as Michael Hart, who named Muhammad as number one in his compilation of the hundred greatest leaders in history. We will consider some insights into leadership from Islamic sources, most notably the Quran and the Prophetic traditions.

## A PRIMER ON LEADERSHIP

The subject of leadership is arguably as old as human history itself. If it was not known by a word before, it was certainly a reality without a name. The Abrahamic faiths recognise the creation of Adam, the first man, as the first leader to be born in human history. And since his creation, his progeny have produced many leaders, some good (i.e. *Habilian*[2] *in nature*) and some leaving much to be desired (i.e. *Qabilian in nature*).

History has produced an abundance of leaders, and the earliest writings attempting to explain leadership include *The Art of War* (Sun Tzu) and *The Prince* (Niccolo Machiavelli), among others. Greek philosophers from Plato to Aristotle also contributed important ideas that influence leadership to this day. Similar works can be found in Chinese and Arab traditions from Confucius to Ghazali and Ibn Khaldun.

However, in recent history there has been a surge in written works on leadership. It is now estimated that well over 90,000 books[3] on leadership have been written to date (some 60,000 are on Amazon alone!), and over a thousand new books are emerging every year. The ideas contained within them vary significantly, with countless models, theories and concepts. Often these ideas have been heavily influenced by the dominant socio-political environment that gave birth to them.

Hence, recent global socio-political trends from communism to capitalism, and competing philosophies from the secular to the religious, have all influenced the ideas captured by numerous leadership thinkers. Major events in recent history from the industrial revolution to the World Wars also had bearings on leadership thought.

Indeed, one of the world's most notable leadership research centres – Roffey Park was founded after the Second World War to serve the socio-psychological needs of the British workforce who were being engaged to rebuild the nation after the immense destruction of war.

Even religious organisations in the East were subject to evolving leadership models drawn from communist ideas during the first half of the 20th century. However, over the decades, what was known widely as the 'command and control' model of leadership and management, shifted to 'business leadership' and the Adairian[4] 'Action-Centred Leadership' approach, which is about managing the interconnected needs of the *teams*, *tasks* and *individuals*, in order to get results. In recent years the 'consensus-based' approach is apparent in a move from 'tell' leadership to 'sell' leadership.

This also correlates with a shift from person-centred to process-centred models, where the command and control of one leader is replaced with a coherent process-driven system that assures the continuity and longevity of the 'business' (here we mean 'business' in very broad terms as 'busy-ness' or 'what you are busy in', hence it applies to both profit and not-for-profit endeavours).

This shift is also reflected in the evolution of definitions of leadership and its choice of words, as ethical leadership philosopher Joanna Cuilla noted. Hence, in the 1920s, leaders 'impressed' their will on those led; in the 1940s, they 'persuaded' followers; in the 1960s, they 'influenced' them; while from the 1990s onwards, leaders and followers 'influenced each other'. This indicated a move towards a non-coercive, participatory and consultative relationship between leaders and followers.

Among well known and evolving leadership theories in recent times (which are by no means exhaustive) are discussions on whether leadership is by *nature* or *nurture (or a bit of both)*; on trait theories, and looking at whether leadership should be defined at the levels of person, position, process, or result; *transactional* versus *transformational* models; on *Fordism* versus *Toyotism*; on what are the most effective leadership qualities (e.g. Covey's 7 habits, 8th habit and Kouzes and Posner's surveys of top qualities), Adair's Action-Centred Leadership framework, Goleman's leadership roles (e.g. autocratic, democratic, consultative), Hersey and Blanchard's situational leadership, and Tannenbaum & Schmidt's leadership continuum, among many others.[5]

More recently, with the passing away of Steve Jobs, the Gates versus Jobs model has been explored, where one leadership approach argued for a research-based functional approach, while the other famously declared *'people don't know what they want until we've shown them'*. As Issacson wrote, Jobs's secret was his leadership, vision and ability to 'marry poetry with technology'. Unique and creative forms of leadership are thus becoming more commonplace.

Emerging trends include distributed leadership (moving from a singular to a collective notion of leadership), and leadership as a cultural construct, where leadership is what happens when you are not there; hence the need to build a culture, such that the organisation performs and moves forward without needing your physical presence.

With such wide-ranging ideas and approaches, it is difficult to arrive at an agreed definition of leadership. Indeed Ciulla highlighted that over 200 varying definitions had been produced by researchers since the 1920s, and they often differ. But what was broadly agreed by all was that: *'leadership is about a person or persons somehow moving other people to do something'*.

However, in selecting from the 200+ definitions out there, Keith Davis[6] offers a very strong definition in our view, when he describes leadership in the following way:

*'It is the ability to persuade others to seek (pursue) defined objectives enthusiastically. It is the human factor which binds a group together and motivates it towards (shared) goals...'*

*'Management activities such as planning, organising, and decision making are dormant cocoons until the leader trig-*

*gers the power of motivation in people and guides them to-
wards their goals.'*

We offer a further explanation by way of demonstrating the difference between managers and leaders, where management is the
process of running and maintaining a ship and leadership is deciding
if the ship is sailing in the right direction. The manager rows, the leader steers.

Indeed, Peter Drucker[7] famously said '*management is doing things
right; leadership is doing the right thing(s).*' Hence the issue of right
and wrong, of morality and ethics, and of good character, emerges
once again, and we will be exploring this further later on.

## SECULAR AND ISLAMIC WORLDVIEWS

Many of the above are Western secular-based ideas, and few are attempting to look at a combination of both Eastern and Western ideas,
or what Professor John Adair calls the 'world body of knowledge',
when it comes to leadership. This book, however, attempts to draw
on both sources, by anchoring on the Sirah and reflecting on contemporary research, to arrive at a nuanced understanding of what good
leadership might look like in today's complex world.

It must be accepted that Western and secular ideas of leadership
have come to dominate most of the discourse in this field around the
world. Hence, research centres and universities in the Eastern world
stock books and resources from the West, but Western universities
do not hold much by way of Eastern resources on leadership.

Some explain this using the current 'world order' or worldview, and
the social, cultural, economic and political successes of the West. According to Jeff Henderson,[8] the former Head of Manchester Business
School, in the past the West would dominate the East by sending in
their armies. Now they send in their TV programmes, in what he called
a 'cultural colonisation' of the East. From science and technology to
education generally, knowledge is sourced primarily from Western and
secular places, in a reversal to the times of Islamic civilisation, when
the world would come to Islamic nations and scholars for knowledge.

However, there is lately an increasing realisation of the limits of
Western, secular and capitalist leadership models, not just in the East
but in the West itself. Scandals and revelations that question the in-

tegrity of leaders have become the norm, which suggests a gap in leadership education and culture. As the head of leadership development, Dr Katalin Illes[9] of Westminster Business School admitted, business schools worldwide should take some responsibility for failing to promote ethical leadership and contributing to a culture obsessed with money and short-term financial performance.

Coupled with this is a rise in interest in history, including the 'Eastern' body of knowledge from Confucianism to Islam. As Joanna Cuilla said, to really understand leadership, we need to put our ear to the ground of history. As such, the likes of Adair, Cuilla and Blanchard have written on these areas, the former having penned works on *'Confucius on Leadership'*, the *'The Leadership of Jesus'* and the *'The Leadership of Muhammad'*.[10]

In the context of issues of integrity, this interest is unsurprising because of the integral part that morality and ethics play in Eastern notions of leadership. This notion includes personal morality, social ethics and humility in character, something that Western notions of leadership have generally neglected,as Adair noted. An exception to this is Professor Patrick Wright of Cornell University, whose pioneering courses have introduced the notion of *'human frailties'* of leaders, where he calls on HR leaders to play a role to mitigate against the human frailties of directors and CEOs. In our discussions with him, he acknowledged the need for the West to consider moral leadership at a time when poor moral character (a fundamental human frailty) is causing huge fractures and loss of trust, and ultimately proving to be bad business – something which matters immensely in Western and capitalist societies.

Also, it is necessary to reflect on pitfalls that exist within some religious leaders who are minorities in the West, which may pose a problem to the wider community. According to Gumusay, these pitfalls include, worldly negligence, non-critical reasoning, exclusivity and claims to divine right. That is, some religious leaders do not take a balanced or middle path approach to their faith, and become neglectful of important worldly engagements, do not develop their education and professional development beyond rote learning hence under-developed in critical thinking, begin to think their understanding is the only exclusively correct interpretation of Islam, and to arrogate some divine right over their limited understandings in faith, leading to rejection of others in the community or even extremism in some cases.

It is worth reminding ourselves at this point that in the post-modern era, the West and East is less about geography and more about ideas and values.[11] Similarly, secularism and *religionism*[12] is not just geographically bound, although secularism does continue to emanate more from geographically Western nations such as Europe and the USA than from other parts of the world.

We are not advocating an abandonment of Western ideas, rather a critical assessment of them, accepting that which does not infringe on one's faith-based values, and leaving that which does. In this endeavour, there is a great need to be careful in order to ensure that the ethics and values of Islam are not lost in the process.

The great Malaysian Islamic philosopher Syed Naquib Al-Attas,in his *Prolegomena to the Metaphysics of Islam,* warns of *'the challenge of an alien worldview surreptitiously introduced into Muslim thought and belief by confused (Muslim) modernists of many sorts, [who have] wittingly or unwittingly come under the spell of modern secular Western philosophy and science ... which have disseminated a global contagion of secularization as a philosophical program.'* He accepts that not all of Western philosophy or science is objectionable, but rightly objects to the uncritical acceptance of them without testing their validity based on Islam's values and worldview.

As such, in the field of leadership, it is important not to *uncritically* accept all 'Western' ideas of what makes a good leader, but to recognise that there is also much to benefit from at the same time. As the narration of Prophet Muhammad teaches us: *'wisdom is the lost property of the believer; he should seek it wherever he can find it'*. (Tirmidhi)

There are many areas where notions of leadership are mutually agreeable from an Islamic and secular perspective; however there are some important differences. Among them is the idea of personal morality and social ethics in a leader, as we alluded to earlier. Western attempts to look at morality, such as John Gardner's *The Moral Aspect of Leadership* mainly focus on the immorality of mistreatment towards staff and followers or citizens, such as cruelty and oppressive leadership practices that disempower, and diminish freedom and human dignity. These are very important; however personal morality or immorality in terms of infidelity or inappropriate gender relations is of little concern. Hence, if we look at celebrated Western leaders from Kennedy to Clinton, their reverence as leaders has not been diminished by their womanising or infidelity.

An Islamic leader, however, would almost certainly find their position untenable if they were to fall short of their constituents' expectations from a personal and social morality perspective in this way. This cannot be explained away by pointing to how large sections of the Muslim community are socially conservative. Rather, it is also because morality and ethics, according to Islamic thought, cannot be compartmentalised such that it is acceptable to be ethical and morally upright in one area but unethical, immoral or unfaithful in another.

Islam's notion of holistic integrity expects a comprehensive application of ethics and values in all spheres of one's life, whether personal or public. A symbolic example of this is an event in early Islamic history when the renowned compiler of prophetic narrations Imam Bukhari famously travelled hundreds of miles to collect a narration from a person, only to reject it when he inadvertently observed the person trick an animal into a pen by luring it with food. While this may be acceptable in farming practices, Imam Bukhari felt that the salience and veracity of prophetic collections were too precious and important to leave it to chance with a person who has shown dishonesty in one area of life, even though it was to an animal. In other words, the existence of trickery and entrapment in the practice of the person may leave open the possibility of dishonesty in relation to the prophetic narration, which was not a risk he was willing to take.

Such a painstaking analysis and expectation of the personal and moral character of leaders is almost non-existent in Western notions, and sadly neglected in Eastern practices today, although Eastern faith traditions are replete with exhortations concerning this. This comprehensive approach to leadership traits, as taken in Islam, is arguably a stronger mechanism to ensure ethical behaviour in whatever endeavour a person may be leading.

However a cursory examination of Muslim leaders, organisations and countries in both the East and West suggests a shortage of education, understanding and application in the area of leadership. This is most unfortunate given the immense wealth of knowledge concerning leadership and character development in Islamic traditions, as we will see.

## ISLAMIC PERSPECTIVES ON LEADERSHIP

Language is a good indicator of whether a concept is well established in a tradition or community. When one considers the language of Islam, Arabic, one finds an abundance of terms for the word 'leader'. This includes *Amir, Imam, Khalifa, Sayyid, Qa'id, Za'im, Murshid, Ra'is* among other words. This suggests that leadership is a notion that is intrinsically contained within Arab and Islamic tradition, and this can be evidenced right from the beginning of human creation.

When God created Adam as the first man and prophet, He not only established the first in a line of prophets and messengers, he also set in motion a long line of leaders (prophets and non-prophets) to come after him from Adam's commencement until the end of time.

We hence find in the Quran, God declaring:

*'Indeed I will place upon the earth a khalifa.' (2:30)*

The word *khalifa* has been translated in many ways, including *vicegerent, divine representative* and *successive authority*, but essentially it is a leadership role involving the leading of other people. The verse continues, where the Angels question whether man will only end up in conflict and bloodshed, but God advises: *'I know that which you do not'*. He hence implies a deep wisdom and vision behind his decision to create and empower man.

This is essentially an honour gifted to man and is implied in this verse:

*'And We have honoured the people of Adam.' (17:70)*

This honour, which is declared with reference to the first man, is hence a primordial role placed upon man, and we must look to the leadership qualities of God's appointed Prophets (who are the ultimate leaders of man) for guidance on what makes a good leader.

All the named Prophets in the Quran were known for certain qualities. Yusuf was known as being *hafeez* and *aleem* – a preserver and manager (and, indeed, because he was an able government minister); Sulaiman prayed for leadership and a unique reign, and was granted the ability to command jinn and animals. Dawud could harness the malleability of iron, as we learn in Surah Hadid. During the time of Sulaiman, Queen Saba was a noted female leader, who led a parliament and was respected for her leadership attributes and nobility. These examples are worthy of further study in the Quran.

Major Prophets such as Ibrahim were noted for demonstrating great intellect, integrity and sacrifice, and Musa is referred to in the Quran as *'Al-Qawi'* and *'Al Amin'* (strong and trustworthy). The Quran further reveals regarding another Prophet:

*'And We had certainly given Luqman wisdom.' (31:12)*

We can hence begin to sense the importance of leadership in Islam, and infer the sort of leadership qualities that are divinely praised.

The concept of leadership is also indicated in another verse in the Quran, where God says:

*'And we raise some above others in rank so that some may command work from others.' (43:32)*

It is thus a natural order of life that one must lead and others follow in any endeavour. However, what makes one deserved of being 'raised' is worth reflecting on. That one's character and capability are of significance in this regard is alluded to when God says:

*'We did indeed offer the trust to the heavens and the earth and the mountains; but they refused to undertake it, being afraid thereof: but man undertook it ...' (33:72)*

This verse further confirms how leadership is at the heart of Allah's creation and divine sunnah. However, the verse interestingly continues by stating that man is *'zaluman jahula'*; in other words, man has wronged himself in ignorance. The exegesis on this suggests that man naively accepted the weight that is associated with entrustment of God's message, which the heavens and the Earth smartly avoided, fearing the pitfalls associated (hypocrisy is highlighted in particular). The verse then indicates that some among men, however, can and do rise to the challenge, having demonstrated the required character to be entrusted with leadership. Given that hypocrisy is singled out in the verse for criticism, it is clear that truthfulness, honesty and integrity must be the praiseworthy leadership characteristics sought.

## PROPHETIC NARRATIONS

Having considered some Quranic references relating to leadership, we note several *ahadith* (Prophetic traditions) on leadership as well. While there is much by way of lessons to be gained from the other Prophets, we recognise the pre-eminence of Muhammad – the leader of all prophets. He was known as *al uswatul hasanah* ('the greatest example') for everyone, whether parents, teachers, community leaders, political leaders or business leaders.

The French historian Lamartine[13] said that *'if greatness of purpose, smallness of means, and extraordinary results were the criteria for human genius, who of the great leaders dare compare with Muhammad!'*

Muhammad was hence not only a noted leader by his example, but also a teacher of leaders, and of leadership. The Prophet famously said:

> *'Each of you is a shepherd, and each responsible for his flock.'*
> (Bukhari)

The great Prophets were known to have been shepherds at some stage in their lives. A simile is drawn from this fact, where the shepherding was a training process to enable the prophets to lead people. This hadith teaches us that beyond the great Prophets, we are all shepherds, one way or the other. Each of us will have someone upon whom we have responsibility or influence. This may be one's spouse, children, relatives, friends, neighbours, colleagues or anyone else with whom one is regularly in contact.

This is quite a powerful notion, as it compels one to assume leadership and ownership of one's actions upon those one has influence over. And it compels one to think long and hard about how dutiful one has been to all the above stakeholders, and that one will be accountable in the next life for that responsibility. Hence, there is no escaping leadership!

In another well-known hadith narration concerning leadership, the Prophet said:

> *'When three are on a journey, they should appoint one as a leader.'* (Abu Dawud)

This is fascinating, as it shows that even in a small group, where one may otherwise have thought that leadership is not required, the Prophetic and hence Islamic exhortation is to still appoint a lead person. This should not only be restricted to a physical journey to a certain destination, but also applied in other endeavours, such as projects and initiatives where one is also on a journey to reach a certain goal or objective.

## CAN LEADERSHIP BE SOUGHT?

A common question arises in light of a hadith where the Prophet advised Abu Dhar *'leadership is not for the one who seeks it'*. Many interpret this to mean that one should never put themselves forward for leadership roles or even run for elections, especially in Islamic organisational settings. I believe this understanding is problematic for two reasons.

Firstly, there is also an alternative interpretation, which has been neglected by advocates of the first view, which suggests that the Prophet was not making a general ruling, but giving private advice just for Abu Dhar. He did not believe Abu Dhar was suitable for the specific role he had sought, hence advised in his eloquent, indirect style that the leadership role being sought was not right for Abu Dhar who was seeking it. In that sense *'leadership is not for the one who seeks it'* takes on a whole new meaning.

Secondly, it is harmful to the advancement of our faith interests, and contrary to the higher objectives of Islam (*maqasid*), if talented and able people sign themselves out from activism, engagement and offering their leadership to solve the many problems facing our *ummah*. There is a desperate need for capable people to step up and take ownership of the challenges facing Muslims and the wider world, but too many able people are choosing to be backbenchers instead.

Interestingly, the Greeks also preached of the disinclination of the virtuous towards leadership; hence, Plato said *'in a land of good men, no one wants to be a leader'*. But he continued by saying that good men must step forward, as the damage of not doing so is to live with the consequences of bad leaders instead.

Having said this, it is equally important for leaders and those stepping forward to ensure that they are keeping their intentions pure, and looking after their spirituality, in order to mitigate against pride, arrogance and other vice which may afflict an unprepared leader. By engaging in regular spiritual acts such as *salah, adhkar, tilawah, qiyam*,[14] and by ensuring good governance mechanisms that promote accountability over centralisation of power, one can achieve this balance, and remain among 'good men'.

## TYPES OF LEADERSHIP

The leadership of the Prophet was comprehensive and all encompassing in nature. Indeed, we noted how the American historian Michael Hart listed him as the most influential figure in human history; this was because he was the only person who successfully combined both political and religious leadership. If we also consider Adair's categorisation of types of leadership, we find that the Prophet embodied all of Adair's three types of leadership, namely:

1. Position/Hierarchy-based
2. Knowledge/Expertise-based
3. Charisma/Inspiration-based

Most leaders fall into being one type of leader; for example, the first type includes line managers, CEOs, prime ministers and presidents, who have hierarchical authority. The second type includes doctors, professors, technicians and specialists, whose direction and instruction are sought due to their knowledge and expertise in the field concerned. The third type includes community leaders, campaign leaders and even celebrities such as musicians, artists, sporting stars and other such figures who people follow by virtue of their charisma, talent or inspiration.

A study of the Sirah of the Prophet makes it clear that the Prophet was a leader in all three senses, hence he holds the foremost hierarchical position over the *ummah*, he is the ultimate human source of knowledge concerning faith and the philosophy of life, and he was able to inspire and attract large swathes of adherents due to his character, personality and charisma.

A deeper look into the life of the Prophet reveals how well-established contemporary leadership models were already being applied over 1,400 years ago. As Badawi aptly explains, Muhammad adapted his style in varying situations and in accordance with the nature of the people, reflecting the now renowned Hersey and Blanchard's 'situational leadership model'. Although they may not have been termed anything in the past, it was a reality without a name then, and perhaps a name without a reality today when you look at the lack of range and ability among contemporary leaders.

## THE 'RIGHTLY GUIDED' SUCCESSORS

In addition to considering Quranic and Prophetic references in relation to leadership, the 'Rightly Guided Successors' are important to consider, in order to gain an insight into Islamic notions on leadership. The immediate four successors of the Prophet, namely Abu Bakr, Umar, Uthman and Ali, occupy a unique theological position compared to subsequent leaders of the Islamic world, and are considered authentic religious references. Their leadership example is particularly important given that it is a key point of creed that there will be no other Prophet after Muhammed, however there is nothing in Islamic tradition to say there will not be another leader like Abu Bakr, Umar, Uthman or Ali. Hence by exploring their leadership approach one can hope to develop oneself to their standards – a more plausible (albeit lofty) aim than reaching the standards of the Prophet.

Abu Bakr, the closest companion of Muhammad, who became the first Caliph (successor) after Muhammad's death, demonstrated a humble approach to leadership after assuming the helm, saying:

> 'O people! I have been selected as your trustee although I am no better than anyone of you. If I am right, obey me. If I am misguided, correct me.'

He hence saw his role as a trust, and did not see himself as being above reproach. The following story provides a great insight into Abu Bakr's leadership. He famously would go out into the desert after Salat al-Fajr but it was not initially clear why. Umar was curious about where he went, so he decided to follow him. He saw Abu Bakr travel and come to a tent. He went in for a while before making his way back to Medina.

Umar went into the tent and found an old woman there with children. He asked her about her situation; she told him that *'I am an old ageing widow who is raising orphan children and I am blind.'* Umar then asked her about the man who visited her. She said *'I have no idea about his name or who he is. He comes everyday and he cooks the food, kneads the dough, bakes the bread, cleans the tent/house, cleans the clothes, milks the goat and then leaves.'*

Umar asked if she paid him anything to which she replied, *'I have no money.'* Umar asked how long he has been doing this and she replied, *'a long time.'* Umar then left the woman, and commented,

> *'You have made it a difficult job for the caliphs (leaders) after you Abu Bakr!'*

Umar ibn Al Khattab (who succeeded Abu Bakr as Caliph after the latter's death) was also known for his modesty, servant leadership, and humility, falling into tears at the scale of accountability he felt he would face before God in the position of Caliph. Under his reign, the Islamic world expanded at astounding speed, and he found himself needing to appoint and train many leaders. Once he was addressing a gathering of his officials and leaders, and said to them:

> *'Remember I have not appointed you as commanders and tyrants over the people. Rather I have sent you as leaders so that the people may follow your example... Do not keep your door shut in their faces lest the more powerful among them eat up (the rights of) the weaker ones. And do not behave as if you are superior to them.'*

Umar was a particularly good example of a responsible leader by Islamic standards. Indeed, Muhammad had endorsed him as an authentic exemplifier of Islamic principles. He was known for his strong sense of justice and simplicity. On one occasion, as Umar entered Jerusalem, the people found him walking and pulling his camel while his servant rode on its back. The people of the city had thought that Umar – the then head of the Muslim world – was riding the camel. What had happened was that Umar insisted on taking turns with his servant-assistant in riding and pulling the camel as they journeyed to the city, and it so happened that it was the servant's turn to ride by the time they had arrived. This unique level of modesty and equality by a great leader and statesman surprised the people of the city, who were more used to the pomp and show of Roman leaders.

Uthman, the third Caliph, was a wealthy individual, and known for his forgiving and merciful leadership approach. Some analysts believe he was perhaps too forgiving and as a leader should have been tougher. This criticism perhaps lends to a masculine and 'strong man' perception of Islamic leaders. However, the fact that someone like Uthman was among the rightly guided successors indicates the accommodation of a diverse range of personalities at the helm of the Islamic community.

Ali ibn Abi Talib was the famous fourth Caliph, and one of the earliest embracers of Islam. He was well known for his bravery and intellect, as we will see later on in the ethical and authentic manner with which he conducted himself in the Battle of the Trench.

He was also known for his wit, and once during his challenging reign he was asked by one of his people why there were so many problems under his leadership compared to the time of Abu Bakr and Umar, to which Ali he said: *'that is because they had followers like me, while I have followers like you!'*

There is a lesson in this response – that good leadership is not just about the leader, but about having good followers as well. And the role of courage, intellect and wit is also not unique to Ali, but a trait that many great Muslim leaders and scholars possessed.

Since the time of the Prophet and the early generations of Islamic leaders, many different leadership models emerged which have a bearing on how ethical decisions got made. Islamic leadership originally sought to merge the political and the spiritual, although that convergence is less existent in recent times.

Models included the dynastic authorities of the Umayyad and Abbasid rulers, as well as the Ottoman model where the Sultan had two key types of counsels – the Grand Mufti (religious advisor) and the Grand Vizier (political advisor) – distinct role bearers who did not always see eye to eye. Such models and dynamics had implications on how decisions and issues of ethics were handled.

In more recent times, two particular models of religious leadership are apparent, one in the form of the well-known *tariqa* system attributed to Sufis, which is a more spiritual model of leadership centred around an individual person or 'shaykh'; the other, the *jama* model, is a more institutionally and/or politically orientated approach centred around an organisation which has elected leaders, and many Islamic parties and missionary organisations adopt this approach. All these models attempt to draw on the leadership lessons and ethics of the Prophet, but manifest it in different ways due to the theological leg-room that allows for different leadership models to exist. Models and formats can vary, but considering which leadership qualities should reside beneath the broader leadership models is arguably more important.

Drawing on the Sirah, a comprehensive list of prophetic leadership qualities would, according to our findings, include *integrity, competence, vision, courage, holistic justice, pragmatic decisiveness, servant-leadership, practical wisdom, resilience, compassion* and *spiritual intelligence*.

These qualities relate to the wider Islamic notion of character development and spiritual development, something of critical importance for leaders and the key to mitigate against corruption and other pitfalls of power. Al Ghazali offers a treasure chest of prophetic guidance on this, which is worthy of further study. In his famous advice to rulers he said:

> *'If a king is upright… his officials will be upright, but if he is dishonest, negligent, and comfort-seeking… officers implementing his policies will soon become slothful and corrupt.'*[15]

## GOOD LEADERSHIP AND RESPECTFUL PLURALISM IN TODAY'S WORLD

The 11 prophetic leadership qualities listed above make for an incredibly good and worthy leader no doubt. Indeed, embodying even half of them would make one stand out in today's leadership vacuum. But cultivating these qualities is not easy, which is why true leadership is ultimately hard won.

The Prophet Muhammad said, *'the best among you are those who are best in character' (Bukhari)*. Hence, we return to the issue of character as outlined in our quotation from Lincoln at the beginning, and note that this is man's greatest frontier. Man's greatness or grotesqueness depends acutely on character and qualities.

While the aforementioned leadership qualities have strong references in Islamic tradition, they are also universal in nature, hence making it globally applicable and useful to any leader, Muslim or non-Muslim.

In today's plural, multicultural and multi-faith environment, universality is gold dust. And there is a desperate need for people to be able to offer leadership across beliefs and boundaries. Muslims need to be able to act as ethical beacons in society, living up to the prophetic (and universal) values. They need to be inclusive and able to serve causes that benefit wider society, not just Muslims.

By the same token, non-Muslims, of another faith or none, need to be inclusive and able to serve causes that benefit wider society including Muslims, not just those who are like them.

One might question whether such boundary-spanning leadership is achievable and whether a religious person can be a mainstream leader, but as Douglas Hicks persuasively argued, it is possible to have religious convictions and lead people who do not share those beliefs – through *respectful pluralism* – that is, to lead with integrity, drawing on the internal inspirations of one's personal faith and belief, and translating that into inclusive and respectful leadership which is accommodative, and gives space and freedom to others of a different belief or worldview.

The beauty of values and qualities such as integrity, fairness and wisdom is that they do not have any religion and they have many religions. Hence, a religious person can apply them universally. It is easy to talk about one's faith or values, but harder to live by them. Hence, our focus needs to be on living up to our values more than preaching them, and this will open up opportunities for mainstream leadership. And this means, one must ensure that one's activities are always subservient to one's values, and not allow 'values' to be subservient to one's activities![16]

Hence, the faith-inspired South African leader Ambassador Ebrahim Rasool said, *'moral ends require moral means'*. He took inspiration from his faith values and provided mainstream leadership. He worked alongside the great Nelson Mandela, a rare leader who embodied the universal values highlighted, such as integrity, courage and patience, helping *Madiba* gain the accolade of one of the most admired leaders in the world (Gallup).

Rasool rightly noted how *'so much of the world today wish they had a Nelson Mandela, instead of... the ideologues that lead them into a cul-de-sac of ideas; instead of the technocrats who offer managerialism rather than leadership'*. He explained how the world saw in

Mandela leadership that was *'principled yet pragmatic, firm yet flexible, decisive yet popular'.* We live in a world today where all of these seem to have become irreconcilable binaries. Mandela offered a template for leadership that can *'balance values and interests, people and markets, environment and growth, freedom and responsibility'.* There are few pairings that are harder to balance than these. And that takes good leadership.

It has often been asked, *'where is the Muslim Mandela?'* It is indeed a pertinent question. In Mandela we see one who embodied many of the prophetic leadership qualities, yet we struggle to find Muslim leaders today who have even some of these qualities. This is of course not just a Muslim problem, as the world in general has not replaced Mandela with an equal.

Muslims believe that there will never again be a leader like the Prophet Muhammad, but there is nothing to say there cannot be another great leader like Abu Bakr, Umar, Uthman or Ali. There is hence certainly no reason why there cannot be another Mandela, if we find it in ourselves to be great people. Let us embody the leadership example of the Prophet, and let the 11 qualities unlock your talent. The world is waiting for you!

# 11 PROPHETIC LEADERSHIP QUALITIES

The life of the Prophet is an ocean and treasure chest of guidance and insight. As Aisha said, *'his embodiment was the Quran'*. He was hence the walking and talking manifestation of God's divine direction. If the Quran was God's outline of the 'what', the Sunnah can be seen as the 'how' of Islam.

The Sirah – life of the Prophet reveals to us hundreds upon hundreds of qualities from which we can begin to think about what might be the most important for leaders throughout the ages. Scholarly analyses vary as to which qualities were exhibited the most, and which were the most important. But a number of qualities emerge as consistently apparent in the life, teachings and conduct of the Prophet.

We have studied the Sirah, analysing it using our leadership lens, and collated numerous scholarly works in this regard from the likes of Badawi, Beekun, Al Attas, Al Buraei, Jabnoun, Baig, Ramadan, Auda and Adair among others, as mentioned in the previous chapter.

What emerged were well over 50 prominent qualities. We then sought to whittle this down to the very apparent and well-evidenced ones. This led us to the top 11 Prophetic Leadership Qualities. They are as follows:

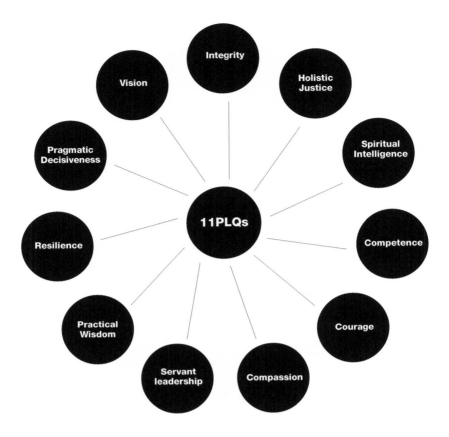

It is not easy to rank these in order of importance, and most of these are arguably as important as one another. But a framework could be built drawing on the Quranic outline of important qualities of the major Prophets, such as Ibrahim, who demonstrated great intellect and sacrifice (which draws us to *spiritual intelligence* and *servant leadership* from the above list), and Prophet Musa, who is referred to in the Quran as '*al-Qawi*' and '*al-Amin*' (which draws us to *competence* and *integrity* from the above list). Given the seal of Prophets Muhammad was known as '*al Amin*' (and also known for his competence). Let us consider these two qualities with some prominence; it is also possible to group the rest of the qualities under these two overarching qualities in the following way:

| COMPETENCE | INTEGRITY |
|---|---|
| Vision | Spiritual Intelligence |
| Pragmatic Decisiveness | Compassion |
| Holistic Justice | Courage |
| | Resilience |
| | Practical Wisdom |
| | Servant Leadership |

Clearly, many qualities are overlapping in nature and could fall under both competence and integrity, but for ease of understanding and memorability, it is a useful way to remember the two overarching Quranic qualities and then seek to reflect on the additional qualities placed under each.

Let us now consider each quality, starting with integrity and competence, followed by the remaining qualities – vision, courage, justice, decisiveness, servant leadership, wisdom, resilience, compassion and spiritual intelligence.

# CHAPTER 1

# INTEGRITY

If there is one quality that could claim the pole position as the most important quality, it is arguably integrity and *amana*.[1] The word *'amana'* is of course more than just integrity, but includes truthfulness, honesty, transparency, ownership and custodianship. It also implies sincerity and authenticity. Given the importance of all these, it is worth devoting some time and detail to this area.

A study by Kouzes and Posner (1995)[2] surveyed 2,615 successful leaders in business and industry, and asked them to put their success down to one quality. Later in 2002, some 75,000 respondents from 6 continents were also asked about what makes a good leader.

The results were fascinating: the top quality was not business acumen or ability to predict future market trends, it was not innovation or a cut-throat hard-headed approach to leadership. Rather, it was honesty and being trustworthy. The results were as follows:

| Rank | Leadership Characteristic |
|------|---------------------------|
| 1 | Honest |
| 2 | Competent |
| 3 | Forward-Looking |
| 4 | Inspiring |
| 5 | Intelligent |
| 6 | Fair-minded |

While this insight was discovered in recent years, over 1,400 years ago we find that of all the titles God could have made the Prophet famous for, he is known in history as '*al-Amin*' – the honest and trustworthy one, or, as John Adair describes, 'the man of integrity'. The prominence of this title and leadership quality is not a coincidence, and God's wisdom is for mankind to first and foremost cultivate this quality.

It is also noteworthy that the top two qualities correspond with the Quranic framework of '*al Qawi*' and '*al Amin*' (competent and trustworthy).

## ETHICAL LEADERSHIP

When talking about *amana* and integrity-based leadership, this is often synonymous with the notion of 'ethical leadership', which was touched on in the first chapter. Ethics and integrity are of course interrelated, and to better understand them let us consider their definitions:

### INTEGRITY:

The quality of being honest and having strong moral and

ethical principles; firm adherence to a code of especially moral values

(Merriam-Webster Dictionary)

## ETHICS:

The discipline of dealing with what is good and bad; the principles of conduct governing an individual or a group; a set of moral principles; a guiding philosophy

(Merriam-Webster Dictionary)

The science of morals, the moral principles by which a person is guided

(Oxford Dictionary)

Hence, we are dealing with fundamental matters of good and bad, and of principles and values. Adair offers a deeper reflection on what integrity is about, stating that it was about more than just honesty. He explains how the Latin origin of the word is about wholeness, soundness and completeness. He continues that it is about loyalty and adherence to standards outside of yourself, especially truth. And this he notes is key because integrity is the quality that creates trust; and when trust breaks down, all human interaction and intercourse comes to nothing.[3]

We would hence describe an Ethical Leader as one who leads with the highest levels of honesty and integrity, builds trust, and is immensely cognisant of his/her need to be a role model, and act based on worthy values and principles that appeal to the higher levels of human nature.

From an Islamic perspective, an ethical leader must act based on the values and principles of the Quran and the Prophetic example (sunnah) by comprehensively integrating these values into all matters and responsibilities that fall under one's leadership role.

## PRIORITISING VALUES-BASED CHARACTER

It can sometimes seem easy to talk about honesty, integrity and ethical behaviour, and even consider certain people as having or not having this quality. But few things test this quality more than power and those things which indirectly give one power, such as wealth, fame and resources.

In our opening we quoted Lincoln's famous words: *'Nearly all men can stand adversity, but if you want to test a man's character (and ethics), give him power'*. We noted that power affects people. They change, and their character changes. Facing an agenda-driven environment, sincerity is forgotten, unethical choices emerge and corruption creeps in.

If we consider some of the global scandals mentioned at the beginning, the corruption among many leaders in politics and industry, and indicators such as Transparency International's well-known Corruption Perception Index,[4] it is apparent that we are in something of an ethical crisis today. Indeed some 69% of countries have major corruption issues, and half of the G20 are included! And the trend overall is going from bad to worse year on year.

Similarly, we note that the Institute of Business Ethics[5] recorded a 10% drop in trust that society felt toward organisations, both business and governmental, or what is increasingly being termed 'the establishment'.[6] This matters, as the moral triumphs and failures of leaders, and those in power, carry greater weight than that of non-leaders, as ethical leadership guru Professor Joanna Cuilla[7] rightly noted.

All this points to the issue of weak human character. Indeed, the Prophet said:

> *'The best among you are the best in character'*. He also said: *'What enables people to enter paradise more than anything is piety and good character.'* (Tirmidhi).

However, in reality, character development is not pursued nor practised, even though it is preached. It is worth reminding ourselves about the sequence of the sirah, and asking whether the Prophet was *al-amin* (trustworthy) first or *al-rasul* (messenger) first. We know he was known as *al-amin* long before he took on the leadership role of *al-rasul*.

This is an important observation, as we often find that people seek to preach a message (*risala*) first without having established their credibility in society or having developed their character to a mature level, commensurate to what is becoming of a leader or person of power and authority. It is hence important to cultivate our character in readiness for future leadership responsibilities that may arise, so that we might be better equipped to cope with the biggest challenge that power poses, which is to compromise our character and integrity.

In developing our character, we need to have a deep sense of our values and higher purpose.

To many, Islam's core has been reduced to a set of rules and 'do's and don'ts'. Some focus on legal rulings at the expense of values and governing principles. They fail to realise that every legal ruling has an ethical, value-driven dimension and it is this legal–ethical harmony which Islam advocates at every level. Every legal requirement should have an ethical and value-driven component. All of Islamic law is subject to higher purposes (al-maqasid), and if there is any law or legal opinion which conflicts with a higher objective or an overarching value, then the law needs to be scrutinised and re-evaluated, leading either to a reconciliation between law and ethics or challenging the legal formulations which are unethical and contradict the higher purposes.

Character development and ethical leadership are predicated on this harmonious reconciliation between our actions/behaviour and higher purposes. The greater the disparity between the two, the likelier it is to lose integrity.

## INTENTIONS AND MORAL RANKING

Even before we enumerate our values, the development of ethical character starts with determining our intentions and purifying our hearts.[8]

As the Prophet said: *'Actions are judged by their intentions'*. The question then is what represents the best type of intentions to pursue and which are lesser types of intentions to avoid. According to Sulaiman Nadwi,[9] the moral ranking of intentions according to Islam are as follows:

## Ethical/Moral Ranking of Intentions

Source:
'Ethics in Islam' from
Shu.Sulaiman Nadwi's
Seeratun Nabi

GOD'S PLEASURE

GAINING PARADISE

SPIRITUAL CONTENTMENT

FEEL GOOD FACTOR

HONOUR, REPUTE, FAME

FINANCIAL OF WORLDLY GAIN

MORAL RANKING

According to the renowned scholar Sulaiman Nadwi, in his work *Ethics in Islam*, a framework around moral ranking of intentions can be argued. Based on evidence from the Quran and Prophetic legacy, it is arguable that worldly benefits have limited moral superiority (although many worldly pursuits are *halal* – permissible and encouraged – as well).  Going up the levels, one might think that spiritual contentment is the highest level. While seeking it is a worthy intention with some moral standing, there is another level above it, which is to ensure our actions are based upon the intention of seeking paradise. However, even that is not the highest level of intention.

When we love someone, we desire to make them happy. When we learn to love God more than anything else in the world, there is nothing we would desire more than to make our Lord and creator happy. Thus, seeking the pleasure of God is the level of intention with the greatest moral ranking, and its pursuit will manifest itself in cultivating the best character in people, leaders and non-leaders alike. The great female mystic Rabia al-Basri expressed this deep motivator of human behaviour in her poem, where she expresses that one should worship God not in order to enter Paradise or to avoid Hellfire but because one is driven by the love God and He alone deserves to be worshiped.

This is clear when we consider the full outline of the hadith of intention as narrated by Umar Ibn Al-Khattab. He heard the Prophet say, *'Verily actions are judged by their intentions, and for every person is what he intended. So the one whose migration was to Allah and His Messenger, then his migration was to Allah and His Messenger. And the one whose migration was for the world to gain from it, or a woman to marry her, then his migration was to what he made migration for.'*

The migration from Mecca to Medina was the context of this hadith. As part of a support system and arrangement, the Meccan Muslims would be given many worldly provisions in Medina, hence the issue of intention became relevant. The Prophet hence advised that if one was just coming to Medina to benefit from the worldly gains, then that is all one will get. But if it is for the greatest intention – that of migrating for the sake of one's love and obedience to God and His messenger – then they will not only gain the worldly provisions, but also spiritual and metaphysical provisions, having proven themselves worthy of reward in the next life – the greatest reward being to be able to stand in the presence of the almighty and be granted the privilege and capacity to actually see Him. This advice was actually prompted by a report of a companion of the Prophet who was migrating but in order to marry someone in Medina.

It might sound simple to elaborate on the pivotal role of *intention*, but guiding our actions by the right intentions is challenging. Many of the classical scholars of Islam have highlighted this in their works on the ethical dimension of intentions:

Yahya ibn Abu Kathir said, *'Learn your intention for it is more serious than the action.'*

Sufyan al-Thawri said, *'I have not treated anything more difficult than my intention, because it keeps changing.'*

Ibn al-Mubarak said, *'Maybe a small action is made great by its intention, and maybe a great action is made small by its intention.'*

## KEY VIRTUES

The process of determining our intentions goes hand in hand with a broader process of purifying our hearts of vice and inculcating key virtues. Some of the most important virtues and values[10] in Islam, as found in the Quran and the Sunnah, include: *ihsan* (excellence), *rahma* (compassion), *ikhlas* (sincerity), *sidq* (truthfulness), *adl* (justice) and *sharh al-sadr* (open heartedness).

The following is a longer list[11] of virtues to pursue, and vices to avoid, in order to build ethical character:

| Virtues | Vice |
| --- | --- |
| Excellence and magnanimity | Violence |
| Mercy and forgiveness | Lying and cheating |
| Sincerity | Pride, show and arrogance |
| Truthfulness | Deceit and betrayal |
| Truthfullness | Slander |
| Humility | Greed |
| Moderation and balance | Cowardice |
| Dignity and self respect | Oppressive treatment |
| Courage | Anger and losing self control |
| Steadfastness | Foul speech and abuse of tongue |
| Contentment | Extravagance and decadence |
| Attitude of gratitude | Selfishness and narcissism |
| Patience | Stirring up conflict |

Many of these will naturally overlap with our selection of top 11 prophetic leadership qualities, given they are sourced from the same place – the Quran and the Sirah of the Prophet. But a useful way to understand this, is that the above is relevant to everyone, leaders and non-leaders, whereas the 11 prophetic leadership qualities are specifically relevant and critical for leadership.

If a leader cultivates their character in light of the above and the 11 prophetic leadership qualities, they will be well positioned to be of benefit to society.

The two dimensions of individual character development and benefit of society are a good way to demarcate the world of virtues/ethics (*akhlaq*) and the world of law (*shariah/ahkam*).[12] The first pertains to the beautification of individual character; the latter pertains to societal rights and protection of people's interests. Some scholars[13] translate law and ethics as *adl* and *ihsan*, reflecting the dimension of legal rights/minimums and the dimension of best practice[14]/maximums and discretionary superior behaviours. There is need to pay attention to both overall, as per the Quranic exhortation, for God 'commands to *adl* and *ihsan*', and this is particularly true for those in positions of leadership. Focusing on only values leads to a soul without a body, and focusing only on legal rights leads to a body without a soul; clearly both body and soul are important.

Leaders hence need to develop their moral character *and* fulfil legal obligations to stakeholders in light of Islamic law – which exists to benefit people and protect their interests (*maslaha*). This is, in short, the *maqasid* (higher objectives, intents and purposes) of Islamic law – something leaders should be versed on. We enumerated the values and virtues above; we will now outline the pioneering framework of Islamic law – *maqasid al shariah*.

Classical scholars from Al-Juwayni and Al-Ghazali to Al-Qarafi and Al-Shatibi pioneered in distilling from the Quran and Prophetic Tradition the higher purposes of Islamic law, hence leading to the emergence of the well-known five *necessities* of *maqasid* which are: the preservation of faith, life, intellect, wealth and posterity. This is illustrated below:

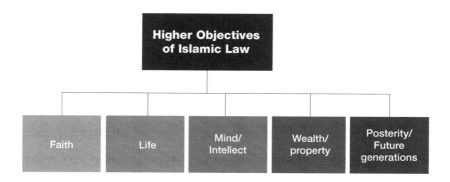

The preservation (and promotion) of these five areas is considered 'absolutely necessary' (*daruriyyat*), while other less critical objectives and obligations are considered needs (*hajiyyat*), such as trade, marriage, transportation – things which are important but not a matter of life and death, and the lowest level of necessity are the 'nice to haves' (*tahsiniyyat*), such as expensive clothes, premium cars or the newest smartphone. Leaders should ensure that in their roles they do not compromise any of the five 'absolutely necessary' areas for preservation, and where possible should support reasonable 'needs', while the 'nice to haves' are down to discretion.

With regard to the five essential areas for preservation, many contemporary scholars felt the need to expand this classical list to include dignity, freedom and justice. These were obvious and evidenced in Islamic history, and perhaps did not need to be spelt out. However, in today's volatile world, where human dignity, freedom and justice are being violated on a colossal scale, there is need to outline these to remind ourselves of all these fundamental objectives and obligations. It is thus the role of an ethical leader to protect and preserve all eight *maqasid* within their roles and capacities, as outlined here:

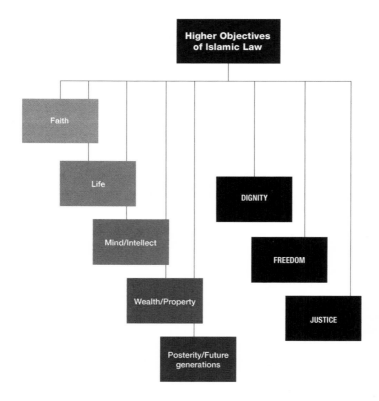

Awareness, application and adoption of all of the above is needed, both the individual character development domain and the benefit/

rights of society domain (i.e. the world of virtues/values/ethics, and the world of Islamic law and its higher purpose), in order to live the prophetic leadership quality of *amana* (integrity and custodianship).

## INTEGRITY IN THE SIRAH

The entirety of the Sirah is a story of prophetic integrity. His life is a reference point and practical example of ethical living according to Islam. Since he was young, he developed a reputation for honesty and good character. Those around him considered him *al-amin*, and continued to do so even after Prophethood, although many did not believe in his message from God.

Enemies entrusted their money to the Prophet due to his integrity and ethical reputation. Indeed, Khadija employed Muhammad when he was young, due to his trustworthiness and competence, and subsequently proposed and married him due to his good character.

This quality of the Prophet is unsurprising given the emphasis on honesty and integrity in the Quran. The following verses make this apparent:

> *'O you who have believed, why do you say what you do not do?'* (61:2)

> *'O you who believe… never misappropriate knowingly things entrusted to you.'* (8:27)

> *'Believers are those who are faithful to their trusts and to their commitments.'* (23:8)

> *'Those who fulfil their commitments when they make them.'* (2:177)

> *'O Believers: Honour your contracts.'* (5:1)

> *'And fulfil every commitment. Surely every commitment will be asked about (on the Day of Judgement).'* (17:34)

Indeed, the longest verse in the Quran (2:282) is also devoted to ethical practices, especially in the context of wealth and finance (a source of power which often can test one's character). God encourages professionalism, and the need to document transactions and honour one's promises. God's direction in this regard is further reflected in this statement of the Prophet:

> '*Whoever from you is appointed by us to a position of authority and he conceals from us a needle or something smaller than that, it would be misappropriation of public funds, and he will have to produce it on the Day of Judgement.*' (Muslim)

Among other noteworthy prophetic statements on truthfulness, there are the following:

> '*The characteristics of a hypocrite are three: when he speaks he lies; when he gives his word he breaks it; when he is given a trust he is unfaithful.*' (Bukhari)

> '*Never do in private what you would conceal from others in public.*' (Ibn Majah)

> '*Whoever advises his brother to take a certain course while knowing that a better course lies elsewhere, has in essence betrayed him.*' (Abu Dawud)

## BATTLE OF HUNAYN: INTEGRITY IN ACTION

One of the most remarkable events in the Sirah is found in the famous battle of Hunayn. It is an event that Adair notes as being an impressive example of managing multiple stakeholder demands with integrity. Hunayn was a difficult and challenging occasion in which the Prophet showed great judgement, astute leadership and arguably all of the 11 leadership qualities in one event. As the saying goes, '*leadership is like a tea bag, you don't know how good it is until its in hot water*'. And in the hot water of Hunayn, the Prophet demonstrated why he was the greatest of leaders.

After the peaceful liberation of Mecca, some neighbouring tribes became enraged at the growth and success of the emergent Muslim community. The Bani Hawazin in particular set out on the warpath in an attempt to destroy the Muslims. The battleground was the valley of Hunayn, near Ta'if, where some 12,000 Muslims would meet some 4,000 enemies.[15] In outnumbering the enemy for once (in contrast to Badr, where Muslims were outnumbered yet won), many among the ranks felt overconfident and complacent, thinking it would be an easy battle.

However, as the Muslims set up camp, they faced a surprise ambush, as the enemy charged forth earlier than expected, leading many of the Muslim soldiers to flee, leaving the courageous Prophet in danger as he continued to stand his ground before the oncoming attack.

As the Prophet and his steadfast companions called the fleeing Muslims to return and stand with the Prophet, the Muslims eventually regained control and overcame the Bani Hawazin. The lesson to be learnt for those who fled was revealed in Surah Tawba,[16] reminding us of the need to both take preparation and rely on God, and not to assume victory solely based on *dunyawi* (physical worldly) and numeric considerations, but to invoke the metaphysical world and seek the help of God as only He can grant success.

The great leadership of the Prophet becomes even more apparent when observing the way in which he managed different stakeholders and emotions in spite of being in the difficult environment of the battlefield. For example, it emerged that one of the captives was Shayma bint Halima – the long-lost foster sister of the Prophet who happened to get caught up in the battle. Her claim of relation was not initially believed, but she asked to see the Prophet and he agreed. When she came forth he did not recognise her until she showed him a bite mark he left on her arm when he was a child. The Prophet then welcomed her warmly and laid down his cloak so they could both sit and catch up – a wonderful example of warmth, patience and emotional intelligence in the midst of the harshness of war.

Another defining moment was when the defeated and captured Bani Hawazins pleaded for mercy from the Prophet. This was difficult for the Prophet to grant, as his soldiers had an established right to the spoils of war, which included booty and captives. However, as Adair notes, he creatively found a win–win approach (Covey concept) by calling upon his men and asking for volunteers to come forward in public and forgo their right (*Ihsan* concept[17]). The opportunity to exchange booty for honour by being recognised by the Prophet before their peers was too good an offer to resist for many, hence allowing the Prophet to grant clemency to those who pleaded. To others, he offered camels and goats in exchange for captives, leaving stake-holders satisfied – a great example of wisdom, integrity and fairness.

However, there remained one group – some of his closest companions from amongst the Ansar – who felt they had missed out completely, gaining little by way of honour or booty. This slight discontentment reached the Prophet, and rather than ignoring the feelings of his people, as some leaders do, he went to find them and ask them about how they felt and why. The hesitant companions eventually expressed how they felt that they had missed out while others gained much, even though they had sacrificed the most. This is where the spiritual intelligence and vision of the Prophet really showed, as he reminded them that while others went home with goats and camels, they, the Ansar, are the favoured ones who get to take Allah and His Messenger home! The companions wept at this great realisation and felt embarrassed at their earlier feeling of discontentment.

The Prophet thus applied great influence as a leader to solve immense challenges with incredible integrity.

## THE WISE OWL MODEL OF ETHICAL LEADERSHIP

Returning to the issue of integrity versus power/influence, we noted how good ethical character is most at threat when power is involved. A useful way to map how this plays out with people is offered by James and Baddeley (1987).[18] They describe a four-sector model depicting people using proverbial creatures known to represent certain qualities. Hence, in teams, organisations, politics and society, one is either a stubborn donkey, innocent sheep, cunning fox or wise owl, depending on where you sit in the spectrum of integrity and influence.

A stubborn donkey reflects those who are liabilities, difficult to deal with, lack credibility and add no value. With low integrity and low influence, they are a burden that needs to be contained, reformed or moved on. Certain fringe and extreme groups that seek to promote intolerance may be considered in this group.

Innocent sheep are good, decent people who have little or no influence, and are often pawns of the powerful. They are prone to being taken advantage of, and have their goodwill abused. Some protest movements, community organisations, and even certain activists, may fall into this category.

A cunning fox is a person who is out for themselves, often at others' expense. They simply want power and influence for the sake of it (even though they may try to convince themselves and others that it is for some greater cause), and are willing to do anything it takes to get it. Hence, principles and ethics are no major object to their hunger for power. As a senior director of one of the world's biggest media channels said: *'people are capable of behaving very badly when power is involved'*.

From amongst the innocent sheep there may emerge some who become frustrated with their lack of influence, and they begin to adopt the unethical tactics and behaviours of cunning foxes in order to 'play the game', only to inadvertently become foxes themselves. Hence, they have exchanged their integrity for influence, and have allowed themselves to sell their values, when in reality it did not need to be one or the other, as both are possible.

It is hence critical to understand how to become the wise owl – one who has both integrity and influence. James and Baddeley describe them as follows:

*'Wise and highly observant, the ... owls are well placed to succeed. They differ from the (cunning) fox in that 'succeed' for them means positive outcomes for both themselves and the organisation. They use their highly developed networking and communication skills to generate support and build alliances. They can take the difficult decisions, but work hard to ensure that the outcomes are not counter-productive. Unlike the foxes, they are overt, and they demonstrate this by listening and disclosing appropriately. They are visible and approachable, yet powerful and focused.'*[19]

Thus, wise owls are ethical and values-based leaders known for their high integrity and influence – they are good people who mean business!

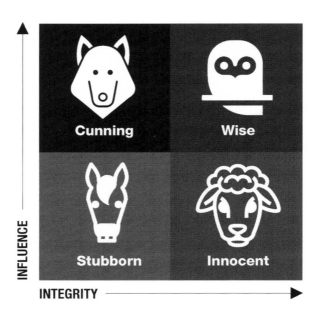

When we look at the life of the Prophet, it is apparent that he completely embodied the above description and more. He overcame powerful corrupt opposition using his political intelligence rooted in values. The battle of Hunayn discussed earlier, and the treaty of Hudaibiyah, which we will look at later, are good examples of wise owl ethical leadership in action. However, if we try to think of leaders today who fit the bill of the wise owl, we will struggle to name many. Among the few names from recent history that do, however, get recognised for being ethical and influential leaders are Nelson Mandela, Mahatma Ghandi, Martin Luther King Jr, Mother Teresa and Pope John Paul. However, it is notable that none of these names are alive today. Among those still alive who also are viewed by many globally as ethical leaders are Jimmy Carter, Justine Trudeau, Desmond Tutu, Dr Rowan Williams, Thuli Madonsela and Jacinda Ardern.

Among contemporary Muslims, some who are considered by many as being wise owl ethical leaders are Muhammad Ali, Malcolm X, Rachid Ghannouchi, Anwar Ibrahim, King Faisal Ibn Saud and Recep Tayyip Erdogan. Also, Ambassador Ebrahim Rasool, Dr Hany El Banna, Dr Muhammad Abdul Bari, Sharif H. Banna and many others are worthy of note for their principled leadership and societal contribution.

It is worth looking at their example to consider how they have navigated a complex world and exerted influence while maintaining integrity.

There are, of course, lesser known leaders whose daily acts of honesty and integrity form the foundation of good leadership, but they are not easy to find. It is rare to find examples like that of a Malaysian chief minister, Nik Aziz, who once had his private road renovated by chance during general infrastructure work but went out of his way to pay for it, as he did not want to gain personal benefit from a state project just because he was a chief minister. He was also known to be disciplined about not using his government vehicle for personal use, among other such ethical choices.

There is desperate need for more people to emerge like the above, and offer ethical leadership in a world where other leaders have failed.

## INFLUENCING SKILLS OF AN ETHICAL LEADER

The wise owl ethical leader is not just a person of integrity and a 'nice guy', but most certainly a person of influence too. There is a need for good people to actively develop themselves and become influencers, as the only thing needed for evil to prevail is for good people to do nothing. And even when good people try to do something, if they have not developed influencing and negotiating skill, they will not achieve much beyond a modest protest or an echo chamber gathering, and they certainly will not see change.

Carnegie outlines some great ways to build influence in his famous work, *How to Win Friends and Influence People.* His approach is not what one might think. He does not take the approach of 'learning how to play the game', or how to be shrewd and Machiavellian to get results, as a cunning fox would. Instead, he takes an ethical approach to influence, outlining how one can develop influence over time through an authentic and genuine engagement with people in a dignified and inspiring manner. He talks about inspiring people, building goodwill and appealing to people's good nature. This was Lincoln's approach, as he sought to unite a nation in the midst of civil war. He said:

*'We are not enemies, but friends. We must not be enemies. Though passion may have strained, it must not break our bonds of affection. The mystic chords of memory will swell*

*when again touched, as surely they will be, by the better angels of our nature.'*

True influence is when your opponents respect you. And even if they disagree with you now, later they may come round to support you, because of that respect.

Mandela was not only a great influencer, but also a smart negotiator. He made a profound point about reconciling firm principles and the need to be flexible in a negotiation situation.

He said, *'when you negotiate you must be prepared to compromise'.* But as Mandela's friend Ebrahim Rasool explained, *'compromise doesn't always mean sacrificing principles. The objective is to know the overarching goals while being pragmatic about the path towards them.'*

His influence was such that he negotiated the terms of his own release while in prison!

## NAVIGATING MORAL DILEMMAS WITH INTEGRITY

Reflecting what we have discussed so far, it may be helpful to consider a couple of scenarios in which a wise owl ethical leader may face a moral dilemma, and how they might navigate such a situation with integrity. A practical checklist will also be offered to help ethical leaders address such challenges effectively.

---

**FIRST CASE:**
*You have a long-serving employee in your team who is not performing well (which is holding the department back), but is a good, loyal and sincere person. You have given them many chances, including training and new roles, but they are still not up to the mark two years on. Your head says dismiss; your heart says keep. What will you do? How do you balance between Excellence (move them on) and Compassion (give them more chances)?*

**Answer:** Give chances beyond legal minimum and prove your integrity in the process, so that if you have to ultimately dismiss them for reasons of maintaining excellence, they will feel that they were given some chances compared to other workplaces.

---

**SECOND CASE:**

*As a humanitarian charity, you have arrived in a war-torn country to deliver aid to famine-struck villages, but the ruling militia want bribery. Do you pay to access the thousands of needy, or apply zero tolerance to bribery which may lead to the needy suffering, and possibly dying?*

**Answer:** Transparency is key. You need to make donors aware of the situation, and consult them on it before paying donor money as bribery. Also, in the end you need to break the vicious cycle. If you keep paying the militia, you maintain the system, and even though you may be accessing poor villagers, this pattern may never change. Hence, you need to break the cycle and do it with transparency and integrity.

## SOME QUESTIONS FOR LEADERS
## CONFRONTING ETHICAL DILEMMAS

Professor Dana Radcliffe, Syracuse and Cornell University, a world expert on the topic of business ethics, formulated an interesting checklist for leaders in navigating moral dilemmas. This includes asking the following questions:

- What are the foreseeable **consequences** of each action and alternative for our various stakeholders, internal and external?
- Given the potential consequences, am I (are we) truly facing an **ethical dilemma** – a choice involving conflicting stakeholder obligations?
- If so, do any of the courses of action **violate** the organisation's *defining values*?
- Among those that do not, does one **more closely align** with the obligation to pursue the organization's mission *effectively* – over the long term?
- If all of the action alternatives require **tradeoffs** among the company values or between its values and its effectiveness, which alternatives would be ***publicly defensible*** to the stakeholders?

This checklist is beneficial in navigating the ethical decision-making process, but perhaps for those driven by a deep sense of spiritual values, they might seek to explore the notion of 'divine defensibility' in addition to public defensibility. To take the right ethical decision is not only determined by what can be publicly defended, but also what can be justified in an theo-ethical framework by attempting to answer the question: 'what would God want us to do?' The answer might be the same or similar to what was reached through a public defensibility reasoning, but space should be accommodated for spiritual reasoning.

---

**To be a wise owl you must:**

- Nurture your character and **integrity**
- Build a **moral compass** and a clear conscience
- Have **public defensibility** for all your internal affairs
- Be **subservient to values**, not make values subservient to you, even when you reach the top
- Build **social and spiritual capital** by articulating shared values which are both universal and faith inspired
- **Offer ethical leadership** in a world where other leaders have failed.

---

| NAME | MUHAMMAD ALI |
| --- | --- |
| BRAND | MUHAMMAD ALI |
| LEADERSHIP QUALITY | INTEGRITY |

Considered the most famous contemporary Muslim in the world in recent times, **Muhammad Ali** was a much-loved personality. Known for his craft in the field of boxing, it was his candid and sincere persona and his ability to talk openly and frankly to anyone that won him adoration.

From his reminders about God, and his calls for being in service of others, to his role in the civil rights movement and conscientious objection to fighting in Vietnam, he was always a person of principle and open to changing his mind. Hence, when he saw how white and black men were dressed the same and equal before God during Hajj, he changed his views about white people and race. And when his Jewish friend Billy Crystal was denied entry to a gentlemen's club where Muhammad Ali used to jog, he decided never to set foot in the club again.

Ali did, of course, court controversy. Outside the ring, he had joined the Nation of Islam – a non-Sunni sect whose founder Elijah Muhammad declared himself a Prophet, and hence a person widely rejected across the Muslim world. And inside the ring, his boxing profession required flamboyance, talking down opponents about how he will defeat them easily, and all the other elements of the spectacle that constitutes boxing to this day.

However, his legacy is his open-mindedness. In a 2004 autobiography, Ali attributed his conversion to mainstream Sunni Islam to Warith Deen Muhammad, who assumed leadership of the Nation of Islam upon the death of his father Elijah Muhammad, and persuaded the Nation's followers to become adherents of mainstream Sunni Islam.[20]

Ali had gone on the Hajj pilgrimage to Mecca in 1972, which inspired him in a similar manner to Malcolm X. Meeting people of different colours from all over the world gave him a different outlook and greater spiritual awareness.[21]

In 1977, he said that, after he retired, he would dedicate the rest of his life to getting 'ready to meet God' by helping people and charitable causes, and uniting people and helping to make peace.[22]

After the September 11 attacks in 2001, he stated that 'Islam is a religion of peace' and 'does not promote terrorism or killing people', and that he was 'angry that the world sees a certain group of Islam followers who caused this destruction, but they are not real Muslims. They are racist fanatics who call themselves Muslims.' In December 2015, he stated that 'True Muslims know that the ruthless violence of so-called Islamic jihadists goes against the very tenets of our religion', that 'We as Muslims have to stand up to those who use Islam to advance their own personal agenda', and that 'political leaders should use their position to bring understanding about the religion of Islam, and clarify that these misguided murderers have perverted people's views on what Islam really is.'[23]

When looking at the above legacy, it is not difficult to see why Muhammad Ali was a person of integrity and principle.

## TIPS　HOW TO STRENGTHEN YOUR INTEGRITY

- Make time to nurture your character, build your moral compass and cultivate a clear conscience. The works of Imam Ghazali, in particular his magnum opus – the *Ihya Ulumuddin* (Revival of the Islamic Sciences) offers one of the best outlines on personal character development, drawing on deep insights from the Quran, the Sunnah of the Prophet and the early generation of scholars.

- Identify and note your five main personal values, and live up to them. Practice what you preach, as people will swiftly notice any discrepancies. Be **subservient to Islamic values**, not make values subservient to you, even when you reach the top. Do not make reference to values as cover for an ulterior motive that you do not wish to share, as this risks your integrity.

- Ensure **public defensibility** for all your internal affairs. Hence, be prepared for your internal meetings and minutes to be made public, then you will be more careful of your actions.

- Increase your self-disclosure to become more transparent. In some innovative companies, all staff including management have their exact current salaries published and available for all to see. Greater transparency leaves less room for hearsay and negative perception and increases trust.

- Welcome scrutiny and governance of your affairs and increase accountability. Consider if your organisation has an ethics/values committee and an audit committee to hold you and the executive to account. For charities and NFPs, a well-functioning and competent trustee board is critical, and there should exist a healthy and honest relationship with the executive leaders.

- *Taqwa* ultimately builds integrity. Studying about God leads to awareness of Him and fear/hope of Him – this is *taqwa*, and leads to honest behaviour and 'divine defensibility'.

- Fast regularly outside of Ramadan. It also builds integrity as you prove to God you are worshipping for him, as it is a form of worship that is not visible to man.

■ Recommended reading: In addition to the Sirah and classical works, read about contemporary leaders of integrity such as Mandela and Malcolm X, to inspire yourself to strengthen your integrity while pursuing influence.

CHAPTER 2

# COMPETENCE

For any leader or leadership framework to be credible, competence is without doubt a foundational quality. An organised, focused, timely and driven leader who has a reputation for delivery is the hallmark of competence, and this inspires confidence among followers and stakeholders. We expect a competent leader to have a vision, be strategic minded, and able to take decisions even when the choices are difficult. We expect them to be driven towards professionalism and excellence.

## THE PROPHET ON WORK AND COMPETENCE

The Prophet made the following noteworthy statements:

> 'Verily God has prescribed ihsan (excellence) in all things.' (Muslim)

> 'He whose two days are equal (in accomplishment) is a sure loser!' (Daylami)

> 'God loves a servant who when performing a task does so with perfection.' (Bayhaqi)

*'God loves to see His servants tired having done an honest day's work.' (Daylami)*

The exhortation to excel is clear, the drive to be better today than yesterday and better tomorrow than today is at the heart of the Prophetic narration. Indeed, being hard-working and exhausted after a day's work is praiseworthy in the sight of God, and competence cannot be gained without hard work.

In more specific terms, the Prophet said concerning competence:

*'Whoever delegates a position to someone when he sees that someone else is more competent, then surely he has cheated...' (Al-Hakim)*

Hence, a meritocratic approach, and the empowering through delegation of a talented and capable person of leadership potential is apparent. We already noted that in the Quranic story about Musa we find the following verse:

*'One (of the two women) said, "Oh father, hire him for surely the best person to hire is one who is strong (competent) and trustworthy."' (28:26)*

Again, competence was among the most apparent and highlighted qualities of one of our great leaders and Prophets.

## COMPETENCE IN THE SIRAH

When we consider the greatest leader and Prophet, we see how he demonstrated skills in key tasks that require competent execution. His skills were diverse and included: people management skills, diplomacy and management of peace and treaties, military strategy, swordsmanship, education and people development, equestrian skills, negotiating treaties, construction (helped build his mosque in Medina), business and trade, communication skills and public speaking (indeed he was known as having the quality of *jawami al-kalim* – *i.e. succinct yet deeply meaningful speech*), and the list goes on. He was even skilled in many domestic duties at home, such as cooking and sewing.

The Prophet's competence and ability to problem solve was apparent even before his prophethood. When he was about 35, the Quraysh decided to renovate the Ka'ba, and in doing so had to remove the black stone. A dispute arose among the tribes over who would have the right to place the black stone back into its correct place. This dispute continued for four days, and became so heated there was a risk of a brawl. On the fifth day, the oldest chief there, Umayy Ibn Mughairah, proposed that whoever was the first to enter the Ka'ba the next day should be accepted as the judge to decide on the black stone.

The next day, that person happened to be Muhammad, and the chief cried '*al-amin* has come!' After the chief assigned him to adjudicate, the Prophet laid his cloak down, placed the black stone on it, then invited all the chiefs to hold a corner of the cloak. They then all enjoyed the honour of taking the black stone to the Ka'ba, and Muhammad completed the task by placing it up on the southeast side of the Ka'ba. Hence, the Prophet was able to manage the situation effectively and solve the problem without conflict.[1]

Muhammad had not only built a reputation for honesty, but also of competence. His capability and trustworthiness were the reasons why lady Khadija hired him to trade on her behalf. He showed a lot of skill and professionalism, which eventually impressed Khadija so much she proposed to Muhammad and soon they were married.[2]

From tradesman and then persecuted preacher, he successfully progressed to statesman and a Prophet with growing power and following. His statesmanship was impressive, from his ability to appoint suitable leaders to his development of the first constitution in Medina, which formed the basis of a multicultural and multi-religious state.

The constitution promoted equality, fairness and justice, protection of the weak, ensured freedom of religious belief, forbad bloodshed, forbad war declarations without Prophetic authorisation, and outlined an inclusive consultative process on key state matters such as foreign policy. This inclusiveness included Muslims and non-Muslims including the Jewish tribes of Medina. Indeed, the constitution specified that 'no Jew will be wronged for being a Jew' and will be treated as one community with the Muslims. This common community was to coexist in peace and share in the good and bad times, in ease and in hardship.[3] Although the period of Medina was a time of growing strength and capability compared to the incapacity of the Muslims during their persecution in Mecca, they regularly faced major challenges as a city state. They had to face down those who would wage war, attempt to invade and seek to wipe out the fledging Muslim community. From the battle of Badr to Uhud and Khandaq, the Prophet showed great leadership capability, military competence and determination.

Towards the latter years of his time in Medina, his negotiating position strengthened, which he smartly leveraged in the famous treaty of Hudaybiyah (which will be explored further in coming chapters). His competent handling of the whole process eventually led to the broadly peaceful conquest of Mecca: an astonishing achievement to take the city at the centre of the aggression towards him, without needing to even wage war. He combined his competence with his values, and hence did not seek vengeance after taking Medina but invited all to live with freedom and in peace.

One of the hallmarks of a competent and professional person is the way their manage their time. The Prophet was known for being very disciplined about his time, and encouraged his followers to use their time productively. For many people 'time is money', but as the Prophet taught, 'time is life itself', hence if you waste time you are wasting your precious life.

The example of the five daily prayers is noteworthy. Even without clocks or alarms, the Muslims were taught to keep a sharp eye on the time, especially for prayer. They were taught how to use the position of the sun to determine the time of day, and advised by the Prophet to pray on time. With all the gadgets and gizmos of today, time management remains challenging for many.

The Prophet relayed the Quranic verse saying that believers are *'those who avoid vain talk'*, and would discourage useless chit chat and gossip. He would warn people about taking their free time for granted, as one day it will disappear.

## COMPETENT SUCCESSORS

The Prophet once said: *'a strong believer is better than a weak believer.'(Muslim)* This applies to physical, intellectual and professional strength. When we seek strong candidates, we seek competent people.

Being a competent and strong leader is one thing, but developing other competent leaders and successors is another. The world may have many of the former but very few of the latter. The Prophet was a true *murabbi* – one who holistically nurtures and develops people. This includes not just their competence but crucially also their character. Indeed, the human resource community today know well that in addition to skillset one needs good mindset. It is not just about aptitude, but attitude. This comprehensive approach to competence and leadership development was the Prophetic hallmark.

He was also known for appointing leaders based on competence. His preference of Abu Bakr to lead prayers when he could not, and indeed to ultimately succeed him as leader, had a lot to do with Abu Bakr's clear competence as a worthy and able leader. Khalid bin Waleed had built a reputation as a capable military leader having demonstrated skills in warfare management, and hence was given many duties in this regard despite the reservations of some of the companions who were senior to Khalid. Bilal Al Habashi had a beautiful voice, and hence was suitable to be appointed the first muezzin. Ja'afar ibn Abi Talib possessed strong diplomatic and communication skills, and hence was sent as a representative and spokesman to Abyssinia. Mus'ab ibn Umayr demonstrated qualities as a gifted teacher and hence was sent to Medina for educational purposes. Muadh ibn Jabal was sent to Yemen for similar reasons, especially his competence to apply good judgement and *ijtihad* (intellectual exertion and analysis). Salman al-Farsi was known for his insights into strategy, and hence was consulted on matters related to warfare. Hassan Ibn Thabit was a competent poet, and was assigned as the Prophet's personal poet, reciting poetry even from the pulpit of the Prophet.

This quality of competency is also evident in many stories from the Prophet's life, notable amongst them is his advice to a companion of his, Abu Dhar al-Ghifari, who once asked the Prophet: *'Will you not appoint me to public office?'* The Prophet stroked his shoulder and replied: *'Abu Dhar, you are weak and authority is a trust. And on the Day of Judgment it is a cause of disgrace and remorse except for one who fulfils its obligations and properly discharges its duties.'* (Muslim)

Abu Dhar also narrates how the Prophet once said to him: *'I see you to be a weak man. I love for you what I love for myself. Don't ever find yourself in a position where you are in charge of two people. And don't ever be entrusted with the wealth of an orphan.'* (Muslim)

Here the Prophet is not undermining nor belittling Abu Dhar, but rather pointing out the need for competency in leadership. Sincerity and good intention alone are not sufficient.

The importance of competent people was something all the Caliphs valued. Umar once said to his companions: *'Wish for something.'*

Someone said: *'I wish that this place were filled with gold so I could spend it for the sake of Allah.'*

Someone else said: *'I wish it were filled with pearls, ornaments, and jewels so I could spend them for the sake of Allah and give them in charity.'*

Umar then said: *'I wish it were filled with men like Abu Ubaydah b. al-Jarrah, Muadh b. Jabal, Salim and Hudhayfah b. al-Yaman!'*

## ACTION CENTRED LEADERSHIP – THE ACL™ FRAMEWORK FOR COMPETENT LEADERS

A competent and effective leader is, according to Adair, one who provides comprehensive oversight in relation to three areas – task, team and individual. Adair outlines this simple yet profound model[4] as follows:

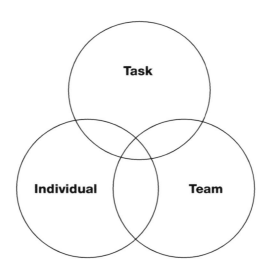

Hence, a competent leader will ensure everyone understands the task (goals, objectives, targets, deliverables, timeframes, lead persons etc). They will ensure the team is cohesive, balanced and work-ing effectively together. And they will ensure each unique individual is taken care of, whether that is supporting their personal needs, re-warding them with fair remunerations and opportunities, or generally keeping an eye on their wellbeing.

The design of the three-circle diagram is important as it shows interdependency. Hence, if one circle is neglected, the other circles are incomplete and cannot fully be realised. Tasks cannot be fully achieved, nor a team fully energised, if some individuals are neglect-ed. Happy individuals will not ensure good teamwork is taking place. A great team environment will not guarantee the job (task) gets done.

Hence, a competent leader must have performance accountability systems in place to ensure that tasks are on track, they should have regular team away days, develop trust and bonds, and swiftly resolve disputes amicably where they arise. And they should have regular one-to-ones to ensure each individual is happy, engaged and thriving.

## THE HELICOPTER VIEW
Once the above three areas are being supported, the leader should step away and create space for their people to perform and succeed. Leaders should not be micromanagers, but empowering agents who facilitate people to succeed. But after stepping away, the leader should not forget about the three areas, but instead take a 'helicopter view', as Adair advised. This oversight and bird's eye view is to ensure the task, team and individual areas are thriving. Where signs emerge that one of the areas is struggling, the helicopter should come down, intervene, take corrective action, then hover back up. A competent leader's life is hence a process of hovering up and down as needed, and this, according to Adair, will deliver results.

## COMPETITIVE EDGE
One of the linguistic connections of the competent is one who can compete and has the capability to be competitive. If your calibre is such that you can compete with other talented people, you are clear-ly competent. It is worth reflecting on how many areas and fields of expertise Muslims are truly competent and competitive in today. The reality is not very encouraging.

When we look at how the prophetic leadership foundations set in motion centuries of research, innovation and creativity, and the subsequent emergence of great civilisations and world-leading scholars in all major fields of science, from Ibn Sina and Ibn Al Haytham to Al Khawarizmi and Al Kindi, it soon dawns on us that reminiscing about our great ancestors will do little to change our current condition of uncompetitiveness.

There is therefore a need for us to find in us the drive and ambition (*himma*) necessary to build one's competence. Ibn al-Qayyim once said: *'Ambition is the seed from which all growth of nobleness proceeds'.* Indeed, it is something from which great leadership can proceed.

Competence development requires a continuous learning attitude and a continuous improvement philosophy. The Prophet hence gave the following pieces of advice:

> *'Seeking knowledge is obligatory upon all Muslims.'* (Ibn Majah)

> *'Pursue knowledge even (if all the way) to China, for its pursuit is the sacred duty of every Muslim.'* (Ibn Abdul Barr)

We also know that one of the *maqasid* (higher objectives of Islamic law) is to preserve the intellect, hence signifying its great importance. Learning and competence development is one of the main things that makes us human in contradistinction to other animals and creatures.

The leading nations in the world are not only politically or economically advanced, but also educationally advanced. There is a clear correlation between them and where the top educational institutions are based. These are nations where personal and professional development is a multi-billion-dollar industry, and where the most talent, expertise and competence can be found.

The equivalent of such a leading nation was the great Andalusian civilisation in what is now known as Spain and Portugal. But few Muslim-majority nations come anywhere near such standing in the world today. If you look at the top 100 universities in the world, there is effectively none from the Muslim world. If you consider the largest and most successful companies in the world, or the biggest brands, hardly any hail from Muslims or the Muslim world. From the cars we drive, and the planes we fly, to the phones we love and the laptops we use, the Muslim imprint is unfortunately minimal.

The world's biggest brand, Apple, has primarily been in computing, but few know that the origin of algorithms (which make the computing field possible) is the great 9th century Muslim scholar Al Khwarizmi, known as the father of Mathematics and Algebra. His legacy lives on thanks to his competence and contribution. The word 'algebra' originates from his book *Hisab al Jabr wal Muqabala*. His very name, Al Khwarizmi, is the root for the word 'algorithm'.

Inspired by the Prophet's leadership and legacy, many other great and competent scholars, thinkers, and leaders emerged throughout Islamic history, whose legacy lives on. This includes Ibn Al Haytham, the father of optics, whose discovery still forms the basis of the modern camera, and Ibn Sina, whose research was the basis for the study of medicine for centuries. To this day, if you go to the Bodleian Library at the University of Oxford, you will find such historic Arabic textbooks by such scholars.

The absence of the same drive for competence and excellence as these ancient Muslim greats explains in large part why the most successful leaders and organisations in the world are non-Muslim. As an indicator, a glance at some of the world's biggest brands, and the handful of companies that own them, paints quite a picture.

## WORLD'S MAJOR FOOD AND CAR BRANDS AND WHO OWNS WHO

Aside from a meagre few companies, such as Proton of Malaysia, it is apparent where the rest of the organisations hail from. *Forbes* magazine once published an article about *The Four Companies That Control the 147 Companies That Own Everything.*[5] This state of affairs may well exist because of many factors, including unethical behaviours of individuals, unfair practices of companies and undemocratic collusions of government. One might even talk of a post-colonial legacy that has contributed to some countries becoming developed and others remaining underdeveloped.

But while ethical questions should be asked, one thing is clear, you cannot get to the top without competence. You cannot have impact without effective skills. And you cannot raise standards without an absolute drive for excellence.

World's Major Food Brands and Who Owns Who

World's Major Car Brands and Who Owns Who

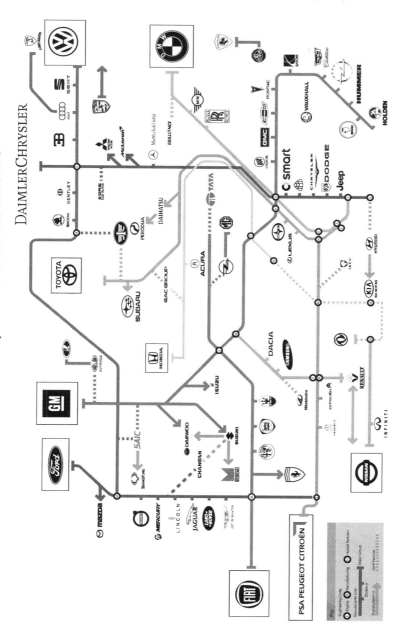

Emergent ethical and Muslim leaders should take up the task to revive the intellectual and industrious spirit of our history and produce world-class competent professionals who add significant value to their organisations, society and the wider world.

## COMPETENCE AND SPECIALISM

In addition to generalist ideas on competence, one needs to consider the unique requirements of one's sector or role, and what qualities and skills are necessary in order to excel. If working in the technological field, innovation and creativity are critical, but if working in accounting, creativity may not be a helpful skill, whereas numeracy, attention to detail and a compliance mindset are more relevant in order to be competent.

However, it is important to note that a leader does not have to be the most technically competent or foremost specialist in everything in their organisation compared to their followers. A respectable degree of expertise is needed, no doubt, but the leader is the one who can get the best out of everyone else. They can have the foremost experts and specialists around them to draw on.

## COMPETENCE WITH A BIG 'C'

Although we have framed competence as a matter of skill and capability (hence, 'competence with a small c'), rather than a deep philosophical notion of values and human qualities that can be projected in the form of leadership qualities (hence, 'Competence with big C'), I would argue that the divine notion of '*al Qawi*' allows, even compels us to view 'Competence' as inherently worthy of being a leadership quality.

When we consider Prophetic leadership in practice, we noted how the Sirah is replete with the Prophet demonstrating a deep commitment to being competent, keen to place the right people in the right role, and was himself deeply committed to being good at a wide range of skills that demand excellence in execution.

From people management and development skills, military strategy, swordsmanship, equestrian skills, treaty negotiations, construction of his mosque in Medina, business and trade, communication skills, and even domestic duties at home, such as cooking and sewing, the Prophet showed the world what Prophetic leadership in practice meant.

| | |
|---|---|
| **NAME** | SHEIKH MOHAMMED BIN RASHID AL MAKTOUM |
| **BRAND** | DUBAI |
| **LEADERSHIP QUALITY** | COMPETENCE |

With the appointment in October 2017 of Omar Sultan Al Olama[6] as the world's first Minister of State for Artificial Intelligence, the Ruler of Dubai, **Sheikh Mohammed bin Rashid Al Maktoum** made a big statement to the world.

It is the only Muslim country globally that has been viewed along-side Silicon Valley in the US, Tech City in the UK, and others as a major global player in the digital and tech space. And that is quite an accomplishment.

Dubai generally, is also the only country in the Middle East that has simplified bureaucracy, and made it incredibly easy to do business in. It is possible to fly into Dubai and within a matter of days set up a business and bank account.

The city has hence been attracting global talent for many years now, and continues to welcome talented and competent professionals from diverse backgrounds from the Muslim world, and indeed the wider world.

From an almost barren desert in the 1990s to a fully functioning global business hub that is shaping the future of AI, in addition to becoming the centre of innovation in multiple other fields, including the Islamic Economy (with due acknowledgement to Malaysia as the long term centre of Halal Industry and Islamic Finance), Dubai has shown what competence and professionalism can achieve for a people, and is hence deserving of recognition under this particular leadership quality.

Under the leadership of Sheikh al-Maktoum, the Dubai International Airport was constructed, developing Dubai as an international aviation hub and tourist attraction. In 2006, he launched Dubai Aerospace Enterprise (DAE), a global aerospace manufacturing and services corporation with $15 billion investments. In 201, he announced the launch of a $1 million global award and the establishment of the UAE Water Research Agency to find sustainable solutions to water scarcity across the world. In 2015, Sheikh al-Maktoum launched the Arab Reading Challenge, a competition with $3 million in prizes to get 1 million Arab children to read 50 million books. In 2017, he launched the Humanitarian Accelerators, a first of its kind initiative in the Arab world, which aims to attract skilled professionals to the humanitarian sector.

Sheikh Mohammed Bin Rashid al-Maktoum writes: *'With each new day in Africa, a gazelle wakes up knowing he must outrun the fastest lion or perish. At the same time, a lion stirs and stretches, knowing he must outrun the fastest gazelle or starve. It is no different for the human race. Whether you consider yourself a gazelle or a lion, you simply have to run faster than others to survive.'*

The transformation of Dubai is a testimony to Sheikh al-Maktoum's incredible commitment to competence and excellence. He once said: *'Whoever convinces himself that he is not worthy of first position has doomed himself to failure from the very beginning.'*

# TIPS HOW TO DEVELOP YOUR COMPETENCE

- Overcome your laziness. Raise your standards and what you demand of yourself. Regularly repeat the supplication: *'Allhuma inni 'awzubika minal kasl (O Allah, protect me from laziness).*
- Have *Himma* (High Ambition). Ibn al-Qayyim said: *'Ambition is the seed from which all growth of nobleness proceeds.'* Build your ambition and drive to achieve something; be industrious to get good at one thing. Push and practice; feel the pain; get comfortable with pain. A bit of pressure is healthy (although stay balanced, as excessive stress is unhealthy).
- Remember, *'we are all better than we know, if only we can be made to realise this, we would never again settle for anything less.'*
- Improve your planning and learn to prioritise. Failing to plan is planning to fail. Adopt a diary, and plan each day and week in advance. Then build up to planning your months and years (recognising that long-term planning may need flexibility and adjusting, but still sets one on a course to perform well).
- Quality training and development interventions help build competence. Attend a quality programme on personal effectiveness. Examples include performance and time management courses, as well as comprehensive Leadership Development Programmes (LDPs).
- Self-awareness is an important step in training, but it is not enough; one needs to do something about that awareness and find practical ways to actually change oneself and one's behaviours.
- Training is valuable, but there is no better source of competence development than practical experience. Get more of it, in terms of depth and breadth, by offering to take on new and challenging tasks in your workplace, or seeking a new role which will develop and grow your capabilities.
- Gain exposure to top people (shadow them), top educational institutions (access or attend courses), top companies and organisations (apply there, shadow or review them). Be with the best to become the best. Go beyond best practice, instead aim to set best practice standards for others.

- Be passionate about your field and be driven to get good at it through learning and practice. Be curious and have a can-do attitude: right attitude will build aptitude; right mindset will build skillset. You have to want something bad enough otherwise you will not do what it takes to deliver and succeed.

- Research shows that leadership and competence is 80% nurture and 20% nature. Hence, the onus is on you to work hard and make it count. Limiting our potential by claiming our lack of natural ability is a weak excuse.

- Realise that not only is life short, your prime is much shorter. For young professionals, count your years leading to 40 and seek to accomplish something significant before then. For senior experienced professionals above 40, count your blessings for the extended life that God has given and delay no further in pursuing worthy goals now that you are in 'extra time', before your health really restricts you.

- Remember the advice of the Prophet to be aware of five before five – *'our health before sickness, our youth before old age, our life before death...' (Al-Hakim).*

- Remember, *'God doesn't change a condition of a people until they change what is in themselves'* (13:11). Until we change something about the way we live life, little will improve. Einstein said that his definition of insanity was to do the same things over and over again and expect different results. Let us not be insane!

- Recognise that changing oneself and getting competent involves four stages: *unconscious incompetence* then *conscious incompetence* then *conscious competence*, and finally *unconscious competence.* Work your way through that process, taking feedback, getting training, practising the skill and gaining experience until you get so good at your chosen endeavour it becomes second nature.

- Recommended reading: *'The Four Companies That Control the 147 Companies That Own Everything'* by Brendan Coffey

# CHAPTER 3
# VISION

A vision is an aspirational idea of what an individual or organisation would like to achieve or accomplish in the long-term future. It is intended to serve as a simple, clear, high-level guide on where one wishes to go, and what kind of world one wishes to help create.

The fundamental significance of this quality in leadership is quite apparent. It is often viewed as among the most important of qualities. Indeed, by definition a leader is one who seeks to take a group of people to a destination, hence the idea of a vision, goal and end game is implicit in the meaning of leadership. A leader without a clear vision will soon run into trouble, and struggle to lead meaningfully, leaving their organisation and people confused about direction and frustrated with the lack of progress.

Not only do leaders need clear visions, but they must excel above their followers in this quality, and have the capacity to see and articulate that which others may not be capable of. The noted leader and spiritual thinker Khurram Murad said: '*Leadership is the ability to see beyond assumed boundaries, and to come up with solutions or paths that few can visualise. The leader must then project this vision for everyone to see and pursue*'.

It is thus widely considered as something essential, whether as a personal life vision, an organisational vision or a leader needing to be visionary in order to succeed. Many people will be drawn to leaders and organisations because of their vision and mission.

However, one may still wonder why a vision is viewed as being so important and whether it really makes much of a difference, or is just a nice thing to have. Let us consider two examples – The Royal Navy of Britain and Coca Cola.

The Royal Navy decided to set the vision 'Britannia rules the waves'. It was a bold vision, and one that was pursued seriously. Parking its problematic history as a colonial power for a moment, the result was that Britain became a vast empire whose influence was at one point second to none. It dominated the seas for centuries, especially in the latter part of its era, between the 17th century and the 19th century, symbolised perhaps most notably by their victory in the battle of Trafalgar in 1815 under the leadership of the famed Admiral Nelson, who effectively ended the Napoleonic Wars. And while the empire is no more, Britain remains one of the world's most influential nations. Indeed, English is the world's main language, and time itself is measured from the GMT baseline (note: Greenwich was the Royal Navy HQ during the days of empire).

Coca Cola is, at the end of the day, simply a beverage. One would not expect a fizzy drink to warrant much by way of a vision. However, its president in the 1920s set the vision 'anytime, anywhere, always Coca Cola'. They envisioned themselves as the company that would, in their words, 'hydrate the world'. We see that implemented today – now as one of the world's biggest brands, the number 1 drink in almost every country, the 84th largest economy (ahead of Costa Rica), and owning some 500 off-shoot drink brands, from the well-known Sprite, to Dasani – a popular still water in Saudi Arabia which many mistake for a local brand. With more than 1.9 billion servings daily in over 200 countries, they are effectively 'hydrating' a quarter of the planet!

While many factors may explain the success of the above organisations, it is clear that vision is one of them – a fundamental leadership quality, and one that sets course for any enterprise that wants to have national or global impact.

One of the deeper reasons why vision can be so powerful is because of its ability to fulfil people's innate desire to have a purpose in life. According to noted motivation researcher Dan Pink,[1] the things that drive people include *mastery, autonomy* and ultimately *purpose*. We can recognize this within Islamic notions of *fitra*,[2] where our need for a purpose in life is divinely created and ordained.

Hence, when people find their sense of purpose through a vision, they will be driven to work hard for that vision. However, it is possible for a person to propose a vision that does not appeal to many people, or for followers not to find their purpose in it. This is why the best visions are those which connect with people at a deeper emotional level, especially their values and things they deeply care about. It is hence important to have universal values shaping one's vision, in order for it to have wider appeal.

## FROM VISION TO STRATEGY

Many leadership frameworks in relation to strategic visioning start with a vision, then a mission, then values, then strategy, followed by detailed action plans backed by key performance indicators (KPIs), timeframes and so on. However, a more powerful argument is to start with universal values, which then shape a desirable vision, which is then followed by mission, strategy and action plans. This is illustrated on the following page (see page 90).

Let us briefly consider what is meant by strategy, particularly in an organisational context. According to Johnson and Scholes, the definition is as follows:

> '*Strategy is the direction and scope of an organisation over the long-term: which achieves advantages for the organisation through its configuration of resources within a challenging environment, to meet the needs of markets and to fulfil stakeholder expectations.*'

Many compare strategy to a game of chess. It is about considering one's options and context comprehensively, and then pursuing one's vision in the smartest way possible.

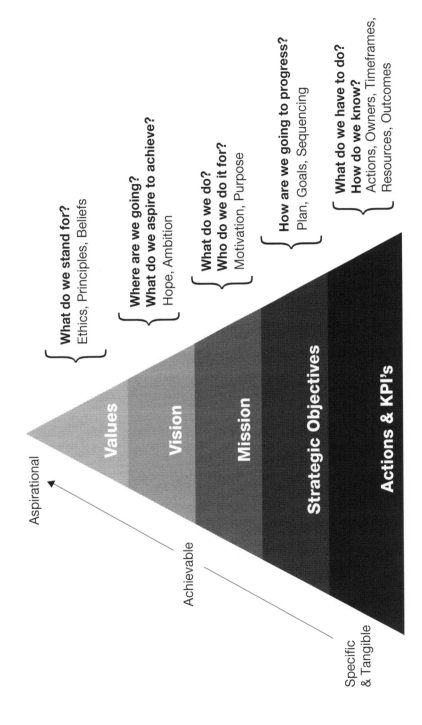

Its about asking important questions, such as: Where are we now? Where are we going? Where do we want to be? How do we get there? And how will we know if we are getting there? Each of these are elaborated in the table below, mapping out strategic actions and interventions associated with each visioning step:

| VISION-ING STEP | ACTION | DESCRIPTION |
|---|---|---|
| STEP 1: Where are we now? | Self Assessment and Evaluation | Review history, records, data; Conduct SWOT & PESTEL analysis |
| STEP 2: Where are we going? | Trends Analysis | Gather trend info and futurist data; Determine possible future scenarios |
| STEP 3: Where do we want to be? | Vision Statement (and Values exercise) | Map out personal and organisational values.Then identify your desired future and the world you wish to create. Use these to shape a vision statement |
| STEP 4: How do we get there? | Mission and Action Plan | Breakdown vision, into three or more mission statements which are about 'how' you will pursue the vision. Determine actions and deliverables that support vision and mission statements |
| STEP 5: Are we getting there? | Implement and Monitor | Ensure there is an implementation plan, and a system to monitor performance regularly, with a mechanism to address any road blocks. |

A detailed engagement of the above will help leaders formulate a powerful vision and strategy, increasing their chances of achieving their goals.

## VISION AND STRATEGY IN THE SIRAH

The Prophet was a man of singular vision and drive. He was a person of focus and determination. It is said that he always looked like he was busy and active in doing something. He moved with purpose and was cognisant of the Quranic question that presents itself to all of us:

*'So, where are you going?' (81:26)*

This divine call questions our direction in life. Where are we headed? What is our purpose in life? What is the end game? The life and leadership of the Prophet stands as a response to the Quranic inquiry, and offers mankind a way to find their own personal and professional vision and direction in life.

The life of Muhammad prior to prophethood was already purposeful and had a sense of direction. He was known for his honesty, helpfulness and desire to make a difference. When the time for revelation and prophethood came, his life and leadership would be shaped by a divine vision and mission.

Aisha the wife of the Prophet narrates this moment:

*'The beginning of the Revelation that came to the Messenger of Allah was good dreams; he never saw a dream but it came true like bright daylight. Then seclusion was made dear to him, and he used to go to the cave of Hira and worship there, which means that he went and devoted himself to worship for a number of nights before coming back to his family to collect more provisions, then he would go back again.*

*Then he would go back to Khadija to collect more provisions. (This went on) until the truth came to him suddenly when he was in the cave of Hira'. The angel came and said, 'Read!' The Messenger of Allah said, 'I cannot read.' He said: Then he took hold of me and squeezed me until I could not bear it any more then he released me and said, 'Read!' I said, 'I cannot read.' He took hold of me and squeezed me a second time until I could not bear it any more, then he released me and said, 'Read!' I said, 'I cannot read.' He took hold of me and squeezed me a third time until I could not bear it any more, then he released me and said,*

*'Read! In the Name of your Lord Who has created (all that exists).*

*He has created man from a clot*

*Read! And your Lord is the Most Generous.*

*Who has taught by the pen.*

*He has taught man that which he knew not.'*

*(al-Alaq 96:1–5)*

*Then the Messenger of Allah went back with his heart beating wildly, until he came to Khadija and said, 'Cover me! Cover me!' She covered him till he calmed down. Then he said to Khadija, 'O Khadija, I fear for myself,' and he told her what had happened. Khadija said, 'Nay, be of good cheer, for by Allah, He will never disgrace you. You uphold the ties of kinship, speak truthfully, help the poor and destitute, serve your guests generously and assist those who are stricken by calamity.'*

Here we find the earliest lessons in Islam, which are at the heart of the Prophetic vision and mission. The divine revelation was a call to submit to the one and only God Almighty and this is at the heart of the prophetic vision. However, Khadija's response also offers insight into Islam's early mission. The Prophet's humanitarian credentials, dutifulness to family and friends, service to others, and honesty are highlighted as evidence of his prophethood. Khadijah did not point to any supernatural or miraculous justification, but to his integrity and moral credibility.

When divine permission for open proclamation of the vision and message of Islam came, the Prophet ascended Mount Safa and shouted: *'Ya Sabahah!'* (an Arabic expression to draw the attention of others to some danger). When the people of Makkah had gathered around him, the Prophet said to them, *'If I told you that horsemen were advancing to attack you from the valley on the other side of this mountain, will you believe me?'*. *'Yes'*, they replied, *'We have always found you truthful.;* The Prophet said:

> *'I have come as a warner to you; and if you do not heed my warning, punishment will fall upon you. I have been com- manded by God to warn you, and I cannot protect you in this world; nor can I promise you anything in the next world, unless you submit to the worship of one God.'[3]*

After this message, the Prophet asked them to save themselves by declaring that Allah was one, and that he, Muhammad, was his messenger. He tried to make them understand that if they clung to polytheism and rejected his message and divine mission, they would face Allah's punishment, but if they accepted it, there was promise of great reward.

The vision of *tawhid* or monotheism was by extension a vision for the betterment of mankind. It was a mission to end oppression and injustice in the world, and promote human rights and dignity. This meant challenging powerful people, and hence faced a negative re- sponse, including from his own uncle, Abu Lahab, who at Mount Safa retorted: *'May you perish! Have you gathered us only for this reason?'*

One of the famous occasions is the time during the Battle of the Trench when the sparks from digging the trench[4] triggered a vision of liberating great lands with the message of Islam.

When the Companions were digging the trench to defend them- selves from an advancing army, they hit a large rock which was too hard for their spades to break up. So, they sought the help of the Prophet.

He stepped forth and struck the rock three times, causing it to break; each time he struck it, bright lights and sparks flew, and in one narration it was like a bright light in the middle of a dark night. When Salman Al Farsi asked him if the lights had a significance, the Prophet said:

*'Did you (also) see that Salman? The first (light) means that God will open up for us the Yemen, the second (light is) Syria and the West, the third (light) the East.'*

Other narrations mention more specifically the Romans of Byzantium (in the West) and the Persian ruler Kisra (Chosroes) in Mada'in (in the East).[5]

It is noteworthy that the Prophet projected a vision of hope and success at a time when the Muslims were under a great siege. He was able to inspire his companions' hope with a vision that inspired them to work harder, even during tough times when many, including the Prophet, had tied stones to their stomachs to contain the feeling and pain of hunger whilst digging the trench in the strong heat. It is with the immense commitment he generated that the Muslims sure enough went on to reach and triumph in the stated lands.

All these countries were conquered just as the Prophet informed Salman. Islam spread to Yemen during the time of the Prophet, and Muad ibn Jabal was sent there to govern it and teach their people. Among the first cities to be conquered after the death of the Prophet was Ancient Syria; it was conquered with a peace treaty during the reign of Abu Bakr, as stated by Ibn Kathir. Umar continued its conquest, and conquered Persia as well. Ibn Sa'd, when speaking about the conquests of 'Umar, said, *'He conquered the entire Iraq, Azerbaijan, Al-Basra, Persia, and ancient Syria.'*

There are many other examples of visionary leadership by the Prophet. He would remind them of their spiritual goals, promise of paradise and the next life, to help them cope with the challenges of this life. He developed long-term orientated followers, and encouraged them to organise their lives in line with the Prophetic vision and divine guidance.

## STRATEGY

In pursuit of the Prophetic vision, the Messenger and his companions would apply themselves to consider the best strategies and approaches. When the Prophet and Abu Bakr escaped Mecca to avoid the Quraysh's murderous plans, they knew they would be pursued. Hence, they took the strategy to escape via an unexpected route not normally taken to Yathrib (later Medina). This threw the pursuers off, and made it harder for them to catch up with the Prophet.

During the Battle of Badr, on advice from his companion Hubab al Jamuh, he positioned his troops near the last available well to the enemy, thereby cutting off their supply and ensuring his companions were hydrated in the searing heat of the desert. This offered some much-needed advantage at a time when they were outnumbered and 'outgunned' by the enemy.[5]

During the Battle of the Trench, when the Prophet discussed preparations with his companions, Salman Al Farsi stood and said: *'O Messenger of God, in Persia when we feared an attack on horse, we would surround ourselves with a trench'.*[6] The Prophet liked the suggested strategy and adopted it, mobilising his companions to commence the digging process in the exposed areas north of the city. This strategy proved highly effective, managing to halt the advance of the enemy.

## FORESIGHT AND STRATEGY AT HUDAIBIYAH

A visionary leader should by implication be strategic and high minded, not narrow and petty, in approach. As Lock (2004) explains, strategy is the *'means by which an organisation continually adapts to meet the changing demands of its environment and exploits opportunities in pursuit of its core purpose – so enhancing its chances of long-term survival and success'.*

We see moves of strategic genius by the visionary Prophet, from his smart departure from Mecca by taking an unexpected route, hence throwing the Quraysh off his trail, and the innovative defence dug out during the Battle of the Trench, to the Treaty of Hudaibiyah[7] (628AD/6AH) – a masterful stroke which initially looked like a bad deal in the short term, but lead to great outcomes long term.

The Prophet had not just wandered down with the believers to try to make pilgrimage, oblivious to the hostility of the Quraysh. He knew what he was walking into. He was progressing his vision and cause – which included establishing their right to make pilgrimage, while throwing down the gauntlet to his detractors by putting them in an awkward position.

By arriving relatively unarmed, it would harm the Quraysh's reputation to attack them. With some 1,400 believers, it was a formidable group to challenge anyway. By blocking their entrance, they would send a message to the world that Mecca was no longer an open hub for pilgrimage, which was bad for business. The Prophet effectively put their legitimacy on the line, by creating a problem situation with limited options, and hence forcing them to a solution he could influence. Cornered, they would be forced to make a treaty.

The terms did not please the Muslims, given that there were clauses such as the need to turn back without making pilgrimage that year, and that any Meccan fleeing to Medina would be returned but any Medinan who chose to leave to Mecca would not be returned.

But the foresight of the Prophet was clear. The very process of forcing a treaty had projected a lot of power in the eyes of the enemy, weakening their resolve against him. He was now recognised as the leader of the state of Medina. He secured a 10-year peace agreement neutralising the hostility of the Quraysh, and enabling the Muslims to work freely to spread their message across the Arabian Peninsula. And, sure enough, their followership and alliances grew.

In the ensuing months, the Prophet strictly adhered to the treaty, being the man of integrity he was. But perhaps he anticipated that the Quraysh would falter eventually. And, sure enough, they did. One of their allied tribes, Banu Bakr, attacked and killed members of a rival tribe that was allied with the Prophet, the Banu Khuza'a. This act of aggression, using resources and support from the Quraysh, effectively breached the treaty.

The Prophet gathered his followers, now much larger in number, and made a surprise and unannounced move by surrounding Mecca. According to some narrations,[8] he projected their visibility further by instructing every follower to light a camp fire. Normally one fire was lit for some ten people, and enemies would use the fires to estimate the numbers of their opponents. This visibility approach made the Prophet's army look ten times bigger than it actually was, overwhelming and breaking the Quraysh's resolve. Eventually, they were able to simply walk into Mecca without a fight.

The strategic genius of the Prophet was complete for all to see. He was determined to avoid bloodshed in the process of victory, and he achieved this by strengthening his negotiating position, thinking long term and weakening his opponents to the point that they eventually found themselves relinquishing Mecca itself to him.

All this was a combination of astute strategic planning, and reliance on God. Planning and activism alone will not lead to success, nor will prayers in the absence of effort. As Beekun notes, strategic planning is simply 'tying our camel', and then we put trust in God known as *tawakkul*.

From the above, it is apparent that the Prophet was hands-on and action orientated with his vision, and not an armchair critic or a passive observer. This combination was critical to his success and impact. As Mandela rightly said, *'action without vision is only passing time; vision without action is merely day dreaming; but vision with action can change the world.'*

## COMMUNICATION

Related to vision and strategy is the crucial area of communication. As mentioned earlier, a leader must 'project (their) vision *for everyone to see and pursue'.*

It is also not enough to have a good vision, strategy or even a detailed action plan. A leader needs to communicate and cascade this vision to their followers, in order to build alignment, support and momentum to work for the vision. Effective communication involves clear, concise and candid delivery of one's message.

We noted earlier how the Prophet was known for the quality of *'jawami al-kalim'*, which literally means condensed or congregated speech, but its meaning is about eloquence and the ability to say a lot in a few words. The Prophet's manner of communication was always clear, direct and succinct. He would choose his words carefully and wisely. According to some scholars, he was also known to never have given a speech for more than about 20 minutes in one go. This is significant, as recent research has shown that people's attention spans wane after about 20 minutes of hearing a monologue.

## CASE STUDY

| | |
|---|---|
| **NAME** | MAHATHIR MOHAMAD |
| **BRAND** | MALAYSIA |
| **LEADERSHIP QUALITY** | VISION |

**Tun Mahathir bin Mohamad** – the Prime Minster of Malaysia – is the world's oldest stateman. At 92 and counting, he spearheaded the victory against his old party – United Malays National Organisation (UMNO) – with help of Anwar Ibrahim's Pakatan Harapan coalition, to return in 2018 as PM once again, after his previous tenure from 1981 to 2003.

Mahathir is well known as one of the pioneers of the tiger economies of Asia. A real visionary and driven leader, he was able to turn an economy that was some 80% agriculture and 20% services into one that was 80% services and only 20% agriculture, a most noteworthy achievement.

Among his contributions include the Islamic Development Bank, whose Vision 2025 was authored by him. However credit must also be given to his once Deputy Prime Minister, the talented Anwar Ibrahim, who showed great character in his many years in prison, but was also able to put his mark on visionary initiatives such as the International Islamic University of Malaysia (IIUM) and the International Institute of Islamic Thought and Civilisation (ISTAC) among others.

Together, brand Malaysia was built, offering the world visionary leadership in Islamic Finance and Halal industry and standards.

Always looking to set the nation apart economically, Mahathir considered that an automotive industry was essential to Malaysia becoming an industrial nation. His government used tariffs to support the development of the Proton as a Malaysian-made car and to limit the capital outflow of the Malaysian ringgit to foreign countries. The 2012 Proton Prevé Sapphire concept symbolised this bold move, unique in the Muslim world.

However, he was not without controversy, locking horns with the likes of Al Gore, William Cohen and Madeline Albright from the Clinton era, and was publicly critical of US foreign policy, particularly during the George W. Bush presidency.

Most notably, his declaration that 'Asians need economic growth more than civil liberties' led to much criticism from the West. And economic growth was his specialism. Indeed, during 1997, the Asian financial crisis which began in Thailand threatened to devastate Malaysia. The value of the ringgit plummeted due to currency speculation, foreign investment fled, and the main stock exchange index fell by over 75%. At the urging of the International Monetary Fund (IMF), the government cut government spending and raised interest rates, which only served to exacerbate the economic situation.

In 1998, in a controversial approach, Mahathir reversed this policy course in defiance of the IMF. He increased government spending and fixed the ringgit to the US dollar. The result confounded his international critics and the IMF. Malaysia recovered from the crisis faster than its Southeast Asian neighbours. In the domestic sphere, it was a political triumph.[9]

Mahathir's visionary streak also extended to the way he developed the infrastructure of his country. From his incredible design of the government city of Putrajaya from barren land, to the Petronas Twin Towers and the surrounding central business district in Kuala Lumpur, these were part of a symbolic testament to Malaysia's phenomenal economic evolution under Mahathir's initial 22-year rule. That visionary leader has returned, albeit this time in partnership with Anwar Ibrahim – a reunion and alliance to save a nation from corruption and a new economic crisis. His visionary leadership quality will no doubt be needed once again.

# TIPS

## HOW TO BE MORE VISIONARY AND GOALS ORIENTATED

- Reflect on your values. List what you really care about more than anything else in life. This will help you consider what kind of pursuit inspires you personally, voluntarily and professionally.

- Lou Holtz said, *'if you don't wake up each morning with a burning desire to do things, you don't have enough goals'*. Ask yourself, do you have enough goals? If not, adopt some.

- Who are your role models that you wish to emulate? Study them. They are also human and had only 24 hours in their day as well. Hence it is possible for you to also achieve great things.

- Leadership is 80% nurture and 20% nature. So do not underestimate your ability to pursue a great vision, and ask yourself what you are doing with your 80%.

- Do not be afraid to fail but also, as the visionary leaders of Google say, 'don't be afraid to succeed' as well.

- Set yourself SMART[18] goals for short and long term in order to make your vision work. This means setting goals which are specific, measurable, achievable, relevant, time bound.

- Use a tracker such as an Excel sheet to map out your goals and monitor your progress. Identify someone to meet with you once a week to review the tracker and discuss your progress.

- Have long-term goals, but also have short-term quick wins to motivate yourself to continue.

- Recruit people to your cause so you can support one another. Communicate your vision with all key stakeholders to gain support and buy-in. This includes your family, your friends, your colleagues and your 'customers'.

- Read sample visions of top organisations to find inspiration, and start thinking about your own personal vision and organisational vision.

- Reading: *See 10 Tips for Goal Setting* by Hilton Johnson.

# CHAPTER 4

# COURAGE

Aristotle called courage the first virtue, as it makes all of the other virtues possible. We usually know what the right thing to do is, but do not necessarily do it. Something stops us, perhaps fear, self-doubt or lack of confidence. Hence, we have to find it in ourselves to overcome those fears, or learn to cope with them in order to find the courage and ability to do what is right. Courage makes it easier for us to live other values and qualities.

In this sense, courage is sequentially the 'first virtue' and quality to conquer, as it opens doors to other virtues, but this is different to being first in inherent importance, which, as we have noted, was integrity and *amana*.

According to the Cambridge definition, courage is 'the *ability* to *control your fear* in a dangerous or *difficult situation*'. It is also 'to be *brave* and *confident* enough to do what you *believe* in'. This relates well to Aristotle's point about virtues.

Also acording to Webster's Dictionary courage is defined as 'mental or moral strength to venture, persevere, and withstand danger, fear, or difficulty'. Courage is the ability to act in spite of doubt or fear. Courage means accepting responsibility, being able to go against the grain, breaking traditions, reducing boundaries, and initiating change. In addition, it means pushing beyond the comfort zone, asking for what you want and saying what you think, and fighting for what you believe.

Effective leaders must have courage to see difficult situations and accept responsibility for the outcomes of decisions and actions. It is not hopefulness and not stubbornness. Leaders will work with others, but if they do not have courage to express their own ideas and feelings they would do injustice to themselves and their followers. Courage is not a typical value or principle like justice or compassion, but it is the key to unlock all the other values.

---

**In practical terms, courage can be viewed in three basic forms:**

- **TRY Courage:** The courage of initiative and action – making first attempts, pursuing pioneering efforts and stepping up to the plate when no one else is coming forward.
- **TRUST Courage:** The courage of trusting others – letting go of the need to control situations or outcomes, having faith in people, and being open to direction and change.
- **TELL Courage:** The courage of voice – raising difficult issues, providing awkward feedback and sharing unpopular opinions. It is also about being able to speak truth to power – a leadership trait found among great leadership throughout history.

---

One may find courage to do one of the above but not another, but a leader needs to learn to be courageous in all three forms. If a leader does not show courage, their followers certainly will not find motivation and self-confidence to do what is needed, and this will affect their entire enterprise being pursued.

## THE PROPHET'S COURAGE

The bravery of the Prophet was well known to his companions.

His fear was only of God, and no other. This steadfast disposition helped him through the 13 difficult years of persecution in Mecca. It is what made him lead from the front and share in the dangers with his people, unlike many of today's leaders and commanders who stand in safety while their followers face dangers alone.

Courage was necessary when the time came for him to openly declare his prophethood and message of one God. He proceeded to climb up Mount Safa to declare his message. It was customary to go there and tear your clothes off until naked to get everyone's attention, then announce an important message. The Prophet followed the basic custom but within dignified bounds, hence symbolically he only tore a limited part of his clothes.

He gained the attention of the Meccans and said: *'O people of Quraysh, were I to tell you that an army was advancing to attack you from beyond this mountain, would you believe me?'* He was essentially gauging the views of the crowd and establishing his credibility before giving his message. He needed to rely on it, as his message was not going to be easy for the Quraysh to accept.

The Quraysh replied, *'yes, why not, we have always found you truthful'*. The Prophet proceeded to declare his message, calling all to the worship of one God and to abandon their idolatry. It must have taken a lot of bravery for the Prophet to step up and announce such an unfamiliar message to the powerful Quraysh and idol-worshipping Meccans. Immediately, he was rebuked, especially by his own uncle, Abu Lahab, who began cursing and verbally abusing the Prophet. When facing abuse for your beliefs and ideas, it can be incredibly disheartening and tempting to give up. It can make one fearful of proceeding and carrying on. But the Prophet remained strong and steadfast, knowing he was on the path of truth.[1]

His courage was evident for all to see. There was once a loud and shocking sound in the middle of the night in Medina. Many were afraid to go and find out what it was, but some brave companions ventured out, to then find that the Prophet was already the first on the scene, having gone straight out to deal with the source of the noise – which happened to be an irate and disorientated horse which needed to be brought under control. The Prophet's willingness to go forth and face the challenge, whatever it may be, gave others the courage to stand strong too. He would remind them: *'Don't be afraid, don't be afraid.'*

The Prophet comforted Abu Bakr whilst they were hiding in a cave and his enemies were approaching: *'Do not grieve, indeed Allah is with us.'*

During his leadership in Medina, and within a couple of years of migration, he was faced with going to war for the first time. He was able to find the inner strength and give his companions courage, despite being under-resourced and grossly outnumbered three to one at the Battle of Badr. But courage and faith in God paid off, as they routed the enemy with minimal losses.

In one battle, at Mount Uhud, the enemy was so strong, and the fighting so fierce and overbearing, that the companions who usually try to shield the Prophet from harm actually hid behind the brave Prophet as he fought the enemy. Ali states: *'When the fighting became fierce and the two armies met, we used to seek the protection of the Prophet.'*

In the most testing times, there was none more steadfast that the Prophet. In the Battle of Hunayn, many of the companions were injured, and many also fled the battlefield, but not the Prophet. He was on his mule, and Sufyan Ibn al-Harith was holding the reins while the Prophet was calling out: *'I am truly the Prophet, I am the son of Abd al-Muttalib!'*

Many great companions were killed during the battles. Perhaps one of the hardest things a leader has to face is the death in service of his followers. What do you say to their families and next of kin? Do you begin to question your cause, and ask if all this loss is worth it? Dealing with martyrs to your cause, whether by physical death, decline in health, adverse financial effects or reputational attacks that come from character assassinations, can take tremendous psychological strength and character. The Prophet faced these challenges with faith and conviction, while constantly seeking the help of God.

On another occasion, the Prophet sought shade under a tree to take a nap, as he was tired because of a battle he had fought in, and so he hung his sword on the branch of a tree. Whilst in this state, a man from the enemy camp approached him and took his sword, and then said: *'Who can save you from me?'* The Prophet looked up to him and replied: *'Allah'*. Out of fear, the sword dropped from the man's hand and the Prophet took his sword and said to him: *'Now, who can save you from me?'*

Many other challenges came during the Medinan era, from the Battle of the Trench where Muslims were under siege, to the journey to face the Romans in Tabuk. In the hardest moments, the Prophet would find it in himself not only to be brave, but also to give his people courage and hope.

While military defence and engaging in battles no doubt take immense courage, the Prophet taught that the greatest struggle is speaking truth to a tyrant. A tyrant rules by fear and uses threats and harsh means to frighten everyone from challenging, contradicting or speaking up against them. Throughout the Prophet's life he had to face such threats, but he never wavered from speaking the truth before all, weak or powerful, benevolent king or brutal tyrant.

Not only did the Prophet lead with courage, but he also mentored a generation of courageous companions. Ali Ibn Abi Talib, his cousin, at the age of only 10 or 11 was able to display such courage as would be challenging for grown adults. Two incidents are noteworthy. The first was when once the Prophet gathered the family members of Abd al-Muttalib for dinner to explain to them his message and mission. Again, it was Abu Lahab who interrupted and ridiculed the Prophet, and the people dispersed. The Prophet invited his family once again and said: *'I know of no man in the land of Arabia who can place before his people a more excellent offer than what I now make to you. I offer you the happiness of this world and that of the next. So who will help me in my cause?'* Everybody kept silent until Ali Ibn Abi Talib came forward and said: *'My eyes are sore, my legs are weak and I am yet a child, but I will follow you and help you in this mission.'*

Ali also displayed great courage during the Prophet's migration to Medina. The Prophet had asked him to sleep in his bed so that the Quraysh would think that the Prophet was still in his house. This was at a time when the Quraysh devised a clever plot to assassinate the Prophet. For Ali to agree impersonating the Prophet sleeping in his bed at the expense of his own life no doubt displayed great courage.

The Prophet also taught a supplication which asks us to seek God's refuge from lacking courage and developing the trait of cowardice: *'O Allah, we seek refuge in You, from incapacity, laziness and cowardice…'*

Courage is not just about being fearless of death. There can often be heard a romanticised clamour towards the seeming glamour to *die* for Islam, but in today's world, courage is needed to *live* for Islam, to represent Islam, and to patiently continue with one's faith and beliefs in a balanced way during difficult times.

Many leaders in recent history were known for their courage. The famous wartime leader and former British Prime Minister Winston

Churchill said: *'Success is not final, failure is not fatal: it is the courage to continue that counts'*. He recognised that courage was needed to live on and move forward in spite of tremendous challenges.

Mandela's words in court are also noteworthy, when he said: *'I have cherished the ideal of a democratic and free society... in which all persons live together in harmony and with equal opportunities. It is an ideal I hope to live for... but if needs be, it is an ideal for which I am prepared to die.'*[2]

As Ambassador Rasool explained, Mandela understood courage in the Kantian sense of the word: courage was the perfect middle between the passivity of the coward and the recklessness of the populist. Courage was the ability to rise against evil in thoughtful ways.

| NAME | SHARIF H. BANNA MBE |
|---|---|
| BRAND | AWAKENING |
| LEADERSHIP QUALITY | COURAGE |

In the world of Islamic music, publications and art, Awakening Worldwide has stood out for some two decades as a pioneer and leader, producing the highest quality talent, music, publications and artwork, and raising standards which others seek to follow.

Led by its CEO, **Sharif H. Banna**, and three co-founders and entrepreneurs, Wali-ur Rahman, Wassim Malak and Bara Kherigi, Awakening has introduced to the global Muslim market household celebrities who have received over 40 platinum awards. These include superstars such as Maher Zain, Sami Yusuf, Hamza Namira, Harris J, Mesut Kurtis, Humood and Raef among others. Starting from a small bedroom in Swansea, Awakening now has offices in five countries and operates in over 120 countries. Multinational brands such as Vodafone, BP, Mercedes and Universal Music have worked with Awakening in the past

Content produced by Awakening is now the most popular Muslim media content online – with over 7.8 billion[3] views on YouTube and 56 million social media followers, leading to recognition of Awakening as the world's leading Islamic media company by the prestigious Dubai Islamic Economy Awards[4] audited by Deloitte.

Without doubt, the stand-out leadership quality on display is *courage*. Far from being held back by community inhibitions, Awakening sets the trend and then the community follows. In that sense, Awakening is the Apple of Islamic Music. Indeed, it was Steve Jobs who said *'people don't know what they want until we've shown them'*[5], and Awakening embodies this spirit.

Hence, they have for many years boldly delivered artists who have enthralled and inspired millions of people worldwide. Their philosophy is to recognise that courage is the ability to act in spite of doubt or fear. They apply courage as a form of accepting responsibility to transform the ummah, to be able to go against the grain, break inhibiting traditions, reducing boundaries, and initiating faith-inspired change. They recognise culture as soft power and have the courage to lead the way.

Awakening's CEO Sharif H. Banna writes: '*Vision can only take you so far, courage is required to realise any dream; the courage to challenge, to defy and to lead. One of the greatest challenges for an entrepreneur is to have the courage to challenge his/her own assumptions and opinions.*'

Awakening is driven by its commitment and courage to go beyond boundaries and push beyond the comfort zone. Many examples of this exist, including their courageous decision to tackle the taboo of music and Islam in Muslim markets, addressing female inclusivity in their videos, engaging with mainstream multinational brands and hosting the biggest ever Islamic music concert in Wembley Arena, London (UK).

As global leaders in their field they recognise the need to have courage to express their own ideas and feelings, without which they would do a great injustice to themselves and their fans (who are the 'followership' from a leadership perspective).

# TIPS  HOW TO FIND COURAGE WITHIN

- Spend time with people braver than you. Get involved in their endeavours and projects.

- As Simon Sinek notes, courage comes from knowing you have people to back you up. The Prophet knew he had God, and later built up a group of able companions. Similarly find your backers, build allies and enlist supporters to your endeavours. You cannot succeed on your own.

- Try the following simple steps as part of a 15–20 minute exercise. Write down what exactly scares you the most from everyday life.[4] Then select one item, and imagine facing it and hypothetically go through the experience of living it, in your mind. After this, you may feel uncomfortable, but take some minutes to process the aftermath. Now recognise you are still OK, stand strong and move forward. The item of fear may feel a little less daunting now.

- Attend a course on positive psychology and positive self-talk. It helps you realise that it really is all in the mind, and its within your power to overcome your demons.

- Take on a challenging task which you fear doing, for example, public speaking. Feel the fear and just do it. Manage your expectations and assume it will not be great but prepare really well anyway. In fact, expect it to go wrong and accept that, then proceed, and you should feel a little more at ease. Start small (e.g. a talk in front of friends or a few familiar colleagues), then build up. I was once unable to talk in front of more than ten people, later building up to speak at a conference of 8,000.

- Attend 'outward bound'[7] programmes and other guided outdoor challenges to build courage. These include abseiling, mountain climbing, kayaking, tree climbing and other feats.

- Build your convictions and commit to some core values to find courage, as convictions carry you forward when the going gets very tough.

- Take (calculated) risks and move out of your comfort zone. Amazon founder Jeff Bezos once said: *'I know that if I failed, I wouldn't regret that, but I knew the one thing I might regret is not trying'*. Similarly, Mark Twain said: *'in 20 years you will be more disap-*

*pointed by what you didn't do than by what you did'.* Ask yourself what you would do if you were not afraid.

■ When feeling anxious or nervous, tell yourself to feel excited instead.[8] The mental and chemical process triggered from anxiety is hard to just think away, hence people saying 'don't worry' doesn't always help. But it is a shorter and easier switch to go from anxiety to excitement, as it channels the chemicals towards a better state of mind. If it is public speaking, then feel excited by the chance to do something special; if it is out of fear of something negative such as a conflict situation or even a loss of a possession or a loved one, then say to yourself, this is life and getting though it will make you incredibly strong. Indeed, there is an excitement to be gained from thinking about the possibilities the future holds for you with your new-found capability to handle immense challenges. Others will turn to you for advice and guidance, and you will have the honour and opportunity to help others when they also face big challenges in life.

■ Read *Feel the Fear and Do it Anyway* by Susan Jeffers. It deconstructs your fears and provides great techniques to overcome your anxieties and build new levels of confidence. It gives rational perspective to overcome irrational fears, and practical ways to deal with your mental hang-ups.

■ Based on a suggestion in this book, say the following ten times every morning and before any daunting task: '*Allah has made me strong and capable'.* While you may sometimes feel like you are just saying it, the brain absorbs the instruction and tacitly strengths your confidence.  Also say to yourself '*I can handle it'.* Our ultimate fear is that we cannot handle it.

CHAPTER 5

# HOLISTIC JUSTICE

The worldwide importance of justice and fairness, especially in leaders, has not changed with the passage of time. It is one of the most universal and enduring human qualities and values most of humanity can agree on.

Few things trigger stronger human emotions than injustice and feeling unfairly dealt with.

As Kouzes and Posner's top leadership qualities survey showed, fairness ranked in the top 10 (6th to be precise) as a quality that leaders viewed as key to their ability to be successful.

Some of the most respected leaders in the last hundred years, from Martin Luther King and Malcolm X to Nelson Mandela and Desmond Tutu, stood out because of their just leadership and their fight for justice in their community and the world.

As Martin Luther King Jr said: *'Injustice anywhere is a threat to justice everywhere. We are caught in an inescapable network of mutuality, tied in a single garment of destiny. Whatever affects one directly, affects all indirectly.'*[1] He recognised that humanity is deeply interconnected, and it is not possible for us to ignore injustice even if it is happening to another community or location to our own.

Injustice also compels us to make a decision about where we

stand. As Desmond Tutu aptly noted: *'If you are neutral in situations of injustice, you have chosen the side of the oppressor. If an elephant has its foot on the tail of a mouse and you say that you are neutral, the mouse will not appreciate your neutrality!'*[2]

## PROPHETIC JUSTICE – A HOLISTIC APPROACH

Being 'just' is one of the best-known qualities of the Prophet and also one of God's 99 divine attributes. It is hence one of the essential values of the Islamic faith.

In the Quran, God speaks about justice repeatedly in numerous verses such as in Al-Ma'ida (5:42), An-Nahl (16:111), Al-Anbiya (21:79), An-Nisa' (4:58), Al-Hadid (57:25), Al-Anbiya (21:47) and others.[3] These are outlined below:

*'[They are] avid listeners to falsehood, devourers of [what is] unlawful. So if they come to you, [O Muhammad], judge between them or turn away from them. And if you turn away from them – never will they harm you at all. And if you judge, judge between them with justice. Indeed, Allah loves those who act justly.'* (5:42)

*'On the Day when every soul will come disputing for itself, and every soul will be fully compensated for what it did, and they will not be wronged.'* (16:111)

*'And We gave understanding of the case to Solomon, and to each [of them] We gave judgement and knowledge. And We subjected the mountains to exalt [Us], along with David and [also] the birds. And We were doing [that].'* (21:79)

*'We have already sent Our messengers with clear evidences and sent down with them the Scripture and the balance that the people may maintain [their affairs] in justice. And We sent down iron, wherein is great military might and benefits for the people, and so that Allah may make evident those who support Him and His messengers unseen. Indeed, Allah is Powerful and Exalted in Might.'* (57:25)

> *'And We place the scales of justice for the Day of Resurrection, so no soul will be treated unjustly at all. And if there is [even] the weight of a mustard seed, We will bring it forth. And sufficient are We as accountant.' (21:47)*

Hence, justice and fulfilment of rights is abundantly found in the words of God and it is no surprise that *'adil'* (the Just One) is one of His 99 attributes.[4] The Prophet was hence compelled to be the ultimate role model of justice in his dealings with people.

However, as we will discover, the Prophet dispensed his role as a just leader in a holistic and nuanced way. He would be cognisant of the long-term implications of his interventions, and consider alternative solutions to problems of injustice, and this is why we have described his leadership quality and approach as 'holistic justice'. This will be further elaborated towards the end of the chapter.

## PROPHETIC JUSTICE IN RACE AND RELIGIOUS CONTEXTS

The Prophet would be just and fair regardless of race, religion or background. This led him to instances where he would adjudicate in favour of a non-believer, if justice demanded it. In one case, a Jewish person was accused of stealing the property of a fellow Medinan. This item was found among the Jewish person's belongings, and hence appeared to have been stolen as accused.

As the Prophet proceeded to rule against, based on the available evidence, God revealed the truth of the matter – that the Jewish man had been framed. As such, the Prophet absolved the Jewish person of guilt and ruled in his favour with the aid of divine justice.[5] As such, the Prophet carried no racial or religious biases, as justice was about truth and evidence.

He always acted fairly with all, Muslims and Non-Muslims, Arabs and non-Arabs, and would reprimand those who behaved unfairly. For example, he reprimanded an Arab Companion who spoke negatively about Bilal Al-Habashi (the Ethiopian), for he applied God's guidance to only judge people by their actions, not the colour of their skin or their ethnicity.

During his last sermon, his message was of racial equality, dutifulness, kindness and justice. The following excerpts are worthy of note:

*'O People, lend me an attentive ear, for I know not whether after this year, I shall ever be amongst you again. Therefore listen to what I am saying to you very carefully and take these words to those who could not be present here today.'*

*'Return the goods entrusted to you to their rightful owners. Hurt no one so that no one may hurt you. Remember that you will indeed meet your Lord, and that He will indeed reckon your deeds. Allah has forbidden you to take usury (interest); therefore all interest obligation shall henceforth be waived. Your capital, however, is yours to keep. You will neither inflict nor suffer any inequity.'*

*'O People, it is true that you have certain rights in regard to your women, but they also have rights over you. Remember that you have taken them as your wives, only under Allah's trust and with His permission. If they abide by your right then to them belongs the right to be fed and clothed in kindness. Do treat your women well and be kind to them, for they are your partners and committed helpers.'*

*'All mankind is from Adam and Eve, an Arab has no superiority over a non-Arab nor a non-Arab has any superiority over an Arab; also a white person has no superiority over a black person, nor a black person has any superiority over a white person – except by piety and good action. Learn that every Muslim is a brother to every Muslim and that the Muslims constitute one brotherhood. Nothing shall be legitimate to a Muslim, which belongs to a fellow Muslim unless it was given freely and willingly. Do not therefore, do injustice to yourselves.'*

The above excerpts capture an array of leadership exhortations and guidance. It is clear that fairness, equality and justice is the core underpinning of his final sermon and his leadership quality.

## PROPHETIC JUSTICE AND WORK–LIFE BALANCE

In his lifetime, he also advised concerning work–life balance, as he taught us that our 'body has a right over us', and that even ritual worship should not be done in extremes. Hence, justice should be done upon our health, and we should be fair and just on what we demand of ourselves and others. The following event during the life of the Prophet comes to mind.

The companion Anas reported that: 'Three men came to the houses of the wives of the Prophet and asked how his worship was. When they were informed, they considered their own worship to be insignificant and said: *'Where are we in comparison to the Prophet when Allah has forgiven his past and future sins?'*

One of them said: *'As for me, I shall offer prayer all night long.'*

Another said: *'I shall observe fasting perpetually, never to break it.'*

Another said: *'I shall abstain from women and will never marry.'*

The Prophet then came to them and said: *'Are you the people who said such things? I swear By Allah that I fear Allah more than you do, and I am most obedient and dutiful among you to Him, but still, I observe fasting sometimes and break it at others; I perform optional prayer at night sometimes and sleep at night at others; I also marry. So whoever turns away from my sunnah is not from me.'* (Bukhari)

Hence, the Prophet demonstrated the need to give everything its due and to act proportionately. While fasting, prayer and abstention were noble acts of worship, if done in extremes this is unjust to oneself and to others you may be neglecting or affecting in the process.

Justice is something that should not only be done, but be *seen* to be done. The perception management role of a leader with regard to fairness and justice is critical, although hard to achieve. The Prophet was keen to avoid a negative perception around favouritism. When he arrived in Medina having migrated from Mecca, there was great fanfare and song at his entrance. People began to pull at his camel and urge him to stay at they their houses. But he said that the camel was under God's guidance, and that people should let the camel choose where to settle. Hence, he avoided personally choosing one house and host over everyone else. Eventually the camel settled upon the house of Abu Ayub Al Ansari.[6]

## GENDER JUSTICE AND WOMEN'S RIGHTS

One of the biggest global campaigns against injustice in the world is that relating to women. Whether in the workplace (gender pay gap, discrimination, and harassment is all its forms) it has rightfully become a matter now featured at United Nations level in their Sustainable Development Goals – Gender Equality.

When we consider the workplace, the fact that women still get paid less than men for doing the same job is a shocking injustice that continues in every country, whether developed or developing. Across the G20 and even G7 wealthiest nations, women continue to go to work, having had to work harder than men to persuade a predominantly male-dominated workforce to get a job, then having to endure the injustice of being offered lower pay to do the same job, often getting greater scrutiny, and having any shortcomings attributed to their gender; all are examples of daily life for millions of women worldwide.

This entire picture is further exacerbated when considering intersectionality – hence, for black and minority ethnic professionals in G7 nations, their race becomes a further barrier to a just workplace. We will consider some data regarding gender pay in the workplace in the latter part of this chapter, after exploring the Prophet's approach to gender justice.

## PROPHETIC JUSTICE AND WOMEN

The Prophet was an advocate of women's rights in a climate where women and their rights were routinely abused. The diminished status of women was unfortunately the norm worldwide. From East to West, India to Athens, woman were second-class citizens, treated poorly, with hardly any rights, and obliged to be enslaved to their husbands. Some even debated whether women even had souls!

A Roman wife was described by a historian as: *'a minor, a ward, a person incapable of doing or acting anything accordingly to her own individual taste, a person continually under the tutelage and guardianship of her husband.'*[7]

In Roman law, a woman was considered a dependent. If she married, her property passed into the control of her husband. As such, the wife was also like a purchased property acquired mainly for his benefit. A woman could not exercise any public or civil office, could not be a witness, tutor or curator; she could not adopt, or make a will or contract.

According to the old English Common Law, all property and land which a wife held at the time of a marriage became a possession of her husband. He was entitled to the rent from the land, and to any profit which might be made from operating the estate during the joint life of the spouses. As time passed, the English courts devised means to forbid a husband's transferring real property without the consent of his wife, but he still retained the right to manage it and to receive the money which it produced. As to a wife's personal property, the husband's power was complete. He had the right to spend it as he saw fit.

Only by the late nineteenth century did the situation start to improve significantly.

The Prophetic ideas on gender justice were viewed as too radical and liberal for the pagan Arab men, whose attitude and abusive practices were no different from the examples from Roman and English law mentioned above.

Lezley Hazelton[8] highlights how the Quranic verses that the Prophet shared, were unique compared to other faiths and traditions in their constant address to men and women, believing men and believing women, honourable men and honourable women. This independent acknowledgement of woman by God is the starting point symbolising the fair and equitable nature of the Islamic faith.

As God revealed:

*'Indeed, the Muslim men and Muslim women, the believing men and believing women, the obedient men and obedient women, the truthful men and truthful women, the patient men and patient women, the humble men and humble women, the charitable men and charitable women, the fasting men and fasting women, the men who guard their private parts and the women who do so, and the men who remember Allah often and the women who do so – for them Allah has prepared forgiveness and a great reward.' (33:35)*

Here, God has not only mapped out praiseworthy qualities for humanity to embrace, but also repeatedly recognised women as equals alongside men in the process. Both are His creation that make up humanity. Both must uphold higher values, both must pursue good deeds, and both are equally deserving of divine reward.

There are many other verses where men and woman are mentioned directly and indirectly by God, as can be seen here:

*'O Mankind, keep your duty to your Lord who created you from a single soul and from it created its mate (of same kind) and from them twain has spread a multitude of men and women...' (4:1)*

*'He (God) it is who did create you from a single soul and therefrom did create his (female) mate, that he might dwell with her (in love)...' (7:189)*

*'The Creator of heavens and earth: He has made for you pairs (man and woman) from among yourselves.' (42:11)*

*'Whoever works righteousness, man or woman, and has faith, verily to him will We give a new life that is good and pure, and We will bestow on such their reward according to their actions.' (16:97, see also 4:124)*

Again, we see the acknowledgement of women, an exhortation of the interconnectedness between men and women, and the opportunity for both to be rewarded for good actions.

In terms of religious obligations, such as the pillars of daily prayers, fasting, charitable obligations and pilgrimage, women are no different from men. In some cases, indeed, women have certain dispensations over men. For example, women are exempted from the daily prayers and from fasting during their menstrual periods and for forty days after childbirth. They are also exempt from fasting during pregnancy and when nursing their babies, if there is any threat to her health or her baby's. Although women can and did go into the mosque during the days of the Prophet and thereafter, attendance at the congregational prayers is optional for them while it is required for men.

One of the most shocking and unjust practices the Prophet had to confront was the burying of young girls who were not considered of value to the family. Despite the social acceptance of female infanticide among many Arab tribes, the Quran forbade this custom, and considered it a crime like any other murder.

> *'And when the female (infant) buried alive - is asked, for what crime she was killed.' (81:8–9)*

Here, God notes that the victims of female infanticide will be given a voice, and a few verses later indicates how those responsible will be made to face up to their actions:

> *'then every soul will know what it has brought about' (81:14)*

Criticising the attitudes of such parents who reject their female children, the Quran states:

> *'When news is brought to one of them, of the birth of a fe-male child, his face darkens and he is filled with inward grief! With shame does he hide himself from his people because of the bad news he has had! Shall he retain her on suffer-ance and contempt, or bury her in the dust? Ah! What an evil (choice) they decide on?' (16:58–59)*

Here, God explicitly calls out the evil culture that was prevalent during the 'days of ignorance'[9] among the pagan Arabs. And it was not just about stopping the killings. Far from saving the girl's life so that she may instead suffer injustice and inequality, Islam required kind and just treatment for all women. Among the sayings of Prophet Muhammad in this regard was the following:

> *'Whosoever has a daughter and he does not bury her alive, does not insult her, and does not favour his son over her, God will enter him into Paradise.' (Ahmad)*

He also said, *'whosoever supports two daughters till they mature, he and I will come in the Day of Judgment as this'* (and he pointed with his two fingers held together).

The good treatment of women was repeatedly promoted by the Prophet. Among the famous sayings of the Prophet are:

*'It is the generous in character who is good to women, and it is the wicked who insults them.'*

*'The best among you are those best to their wife.'*
*'Paradise is at the feet of mothers.'*

Gender justice and women's rights also applied in education. The right of women to seek knowledge is not different from that of males. Prophet Muhammad said:

*'Seeking knowledge is mandatory for every Muslim.' (Bayhaqi)*

'Every Muslim' is used here to mean both males and females. In some variant narrations of the hadith, it more explicitly states, *'Seeking knowledge is mandatory for every Muslim, male and female.'* As the saying goes, 'educate a man, you educate a person; educate a woman, you educate a nation'. This was certainly a notion supported in Islam. The renowned contemporary scholar of Hadith, Dr Akram Nadwi, has written and devoted multiple volumes charting the history of female scholarship throughout the centuries of Islamic civilisation.[10]

The rights of women in marriage is another area where the Prophetic direction gave greater rights than women previously had. According to Islamic Law, women cannot be forced to marry anyone without their free consent. Their parents cannot force a marriage on them just because they are parents.

Ibn Abbas reported that a woman came to the Prophet, and she reported that her father had forced her to marry a man without her consent. This immediately shows how women found the Prophet approachable about their rights and needs. The Messenger of God was very supportive, and gave her the choice between accepting the marriage or invalidating it. The woman then said: *'Actually I accept this marriage, but I wanted to let all women know that parents have no right (to force a husband on them).'* Hence, she wanted to make the point that her consent should have been sought, and once she was given the choice she happened to decide on staying married to her husband.

This was a change from the norms of the times, where a woman's consent was not considered, and she was passed around like properties and possessions. In Islam, a woman is secure financially and is far less burdened with any claims on her possessions. Her possessions before marriage do not transfer to her husband and she even keeps her maiden name, unlike today, where in many countries women continue to take their husband's surname.

In another well-known verse, the Quran states:

*'... And they (women) have rights similar to those (of men) over them, and men are a number above them.' (2:228)*

Similarly, in the Quran in 4:34, the verse begins by stating that *'men are responsible for women ...'*. The idea of a degree or number above women has different interpretations, but as Badawi notes, the Quranic word *'Qawwamun'* is about the responsibility of maintenance and protection. This refers to that natural difference between the sexes, which entitles the physically weaker sex to protection. It implies no superiority or advantage before the law or moral standing.

## JUSTICE AND THE QUESTION OF FEMALE LEADERSHIP

It is clear that Islam views men and women as equals, and exhorts justice. However, it is also true that the Islamic view on what equality and gender justice looks like can vary with other philosophies and worldviews. Does equality mean sameness? Do biological differences necessitate differences in roles? Do women need to do everything men do, and vice versa, in order to achieve equality and justice? The answers to these questions will not only vary between Muslims and non-Muslims; it is also a hugely debated area among Muslim scholars themselves, and is outside the scope of this work.[11]

However, one issue that is relevant to raise is that of female leadership in Islam. Scholars debate this, with many suggesting that primary leadership roles should be for men only. Whether driven by cultural and patriarchal tendencies or their interpretation of certain Quranic verses and narrations of the Prophet, this view is found among many Muslims. One of the prophetic narrations cited is the following:

*'The people who appoint a woman as their leader will not be successful.' (Bukhari)*

An uncritical and literal reading of this can understandably lead one to conclude that this was the Prophet's advice. However, the noted scholar Jasser Auda offers a deeper look at the context of the narration, which offers a completely different view.

Firstly, question marks exist in relation to the person who relays this narration, and why it took 25 years to share it after he claims to have heard it from the Prophet. It was, in fact, shared at an opportune moment during the Battle of the Camel, when the Prophet's wife Aisha led male companions to war against other companions led by Ali. Parking that unfortunate civil war for a moment, it is interesting to note that many men and companions of the Prophet were happy to be led by Aisha, and her gender was not an issue. And it appears opportune for the companion standing in opposition to Aisha's camp to declare he suddenly remembers a saying of the then-deceased Prophet some 25 years later that a people who appoint a woman leader will not be successful.

Secondly, assuming the narration is valid, as many scholars believe, the context of the narration itself cannot be ignored. The Persians during the time of the Prophet had appointed the daughter of their deceased king as leader and queen. She was a teenager, thrust too young into leadership after they ran out of male heirs, and was effectively set up to fail, having been asked to step in to run an already crumbling empire rife with internal disputes. Her male predecessors had been in receipt of the Prophet's invitation messages to embrace Islam, but had torn the invitation scrolls and executed the Prophet's emissaries. The Prophet hence condemned the Persians to failure and on hearing their latest appointment, spoke of how this empire will not succeed, making reference to the new ruler, who happened to be female. The prophecy of failure was not to do with gender, but to do with the corruption of the Persian rulers, the killings by the male kings, and the insulting manner of their rejection of the Prophet's message.

Turning to the Quran itself, the verses relating to the leadership of the Queen of Sheba are most noteworthy (excerpts from 27:29–44):

*'When the Queen (of Sheba) read Solomon's letter, she said "oh you nobles! A truly distinguished letter has been conveyed unto me. Behold it is from Solomon, and it says, 'In the name of God the most Gracious, the dispenser of Grace:*

*God says: Exalt not yourselves against Me but come to me in willing surrender.'"'*

*'She added: "Oh you nobles! Give me your opinion on the problem with which I am now faced; I would never make a weighty decision unless you are present with me". They answered: "we are endowed with power and with mighty prowess in war – but the command is yours; consider then what you would command."'*

*'She said: "verily, whenever kings enter a country they corrupt it, and turn the noblest of its people into the most abject. And this is the way they always behave. Hence, behold, I am going to send a gift to those people, and await whatever answer the envoy brings back."'*

*'... Solomon said to his nobles: "she has arrived at the truth without any help from us, although it is we who have been given divine knowledge before her, and have long ago surrender ourselves to God."'*

*'... She cried: "Oh my Sustainer! I have been sinning against myself, but now I have surrendered myself, with Solomon, unto the Sustainer of all the worlds!"'*

Taking the unique Prophets aside, the Queen of Sheba is the only good example of a political leader mentioned in the Quran, and is a woman. This itself should cause us to reflect when thinking about female leadership. It is interesting to see how God highlights her leadership positively and reveals how she was fair and considerate when seeking the opinions of others. Her intelligence and good judgement are made apparent, as is her humility despite her immense power, as she chooses to accept Solomon's invitation and submit to God Almighty.

There are many more examples to note, from the role of Khadija as a businesswoman who employed Prophet Muhammad in his youth, to the fact that the greatest authority in the narrations of the Prophet is Aisha, upon whose words and veracity the very basis of Islam is founded more than upon any other single companion of the Prophet.

When we consider all of the above, the issue of female leadership has completely new possibilities. It inspires the whole *ummah* – men and women – to come together and work to build justice on earth, allowing for the appointment of anyone – man or woman – on the basis of merit. To diminish such possibilities is to hold back the talent of half the entire *ummah*.

## GENDER JUSTICE TODAY

It is hopefully fair to say that there have in recent decades been some improvements in terms of women's rights and status in countless countries today, although abuse of those rights and mistreatment of many kinds remains present worldwide.

While Muslims have for centuries upheld a more enlightened approach to gender justice and women's rights, we have arguably fallen back in recent decades, while others have taken over in championing this cause. It is not enough to cite our past successes to cover over our present failures to champion women's rights and to protect them from mistreatment. And it is fair to say that a person in a leadership position today cannot succeed long term if they do not uphold gender justice and treat women and men fairly. Mistreating half the talent of the planet can never lead to any true form of success or positive outcome.

## CIPD DATA ON THE GENDER PAY GAP

The issue of equal pay is now a global workplace matter that reflects how women continue to be mistreated even in major developed countries (note: we recognise there are a plethora of issues and injustices faced by women worldwide from FGM to sexual harassment that also deserve attention).

Let us consider the analysis of the renowned Chartered Institute for People and Development. According to data filed by more than 10,000 organisations:[12]

- A staggering 77.8% pay men more than women (up by 0.6%)
- Only 8.6% pay women the same as men (down 0.2%)
- Only 13.6% pay women more than men (up 0.4%)
- Men paid 9.6% more than women in 'median hourly pay' (up 0.4%)
- Men paid 13.1% more than women in 'mean hourly pay' (down 0.3%)

The fact that such statistics can be found in G7 developed countries, and so many workplaces, underlines just how much more work needs to be done to address the continuing injustice women face every day in every country in the world.

Beyond the global and general need to continue to fight for gender justice everywhere, there is an urgent need for the Muslim community to return to its former position of championing women's right, just as the Prophet did. While examples of this are still limited, it is praiseworthy to see some new initiatives which are emerging to challenge the mistreatment of women and promote gender justice. These should be supported and replicated worldwide.

## HOLISTIC JUSTICE AND *IHSAN*

As indicated before, the Prophetic approach of justice was incredibly nuanced and holistic, and carried deep perspective with regard to the impact of the approach taken. It takes something deep and holistic to achieve great outcomes, hence our framing of this leadership quality in this way.

In Surah Al-Nahl, God points to another dimension that needs to accompany our understanding of justice when he says, '*God commands to adl (justice; fairness) and ihsan (excellence; forgiveness, magnanimity)*' (16:90).[13]

Thus, the concept of *ihsan* divinely comes into play when talking about justice, and it is worth understanding properly. It is a dimension that can help one move beyond the baseline of 'legalistic' justice to consider alternative and holistic solutions to problems of injustice, which can help take us from legal justice to a broader level of *adl*, which we may call *fairness*. It is an awareness that helps balance between law and spirit, and seeks the fairest outcome.

## WHAT IS *IHSAN*?

*Ihsan* as a broad concept and can be translated as 'goodness', 'excellence', 'forgiveness', 'magnanimity' or even 'deep spirituality'. We mentioned *ihsan* earlier (in the chapter on competence) in the context of excellence and perfection in one's performance. Here we explore its other dimensions, especially magnanimity and mercy – which are also in their own way excellent and praiseworthy.

The Prophet said of *ihsan* that:

*'It is to worship Allah as though you are seeing Him, and while you see Him not, truly He sees you.'* (Muslim)

This is a profound way to describe *ihsan,* as it frames it in a manner that would lead to a person acting in the most appropriate manner possible, given, clearly, that if we could see God, we would not be unjust or unfair in our behaviour. But the fact that we cannot see God does not change the fact that He can see us, and hence our behaviour should continue to be excellent and full of goodness and mercy.

The idea of *ihsan* is not viewed as an optional or 'nice to have' virtue, rather it is essential. Indeed, the verse in Surah Al-Nahl speaks of God's 'command' in this matter. We also find in Surah Baqarah:

*'Pursue ihsan!, Surely God loves the one with ihsan.'* (2:195)

Similarly, the famous Prophetic saying mentioned earlier states that:

*'Verily, Allah has prescribed ihsan towards everything.'* (Muslim)

Hence, we should apply excellence, goodness and mercy in everything we do in our life, personally and professionally. God also seeks to motivate and incentivise the pursuit of *ihsan* when He says:

*'And God brings rewards of this life and the Good rewards of the afterlife. Surely Allah loves the one with ihsan.' (3:148)*

The proposition here is that *ihsan* gives you the best of both worlds – success in this life and the next. In another verse, God says:

*'Is there any reward for (your) ihsan, other than with (God's) ihsan?' (55:60)*

Here, God is saying that when we pursue excellence and goodness, he will reward us with divine excellence and goodness, and such a promise is a reward beyond imagination.

The interplay between justice and *ihsan* in the context of a crime, or the suffering of a detriment, is interesting. In the following verse, it is noteworthy that even in the context of severe injustice and wrongdoing, God encourages the option of not reverting always to legal rights but to consider magnanimity:

*'The recompense for a detriment is a detriment like thereof: but if a person forgives and makes reconciliation, his reward is due from Allah...' (42:40)*

*'Let them forgive and overlook; do you not wish that God forgives you?' (24:22)*

Thus, while the principle of 'an eye for an eye, a tooth for a tooth', and a detriment for a detriment may be considered just, there is scope for a most excellent act of forgiveness and reconciliation, which was often the preferred choice of the Prophet. Hence, by combining justice and *ihsan,* one can achieve fairness as a leader.

## HOLISTIC JUSTICE: PROMOTING A MAGNANIMOUS CULTURE

It is well established that the Prophet was inclined to forgive and overlook people's wrongdoing where possible, especially where there would not be greater evil generated by its forgiveness.

If we consider the occasion when a woman came to the Prophet to admit that she had committed a major sin, we find that the Prophet tried to steer away from the person and the conversation to avoid being compelled to apply the severe punishment that would be deserving of that crime. When the Bedouin[13] man urinated in the mosque, rather than punishing the person, the Prophet stopped his companions from angrily intervening, and instead allowed the Bedouin to finish and then went over to advise him of his error.

The case of Thumama Ibn Uthal is also interesting. The Prophet was expected to apply the death sentence, given that Thumama was responsible for assassinating many Muslims, but instead the Prophet was able to appeal to Thumama's heart, leading to his conversion to Islam – which in turn wiped away his sins, and turned him into an important asset and contributor of the Muslim community.

Countless more examples exist, where the Prophet could have punished or even executed people, but facilitated forgiveness, leading to a greater outcome. Aisha said that the Prophet never took revenge on his own behalf, even though it may be his just right.[14]

It is also apparent that the Prophet would promote responsibilities over rights, which in a sense is a case of preferring *ihsan* over a limited notion of legal justice. For example, in the battle of Hunayn, he encouraged his army to free the captives of Bani Hawazin even though it was their right to keep them in captivity. He would seek buy-in from his companions to give more and more of their wealth in God's cause, even though it was their right to keep their wealth, over and above the legal minimum of Zakat. This advice was best exemplified by Abu Bakr and Umar, who would often have healthy competition in good deeds.

Once, in response to the Prophet's call for the companions to donate their wealth and possessions for an expedition, Umar noticed that he was bringing more to the table than Abu Bakr. He hence rejoiced that for once he would outdo his friend Abu Bakr in good deeds, only to discover that while he had brought literally half of everything he possessed, Abu Bakr's smaller pile represented everything he had by way of possessions, and hence was superior in sacrifice. As such, they were less preoccupied about the rights over their possessions, but more interested in forgoing their rights for a greater good, and this is *ihsan*.

The Prophet's approach to justice cultivated a positive and magnanimous culture among the companions. A heart-warming incident during the preparations for the Battle of Badr is worthy of note. The Prophet was walking up the line to straighten it using his arrow to gently prong people as part of their formation. One of the companions, Sawadi Ibn Ghaziya, was somewhat out of line, so the Prophet proceeded to prod him on his body with his arrow. Sawadi appeared to overreact, saying *'you have hurt me, oh Messenger of God'*. He continued, *'God has sent you to teach us about right and justice, so please allow me to retaliate'*.

The just Prophet did not object or protest at this demand. He did not reprimand Sawadi for challenging the Prophet himself. He obliged with the request in the name of justice, smiling and saying, *'take your retaliation'*, while making his chest and belly unguarded and ready to accept a hit. Sawadi proceeded by kissing the Prophet's body, and then hugging and embracing him.

He then explained: *'O Messenger of God, you see what is before us* (i.e. the Battle of Badr), *and I may not survive the battle, and as this may be the last time with you, I want the honour of my skin touching yours'*. The Prophet smiled, and blessed Sawadi. As Adair notes, with followers and soldiers like these you tend not to lose battles, and sure enough they proceeded to Badr outnumbered three to one, and triumphed.[15]

We learn here about how just leadership need not simply be a statutory affair about upholding the law or rules, but can be about engendering a culture where justice can be demanded at any time and from anyone, but magnanimity is abundant and goodwill is the basis of relations.

## HOLISTIC JUSTICE: BROADENING OUR NOTION OF JUSTICE IN CONFLICT AND MEDIATION

There is a need to take a nuanced approach when thinking about justice as a leader. Like the Prophet, we should try to forgive and overlook faults where possible, and incline away from punishing people unless absolutely unavoidable.

Fair leaders should also be anticipating and avoiding situations which lead to the need for punitive action, and considering if the person in question was set up for failure in some way. Context is hence incredibly important, otherwise a cold legal approach to justice can lead to long-term resentment and a feeling of unfairness.

Of course, if one is adjudicating over a conflict between two people, one needs to apply a correct and just process and cannot force one to forgive another. But there certainly is room to forgive and apply *ihsan* between you and others, as the Prophet did. As the Quranic scholar Ragheb al-Esfhani noted, *'in that sense adl is about taking your right and ihsan is sometimes about forgoing your right'*. And great good can come from foregoing one's legal right and choosing forgiveness.

*Ihsan* gives us an awareness that helps balance between law and spirit. and seeks the fairest outcome with the long-term implication in mind.

However, clearly justice cannot be waived where it sets the sort of precedent which would lead to more evil or harm. Hence, experience and good judgement is a key skill to accompany the just leader.[16]

It is difficult to think of a leader in recent times who understands this approach to justice, but among the few must be Mandela and, in particular, his *Truth and Reconciliation Commission.* Although controversial, it was a unique attempt at solving issues of injustice and human rights abuses during apartheid in a way that would facilitate national unity rather than vengeance. Hence, a good leader must learn to apply justice and fairness in a way that keeps in mind the future of his or her people, whether within an organisational, community or national context.

## CASE STUDY

| | |
|---|---|
| **NAME** | SAYEEDA WARSI |
| **BRAND** | FORMER CO-CHAIR OF THE CONSERVATIVE PARTY AND FIRST BRITISH MUSLIM CABINET MINISTER |
| **LEADERSHIP QUALITY** | JUSTICE |

**Sayeeda Warsi,** (also known as Baroness Warsi) is a British lawyer, politician and member of the House of Lords. From 2010 to 2012, she was Co-Chair of the Conservative Party.

She served in David Cameron's Cabinet, first as the Minister without portfolio between 2010 and 2012, then as the Minister of State for the Foreign and Commonwealth Office and as the Minister of State for Faith and Communities (styled as 'Senior Minister of State'), until her resignation in August 2014.

On 5 August 2014, Warsi resigned from the Government, citing concerns that she was no longer able to support the Cameron Government's policy on the escalation of violence in the Israel–Gaza conflict, describing the Government's position as 'morally indefensible'.

In her resignation letter, Warsi wrote that the UK Government's *'approach and language during the current crisis in Gaza is morally indefensible, is not in Britain's national interest and will have a long-term detrimental impact on our reputation internationally and domestically' and that it was 'not consistent with the rule of law and our long support for international justice.'*[17]

Warsi criticised the British Government by saying it could 'only play a constructive role in solving the Middle East crisis if it is an honest broker, and at the moment I do not think it is.' She explained: *'Our position not to recognise Palestinian statehood at the UN in November 2012 placed us on the wrong side of history and is something I deeply regret not speaking out against at the time.'*

Warsi led on the all-parliamentary group looking at introducing a comprehensive definition of Islamophobia, In May 2018, Warsi, stated that Prime Minister Theresa May should publicly acknowledge that Islamophobia is a problem in the Conservative Party, and that the party was in denial about the problem.

In a statement she said: *'Up to now, sadly, there are certain parts of the party that have been in denial about this issue.'*[18] She told Business Insider: *'It's very widespread. It exists right from the grassroots, all the way up to the top'*, and claimed that Conservative leaders are not taking the problem seriously because *'they don't think it is going to damage them because that community doesn't vote for them in any great numbers.'*[19]

Her principled stance against the government, saying that it failed to act neutrally over Gaza, her efforts to protect Muslim rights in the UK, and her philanthropic work to promote equality and religious understanding make her well placed as an internationally recognised leading Muslim figure who stands for justice and fairness.

## TIPS HOW TO BE MORE FAIR AND JUST

- Attend court cases, judicial mediation, internal investigations and shadow mediation meetings to gain exposure to complex disputes and understand the legal and moral considerations involved to finding a fair judgement and resolution.

- Take on a dispute case as investigator/mediator and practise your skills of fair judgement. Take guidance from a trained mediator or human resources professional along the way.

- Be aware of 'halo and horn' effects when judging people. Hence, avoid allowing your perceptions, past history, the person's gender, ethnicity, age, social background etc to play any part in forming your judgements. Adjudicate instead based on the facts available.

- Be fair in the way you treat your team. Reward your staff fairly (whether financially or otherwise), bearing in mind performance, attitude and hard work. Do not limit yourself just to your favourite top performers or 'who brings in the business'.

- Imagine an occasion where you were the victim of some level of favouritism or nepotism: how did you feel? This memory should make us shy away from being unjust in the same way to others.

- Fear God and remember his attribute as the ultimate judge and the most just. If you are unjust, God may subject you to full justice and no mercy, and without God's mercy you have no chance of salvation or reward.

- Consider a checklist method for fairness when judging a situation, dispute or investigation:
  - *What is the context of this situation? What caused this to happen?*
  - *What are the legally possible avenues here?*
  - *What are the morally acceptable avenues and options in this case?*
  - *What might be the implications of my decision?*
  - *Is there any win-win outcome possible?*
  - *Is there an Ihsan based solution possible?*
  - *Have I compromised any values in the process?*
  - *Have I considered all the arguments?*
  - *Will my decision create a precedent? Is that a good*

*thing?*

- *Have I remained open to all conclusions and sides?*
- *Have any strings unduly influenced my decisions?*
- *Is my conscience clear at the end of the process?*
- Read about the *Truth and Reconciliation Commission* set up by Mandela, and how it sought to strike a difficult balance between justice and forgiveness.

# CHAPTER 6

# PRAGMATIC DECISIVENESS

One of the defining qualities of leadership according to many leadership thinkers is the ability to make decisions. The Cambridge definition of decisiveness is '*the ability to make decisions quickly and confidently*'

It is the quality and ability of deciding and is characterised by displaying little or no hesitation in making a choice once the required information is available to be decided upon. It is about being resolute and determined as a leader.

An *indecisive leader* according to many is an oxymoron, and reflects someone unworthy of leadership. Indeed, some say it is better to make a bad decision than to make no decision at all. While this might not always be true, one can understand the general point being made. Indecisiveness rarely leads to good outcomes.

In the life and leadership of the Prophet, there is an abundance of occasions where decisions were being made, sometimes in very difficult situations.

The great Muslim philosopher Syed Naquib Al Attas enhances our view on this prophetic quality by calling it '*pragmatic decisiveness*', to distinguish from leaders who are rash and inconsiderate decision makers. The Prophet was a deeply cognisant and imaginative decision maker.

## DECISION MAKING IN THE SIRAH

Let us begin with the Ka'ba stone dilemma as an example of pragmatic decisiveness which helped to deliver an agreeable decision. When the Quraysh demolished the Ka'ba in order to reconstruct it, a dispute arose in relation to who would have the right and honour of placing back the Black Stone; this was about five years before the prophethood. They could not agree who was eligible to restore the Black Stone to its original place, and tensions rose, with the risk of a civil war. But Abu Umayya Ibn al-Mughira, their elder, asked the Quraysh to agree on the judgement of the first person to come through the Bani Shaiba gate, and they all agreed to this suggestion. The first to come through this gate was the Prophet.

He put the Black Stone in the middle of a piece of cloth, and asked a representative of each tribe to hold one of the edges of the cloth and raise it close to its place. Then the Prophet picked it up with his own noble hands and restored it to its original place, with everyone's support. By facilitating all parties to partake in this honour, the Prophet prevented a war from breaking out among the Quraysh and helped them reach a pragmatic decision instead.[1]

During the challenging years of persecution in Mecca, the Prophet went to Taif to see if the people there would be more receptive. After he was attacked and driven away, the angel Gabriel came and presented him with an offer to punish and destroy the people of Taif between two mountains. The Prophet decided not to destroy the people. A decision to spare someone, made from a position of power when one has been wronged is not easy. But this was part of his pragmatic decision making, as he considered that little would be achieved by destroying them, and perhaps one day future generations will heed his call and message.

Soon after the Taif incident, the Prophet was honoured and raised to the heavens on a winged horse-like creature in an event known as *al Isra wal Mi'raj*. This event was not witnessed by anyone, and hence would be a far-fetched proposition to share with others. It would have been easy to not want to tell anyone, especially as it could lead to ridicule and questioning of his message. But he decided to share it and talk about it nevertheless. Great leaders can make decisions which are not easy to make for most other people.

In situations of war and military preparation, he was most focused and decisive. Once, as he was making personal preparations and putting on his armour for a military expedition, a companion came to question the plans in relation to the military move. The Prophet knew when it was time for discussion and when it was time for action. He said to the companion, when a Prophet puts his chainmail on, there is no turning back.

His pragmatic decision-making skills were visible in the Battle of Hunayn and the Treaty of Hudaibiya mentioned earlier. In Hudaibiya, he had to decide on signing a treaty with the Meccan enemy despite his close companions strongly objecting to it because they saw it as a big compromise, while the Prophet knew it was pragmatic and good in the long term. Despite their disappointment, the Prophet had enough respect and loyalty among his followers for them to stick with him. Being able to carry your team through a contentious decision is part of the role of an effective leader. As the saying goes, *'leadership is (sometimes about) disappointing your own people at a rate they can absorb.'*[2]

In the Battle of Hunayn, after overcoming the enemy, the Prophet faced a tricky decision in choosing how to meet the conflicting demands for booty and prisoners coming his way from his various companions and the plea for mercy coming from the defeated army of the Banu Hawazin. As mentioned before, he was able to creatively find ways to replace the demands for booty of his followers with alternative forms of compensation – whether in the form of goods from other sources outside the Bani Hawazin, or by offering a recognition and honouring process, or a spiritual reward, as he offered to some of his closest companions of the Ansar.

The Prophet would often be asked if his suggestions and decisions were from his own deduction or from divine revelation. If it was the former, he would welcome advice from others, as he accepted that he may not have all the answers when there was no direct revelation available. Once he was asked about an agricultural matter and decided to provide a view. However, as the season progressed, the crops suffered. When the people informed him of this, he advised that this was not his religious instruction or based on divine guidance but his own personal opinion, and acknowledged that he was not an expert in agriculture. It is important for leaders to know where their expertise lies, and to admit where they do not have expertise, just as the Prophet did.

Pragmatism is an important feature of Prophetic decision making, but this does not mean that swift and strong decisions cannot be made when the situation dictates this. Situational leadership is needed in order to give space for debate and discussion on some matters, or to take an executive decision and move on an issue in other situations. Hence, if we look at the best followers of the Prophet, such as Abu Bakr, he decided to moved fast against those who began to betray their oath, loyalty and commitment to the Muslim community by refusing to pay zakat the moment the Prophet passed away. Being indecisive here risked the very future of the hard-fought Muslim community they had built.

## ON CONSULTATION-BASED DECISION MAKING

The importance of consultation, discussion and deliberation is well established in Islam. From the very beginning of our known divine narrative, when God mentioned to his angels concerning the creation of mankind, a conversation and discussion emerged as follows:

> 'And (remember oh Prophet) when your Lord said to the angels: "Verily, I am going to place a successor on earth." They said: "(How) can You place therein those who will make mischief and shed blood, while we glorify You with praises and thanks and sanctify You." He (Allah) said: "I know that which you do not know."' (2:30)

Here we see how God is engaging in a discussion with His angels about His plans to create mankind. The angels raise their concerns about the plan, which God allays, reminding them that He knows the implications of his decisions. The renowned Quranic scholar Ibn Ashur notes how this is a kind of consultation by God himself, who is affording the angels courtesy and honouring them by discussing His plans.

The following are perhaps the most wel-known verses in the Quran in relation to consultation:

*And those who have responded to their lord and established prayer and whose affair is [determined by] consultation among themselves, and from what We have provided them, they spend. (42:38)*

*So by mercy from Allah, [O Muhammad], you were lenient with them. And if you had been rude [in speech] and harsh in heart, they would have disbanded from about you. So pardon them and ask forgiveness for them and consult them in the matter. And when you have decided, then rely upon Allah. Indeed, Allah loves those who rely [upon Him]. (3:159)*

The first verse outlines the actions of those who are favoured by God, and it is noteworthy that consultation is placed alongside a pillar of Islam – that of prayer itself. Mutual consultation is hence highly encouraged, especially on matters that affect others beyond oneself.

In the second verse, we also find the divine instruction to the Prophet and by extension to all Muslims to consult with one another. The Prophet used to ask his Companions for advice about various matters, to enrich his decisions, to encourage their hearts, and so there was buy-in and active implementation of the decision they reached. The verse continues, saying that once a consultation-based decision has been made, one should be focused on it, not waver, and place trust in God.[3]

During the Battle of Badr, on the advice of his companions, he positioned his army near the wells to deprive the enemy of the water source. Concerning the Battle of Uhud, the Prophet asked the Companions if they should fortify themselves in Medina or go out to meet the enemy, and the majority of them requested that they go out to meet the enemy, and he did.

During the Battle of the Trench, where an immense enemy were heading straight for Medina, he gathered his companions once again to consult on the best way to prepare for the attack. After listening to a lot of suggestions, he decided to adopt Salman's novel tactic of trench warfare, which the Arabs had never come across before. He was hence open to ideas and creative in decision making. In the same battle, he also consulted them about conducting a peace treaty with some of the tribes of Al-Ahzab (the Confederates), in return for giving them one-third of the fruits of Medina. He was hence willing to get the advice of his companions on the most complex of matters, as such treaties were a life and death issue.

The Prophet also asked them if they should engage the idolaters of the Quraysh in battle, on the Day of Hudaibiya, and Abu Bakr disagreed, saying, *'We did not come here to fight anyone. Rather, we came to perform umrah.'* The Prophet agreed, and decided accordingly.

Consultation-based decision making generally yields better results and more buy-in, but to facilitate genuine consultation it is essential to ensure that there is freedom of thought and conscience, and space for people to speak honestly and freely.[4]

The Prophet was very approachable and welcomed people's views, as we have noted above. His successors also did the same, albeit in their own ways. When Umar became ruler, he had a circle of trusted advisors both young and old who had knowledge, expertise and the willingness to speak truth to power. There are many accounts where people spoke their views to him, even though he found them uncomfortable at times.[5]

The evidence of the benefits of consultation can be found in many places, and research also shows this to be the case. For example, some of the leading business schools and leadership development firms today use the 'Schefferville exercise' in their team-building activities. This simulates a survival challenge following a plane crash in the middle of a deserted Canadian sub-Arctic region on the northern Quebec-Newfoundland border. Here, each of the team members (who are the survivors) are given a list of 15 items they have hypothetically salvaged from the crash, which they have to rank in order of importance for their survival. Initially everyone makes their own ranking. Then they park their own scores and engage in a group consultation process to come up with a collective ranking. The individual and collective rankings are then compared with a specialist survival expert's outline.

On well over 90%[6] of occasions, the collective rankings are closer to the expert's ranking, while each individual's score was far off. This suggests that the group would most likely survive when working together and in consultation, while unilateral individuals doing their own thing are likely to die.

This is in line with the advice of the Prophet, who once said *'no*

*one was ever happy by making decisions on his own; and if you con-
sult others, you will not be miserable.'*

## AL FATIH'S DECISIVE MOVE

In Islamic history, we also find leaders whose decisiveness yielded
impressive results, from Salah Uddin Ayubi to Sultan Muhammad
Al Fatih. The latter's famous determination and leadership to get his
advancing ships around the impenetrable Byzantine sea chains was
viewed as one of the history's most audacious feats.

As a young boy, he was always motivated by his mentors that he
will become the person who was mentioned by the Prophet in his
authentic hadith narrated by Imam Ahmad in al-Musnad: *'Verily you
shall conquer Constantinople. What a wonderful leader will its leader
be, and what a wonderful army will that army be!'* Muhammad Al Fatih
was wishing to become that person mentioned by the Prophet. Soon
after he was crowned sultan at the age of 21, he set about making
plans to take Constantinople.

In 1453, Al Fatih commenced the siege of Constantinople (now
Istanbul) with a huge army, and a navy of over 300 vessels. The city
was surrounded by sea and land, and Al Fatih's fleet at the entrance
of the Bosphorus sea was stretched from shore to shore in the form
of a crescent. In early April, the Siege of Constantinople began. After
several failed assaults, the city's walls held off the Turkish advance
with great difficulty, even with the use of the innovative Ottoman Or-
ban's bombardment – a cannon of fearsome reputation. The harbour
of the Golden Horn was blocked by a boom-chain and defended by
28 warships, making it impossible for Al Fatih's ships to get through
and topple the Byzantine rulers. Al Fatih had a decision to make:
either to pull back, given the impossible situation, or to make the big
decision to push forward and not give up.

He decided to make a big decision, which was also bold and strategic.[7] It was a tremendous move, which even by today's advanced
military and technological standards seems impossible. On 22 April,
he initiated the transportation of his lighter warships overland, around
the Genoese colony of Galata and into the Golden Horn's northern
shore. Some 80 ships were transported from the Bosphorus, after
paving over one mile with wooden logs as rollers underneath. The
ships were now through to the other side of the boom-chain block-

*A portrait depicting the creative decision of Al Fatih to transport ships over land*[8]

ade! This unexpected move stretched the Byzantine troops to their limit, as they were now forced to fight on multiple fronts. A little over a month later, Constantinople fell, and Al Fatih was victorious.

## CASE STUDY

| | |
|---|---|
| **NAME** | RECEP TAYYIP ERDOGAN |
| **BRAND** | AKP AND TURKEY |
| **LEADERSHIP QUALITY** | DECISIVENESS |

If there is a Muslim leader in the world today who knows his own mind, it is **Recep Tayyip Erdogan**, the President of Turkey. A leader who no doubt can be attributed with many other leadership qualities however what is distinctively his consistent leadership quality is his ability to be decisive during key moments especially crises.

Erdogan has time and time again shown his ability to make tough decisions in crisis situations, where others would hesitate. A number of examples are worthy of highlighting.

His decision to fly into the danger zone of Istanbul and rally public support on 15 July 2016, in the midst of a coup d'état that was attempted by sections of the military, with aims to remove Erdogan from government, is worthy of note. He had just escaped an attempt to directly apprehend him in his holiday but decided to fly into Istanbul and turn the coup attempt on it head.

Secondly, deciding to abandon openly Islamist politics and established the moderate conservative AKP in 2001 was a significant decision which will have courted controversy across multiple political fault lines. He sought to bridge the divide between secular and Islamist ideologies by introducing a form of secularism that gave freedom and space to all, whether religious or otherwise

Thirdly, deciding to go after the influential Fethullah Gulen's movement, who he was previously allied with, for masterminding and orchestrating the coup attempt was a very big decision. All of the sudden his allies became the main opposition MHP, and now it was another 'Islamic' group that became his enemy, indeed being proscribed by the Turkish government as a terrorist organisation.

Fourthly, deciding to take in over 3 million refugees into Turkey and offering to 'share even one loaf of bread', demonstrated his humanitarian commitment, however it also risked domestic strains as the impact of such a large intake is undeniable. It could not have been a straightforward decision for him, but as a nation that matches the US in annual humanitarian aid even though it is not as wealthy as the USA, he will have accounted for the giving nature of Turkish citizens, to believe it was a decision he can afford to take.

Erdogan's achievements in his over 11 years as prime minister are equally impressive. Since AKP came to power in November 2002, economic growth has averaged some 5%. Inflation has been tamed. The army has been brought under greater civilian control. Erdogan has made more progress than any previous political leader in giving Turkey's Kurds greater rights. In 2005 he achieved something that had eluded all his predecessors: the start of membership talks with the European Union. Despite the current challenges faced by Turkey, President Erdogan's decisiveness has transformed Turkey into a powerful nation which not only seeks to provide moral global leadership by championing the causes of the voiceless but also challenges the global political status quo. President Erdogan states: *"Our motto 'the world is bigger than 5' is the biggest-ever rise against global injustice. We will maintain this objection of ours, which draws larger support each passing day, until a more just global order of government is established."*

Perhaps the roots of President Erdogan's leadership quality of decisiveness can be traced back to his tenure as Mayor of Istanbul from 1994-98. During his tenure as Mayor of Istanbul, he tackled many chronic problems in Istanbul including water shortage, pollution and traffic chaos.

The water shortage problem was solved with the laying of hundreds of kilometres of new pipelines. The garbage problem was solved with the establishment of state-of-the-art recycling facilities. While Erdogan was in office, air pollution was reduced through a plan developed to switch to natural gas. He changed the public buses to environmentally friendly ones.

The city's traffic and transportation jams were reduced with more than fifty bridges, viaducts, and highways built. He took precautions to prevent corruption, using measures to ensure that municipal funds were used prudently. He paid back a major portion of Istanbul Metropolitan Municipality's two billion dollar debt and invested four billion dollars in the city.

Erdogan went on to initiate the first roundtable of mayors during the Istanbul conference, which led to a global, organized movement of mayors. A seven-member international jury from the United Nations unanimously awarded Erdogan the UN-HABITAT award.

This mayoral period of 'pragmatic decisiveness' is amongst one of President Erdogan's finest and most constructive periods of all, as his industrious approach to infrastructure development, problem solving and zero tolerance of corruption was most reflective of the prophetic leadership quality concerned.

## TIPS HOW TO BE MORE DECISIVE

- Build your life, career and work experience so you can make better decisions.
- Take on responsibilities, such as a project manager for a team, responsibility for a budget, an investigation or a review which requires you to make challenging decisions.
- Get off that comfortable fence! The longer you stay there, the more apparent it becomes that you are not a leader.
- Moving from indecision to decisiveness often means letting go. Consider a dilemma and play out a decision process in your mind. Hypothetically let go and make a decision, then experience the implications of that decision, process this and accept the outcome even if it was not perfect or ideal. Sit and reflect as the decision maker who made a call on an issue. This is now you. Go forth and be decisive in reality!
- While one must strive to make good decisions, a bad decision is often better than no decision at all.
- Play timed quiz games that compel a quick decision to practice this skill.
- Find a mentor who can sit with you monthly and hold you to account on your goals and plans. Pursing your goals needs constant decision making, and a good mentor will press you to be more decisive, and also guide you on making better decisions.
- The decision-making process should involve the following: Identify the problem/issue, gather information, identify options and alternatives, weigh up the pros and cons based on evidence, make a decision and choose an option, implement the decision and action, evaluate the result and impact. Then make adjustments to your decision if the results demand it. Each step should be done within a reasonable time frame and not drag on. Try to consult regularly but apply judgement on when and how much consulting is helpful. Use the Tenenbaum and Schmidt model on the 'leadership continuum' to consider your approach.
- Reading: *Effective Decision Making* by John Adair, and *Creative Decision Making* by Edward De Bono

CHAPTER 7

# SERVANT LEADERSHIP

In today's age of individualism, consumerism and narcissism, it becomes difficult to cultivate an altruistic quality such as servant leadership. But it is needed today more than ever. Many of society's problems, and arguably the world's biggest conflicts, stem largely from this issue of serving yourself and not caring about others. Think of any war, political conflict, or even bring it down to the level of an office argument: this is invariably the case.

There is hence a desperate need to revive altruism, selflessness and a service-orientated spirit in order to build a more peaceful and harmonious world. And this approach needs to be role-modelled from the top, at the highest leadership levels, if it to translate into culture change among followers and stakeholders.

In addition, the nature of today's followership, whether staff in organisations or society in general, are less receptive to dictatorial and self-centred styles of leadership. As mentioned in our opening chapter, the global evolution of leadership in the past hundred years alone indicates a shift from 'tell' leadership to 'sell' leadership. Hence, buy-in is critical, and leaders rely much more on the goodwill of their followers; this is something that can be cultivated with a servant leadership approach.

The phrase 'Servant Leadership' was coined by Robert K. Green-leaf in 'The Servant as Leader', an essay published in 1970.[1] There he said:

> 'The servant-leader is servant first... It begins with the natural feeling that one wants to serve, to serve first... That person is sharply different from one who is leader first, perhaps because of the need to assuage an unusual power drive or to acquire material possessions... The leader-first and the servant-first are two extreme types.'

Greenleaf is making the distinction very clear, framing the servant leader as one who goes strongly against the power-hungry or wealth-obsessed characters that often occupy leadership positions in the world. We see such narcissistic leaders covered day in day out in the media, which has perhaps shaped the average person's idea of what leadership looks like. The presence of such leaders does not bode well for the future of any nation, and hence needs to be challenged through the promotion of servant leadership.

Let us understand this key leadership quality further in light of the Sirah.

### SERVANT LEADERSHIP IN THE SIRAH

In a defining statement, the Prophet famously said: *'the leader of a people is their servant'* – as such a leader should not be self-serving or treat his followers as servants, rather a leader should take an approach where they are seeking to serve others.

This significant statement and lesson in servant-leadership pre-dates Greenleaf by some 14 centuries. It is a principle that the Prophet lived by, and an approach that has marked the greatest of leaders in history since.

In another narration, the Prophet said: *'God will continue to assist His servant, as long as the servant is assisting his brother'.* Hence, a person is deserving of God's help and support when they are in service of others.

There are many examples[2] of how the Prophet served people and would get his hands stuck in. For example, after migrating to Medina, he personally engaged in the building work of the Masjid al Nabawi, rather than leaving it to others. During the Shibh-Abi Talib (the harsh sanctions on the Muslims by the Quraysh during the Meccan era), the Prophet suffered with his people and went hungry alongside them. In the difficult battle of Uhud, he faced the same danger as his people, and indeed was seriously injured such that some thought he had died.

Unlike many kings who sat upon lofty thrones, it was said that a stranger could walk into the gathering of the Prophet, and not immediately know who from amongst the companions the Prophet was, as he sat amongst is people as one of them. He never reaped wealth while his people were poor, and he slept on a rough mat that left marks on his back. He would help his wives with housework, and would sew and repair his clothes.

He even served those who treated him poorly, such as the elderly woman who would leave rubbish in his walkway, much to his discomfort. One day when this mistreatment stopped, the Prophet went out of his way to find out what happened to the lady and found she was unwell. He then proceeded to care for her, and personally cook for her, much to her astonishment and embarrassment.

The Prophet did not shy away from domestic chores or what might seem like menial tasks. *'I am a worker'*, he once declared, and this was visibly apparent to those around him. He was not one to sit back while others laboured away. Once, he and his companions were journeying through the desert, and stopped in the evening to rest and replenish. The companions started talking about buying a sheep locally, some offered to slaughter and cook it. As for the Prophet, he was already on his feet and in action – collecting firewood and thorn bushes in preparation for the campfire that would be needed to cook the sheep. Although his companions urged him to rest, he insisted he would not sit idle while everyone else was preparing to work.[3]

Being around the Prophet was not just an experience in seeing a servant leader in action, but to be served personally by him as well. Anas ibn Malik, who worked for the Prophet as an assistant and servant, once said: *'he served me more than I served him'*. He continued: *'he was never angry with me; he never treated me harshly'*.[4]

His followers could see for themselves that their leader and Prophet 'walked the talk', was a man of the people, and was willing to strive and face every challenge together with them. They could see that he did not ask them to sacrifice or do anything he was not prepared to sacrifice or do himself. They could sense the sincerity, see his toil, and observe his full commitment to serve God and work for the betterment of mankind.

As Adair observed, Muhammad shared *'in the labours, dangers and hardships of his people'*, and thereby *'exemplified a universal principle of good leadership'*.[5] Being with the people during both good and bad times confers moral authority[6] on the leader in a way that very few other actions can. This moral authority transcends conventional hierarchies and transforms the nature of the relationship between leaders and their followers. It forges a powerful psychological contract[7] which allows leaders to not only attract and retain good people, but also to harness a tremendous level of passion and commitment from their followers, far beyond what could be achieved by a legal contract or other means.

## CARE AND COUNSEL

The Prophet deeply cared for humanity. He would often say *'Ummati Ummati'* (my people, my people), praying and constantly thinking about the salvation of all people across the world and across the ages, not only for the men and women of his time. He was praying for humanity – past, present and future. He also taught others to care for one another, as noted in the following counsel:

*'None of you truly believe until you love for your brother what you love for yourself.'* (Bukhari)

*'Love for humanity what you love for yourself.'* (Bukhari)

It is worth asking if we and those around us exhibit this approach of truly wanting for others what we want for ourselves. In a similar vein, he gave this wonderful piece of advice:

*'Abandon desire for this world and God will love you. Abandon desire for what people have and people will love you.'* (Ibn Majah)

In two simple sentences, he has outlined a profound formula and approach which can transform one into a servant leader worthy of admiration. This does not mean a servant leader should literally have nothing; rather, one can hold the '*dunya*' (world and its possessions) in one's hand and harness it for good, as long as it stays in one's hand and not in one's heart.

The importance of *servant leadership* in Islam is perhaps unsurprising, given that a central part of the Prophet's counsel to us was the idea of '*ubudiyyah*' (servitude). He relayed the well-known verse in the Quran:

> '*We have not created jinn or mankind, except to serve (me).*'(51:56)

Hence, the idea of service and servanthood is ingrained in Islamic teachings. The higher service being for God, through faith, worship, and the day-to-day service of one's fellow man.

## SACRIFICE OF SERVANT LEADERS

For a servant leader, leadership is a burden not a privilege. It is a deep sense of duty to others, rather than being about a benefit to them. Unlike contemporary political leaders, who celebrate their election victories, Umar wept at his appointment due to the realisation of the heightened burden of accountability before God over his duty to his people that he had to face. But like Umar, one must not run away from the responsibility, just because it is a burden.

It is curious to observe the euphoria and triumphant demeanour of election victors nowadays. Are they happy because they can make a difference to others? Are they celebrating their chance to build a prosperous nation for all?  Or are they glad they finally get access to all the perks and privileges that come with victory?

It is, of course, possible to celebrate leadership for the right reasons, but a true servant leader will at some level, perhaps a personal and private level, feel a deep sense of responsibility and have little time to think about their rights and privileges.

Below is a useful illustration of how a servant leader's notion of rights and responsibilities should change depending on where they are in the spectrum of leadership, authority and power:

## THE COST OF LEADERSHIP

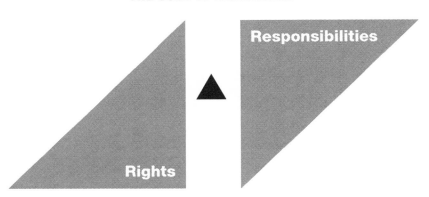

As you rise in leadership, resonsibilities increase and rights decrease

According to the servant leadership philosophy, the higher you are in leadership, the greater is your responsibility and the lesser is your scope for, or preoccupation with, seeking rights and privileges. Whereas the lower down you are, your rights should increase, given that your responsibilities are much less. Indeed, those with less power are in greater need for their rights to be protected, and provisions should be made to ensure this.

Interestingly, a dictator's profile is an inverted version of the above, where one seeks more rights and privileges as they gain power and leadership over others, while the weak and less powerful are landed the burden of responsibility to serve their leaders, with their rights diminished. This reduces people to *servant followers*, with the leader positioning themselves as a king, master, or even godlike figure. The days of such leaders are fading, and remnants that live on today should be challenged and reformed.

However, we are not advocating that a leader should have no rights, or that senior management should not have higher salaries than junior staff, for example. A leader has the right to be respectfully engaged with, and indeed can have the right to earn a fair and legitimate income based on credentials and level of duties.

However, a leader should not consider themselves somehow superior to their followers, nor think that getting involved in operational tasks at junior level is beneath them. They should also try to limit some of the symbolic privileges that may signal a sense of superiority, whether it is private squash rooms in the workplace or an exclusive senior management cafeteria where junior staff are not allowed access. This certainly is problematic for not-for-profit organisations, and where public or donor funds are involved, such as in government or charities.

But many companies and businesses are also realising that this 'gravy-train' approach does not engender goodwill and confidence among followers and employees, and hence have done away with many of the above, which is noteworthy. Open-plan offices have also proliferated around the world, and are a reflection of a more transparent approach, signalling equality and non-superiority.

## HUMILITY AND SERVANT LEADERSHIP

There are certain human traits that are helpful in cultivating a disposition towards servant leadership, and one of the most important ones is humility. The Prophet said:

> *'Practice humility until no one oppresses or belittles another.'* (Muslim)

A humble person will not see themselves as superior, nor see it as beneath them to help others. The rightly guided successors[8] of the Prophet are among the greatest examples we find in humility. They are important examples to consider, as they role modelled how one should follow the Prophet and live by his teachings.

Abu Bakr, on becoming the leader, once said:

> *'I have been appointed as ruler over you although I am not the best among you. I have never sought this position nor has there ever been a desire in my heart to have this in preference to anyone else...*
>
> *If I do right, you must help and obey me; if I go astray, set me aright... Obey me so long as I obey God & His Messenger. If I disobey them, then you have no obligation to follow me.'*

This was a great example of humility and sincerity on Abu Bakr's part. It is also noteworthy that he pointed to something higher than himself as the standard to be judged and governed by. Servant leaders similarly must point to higher values and standards that they must be held to account over, rather than thinking that their decisions and actions are always unquestionable.

Abu Bakr's humility and servant leadership is further demonstrated by a touching discovery that Umar made. When Abu Bakr was caliph, after Salat al-Fajr, he would go out into the desert. Umar was curious to know where he went, so one day, he decided to follow him. He saw Abu Bakr travel and come to a distant tent. He went in and stayed for a while, before making his way back to Medina.

Soon after, Umar went into the tent and found an old woman there with children. He asked her about her situation; she told him, *'I am an old ageing widow who is raising orphan children and I am blind.'*

Umar then asked her about the man who visited her. She said, *'I have no idea about his name or who he is. He comes everyday and he cooks the food, kneads the dough, bakes the bread, cleans the tent, cleans the clothes, milks the goat and then leaves.'*

Umar asked if she paid him anything, to which she replied, *'I have no money.'* Umar asked how long he had been doing this, and she replied, *'a long time.'*

Umar then left the woman and said to himself, *'You have made it a difficult job for the caliphs after you Abu Bakr!'*

Abu Bakr had set the bar so high that even the great Umar was struggling to envisage how anyone could follow in such footsteps. It is interesting to see how an act of service was viewed as a leadership standard. It was not a brave military move or a bold strategy that triggered such a comment. Perhaps those seemed easier in comparison to the formidable Umar, who was in no doubt of the importance and difficulty of being a servant leader who can even remember to look after a poor blind old lady and her family.

## UMAR ENTERS JERUSALEM

When Umar became leader, his era ushered great expansion, and a vast empire emerged under his leadership. Yet he remained humble and lived a simple life, often wearing patched-up clothing and sitting under a tree, to the surprise of visitors expecting to find a king-like leader on his throne. He maintained his servant-leadership nature, even as his influence and rule grew.

In 637AD, Khalid Ibn al-Walid and Amr Ibn al-As came to Jerusalem, following an earlier expedition and siege. Jerusalem and Al-Aqsa were naturally in the minds of the Muslims, who only a few years earlier had been prostrating in prayer towards it, before it was shifted to the Ka'ba during the early days of Medina.

Patriarch Sophronius was in charge, but willing to accept Muslim rule if Umar personally came to see him. Umar, although in a position of strength agreed, and came to Jerusalem. Umar travelled with simple provisions and with the accompaniment of an assistant. Given they had only one mule between them, they would take turns to ride it while the other walked. Umar's sense of consideration for others was greater than any sense that he should have the sole privilege of riding the mule.

As he reached Sophronius, he was walking as it was his assistant's turn to ride the mule. He was also dressed in no more than simple robes and was generally indistinguishable from his assistant. This projected Umar's servant-leadership approach to Sophronius, who will have no doubt noticed.

The Muslims assumed authority of Jerusalem, and Umar ensured that people were treated well. Indeed, the previously persecuted Jewish community were liberated under Muslim rule. When Umar addressed the people of Jerusalem, he did not do so as a king-like victor, but introduced himself simply as a 'servant of God'.

We find many other such examples of prophetic leadership in practice in the life of Umar. Once, in a gathering in Medina, after Umar was providing instructions, a person stood up and declared 'we hear but will not obey'. This was now a challenge to his authority as a leader. However, Umar remained calm and asked the person to explain his reasons. It then transpired that the person was upset about a perceived inequality and alleged inequity in the distribution of clothes that had taken place among the Muslims, as he pointed to how everyone gained one item of clothing, but Umar appeared to have two.

Such a small matter would easily be tolerated in many other societies and organisations, but this incident points to the strong spirit of equality and resistance to privilege among the early Muslims. Umar called his son to come forward who clarified that the second garment was his, and hence Umar also personally received one item of clothing also, but was sharing with his son. This satisfied the aggrieved person who had spoken out.

This incident also shows how Umar reacted when challenged, and it is worth us reflecting on how we react when challenged. We should observe whether we get angry, defensive or upset, or whether we rise above our emotions and our pride, and humble ourselves before people – as servant leaders.

The servant-leader approach is powerful in binding followers to their leader, and an important ethical anchor that Islam exhorts upon leadership.

It is a prophetic leadership quality that is universal and timeless in nature, which is apparent in its manifest relevance and rising popularity today. An example is the great servant leader of recent times, a man who ran the world's largest voluntary ambulance service for the poor – Abdul Sattar Edhi. He was not only much loved nationally by his fellow Pakistanis and beneficiaries for his services, but was even recognised by Google, who informed the world of Edhi's death on their search engine homepage in 2016.

Perhaps a more widely known and iconic servant-leader of recent decades is the Albanian-Indian nun Mother Teresa, who died in 1997. Her life was humble, frugal, and one that was dedicated to the poor and most desperate in India and worldwide. Her contribution and service was so noteworthy that the Vatican decided to honour her in 2016 as a saint.

Leaders and professionals worldwide can expect to achieve great buy-in, engagement and motivation from their followers and stakeholders if they embrace this quality.

## CASE STUDY

| | |
|---|---|
| **NAME** | ABDUS SATTAR EDHI AND BILQUIS EDHI |
| **BRAND** | EDHI FOUNDATION |
| **LEADERSHIP QUALITY** | SERVANT LEADERSHIP |

**Abdul Sattar Edhi** was a Pakistani philanthropist and humanitarian who founded the Edhi Foundation, which runs the world's largest volunteer ambulance network, along with homeless shelters, animal shelters and orphanages across Pakistan.

Edhi's charitable activities expanded in 1957, when an Asian flu epidemic swept through Karachi. Donations allowed him to buy his first ambulance the same year. He later expanded his charity network with the help of his wife, **Bilquis Edhi**.

In his own words, at the start of his work, Edhi 'begged for donations' and 'people gave'. This allowed him to convert a tiny room into a medical dispensary.  He also bought an ambulance that he drove around himself. Raising more donations and enlisting medical students as volunteers, his humanitarian reach expanded across the country.

Over his lifetime, the Edhi Foundation expanded, backed entirely by private donations, which included establishing a network of 1,800 minivan ambulances. By the time of his death in 2016, Edhi was registered as a parent or guardian of nearly 20,000 children. He is known as the Angel of Mercy, and is considered to be Pakistan's 'most respected' and legendary figure.[9]

In 2013, The Huffington Post claimed that he might be 'the world's greatest living humanitarian'.[10]

Edhi maintained a hands-off management and leadership style, and was often critical of the clergy and politicians. He was a strong proponent of religious tolerance in Pakistan, and extended support to the victims of Hurricane Katrina and the 1985 famine in Ethiopia.

He was nominated several times for the Nobel Peace Prize, including by Malala Yousafzai. Edhi received several awards, including the Gandhi Peace Award and the UNESCO-Madanjeet Singh Prize, which named him 'Pakistan's Father Teresa' for adopting tens of thousands of orphans.[11] Even when he was critically ill, he was offered treatment abroad, but insisted on being treated in a government hospital at home. The selfless efforts and sacrifices by both Abdus Sattar Edhi and Bilquis Edhi for a better humanity are ideal examples of servant leadership.

## TIPS — HOW TO NURTURE YOUR SERVICE AND GIVING ORIENTATION

- Martin Luther King Jr once said *'not everyone can be famous but everyone can be great, as greatness comes from serving others'*.
- Find practical ways to serve others.
- Find a hospice or any charity, and volunteer with them. Perhaps paint a wall, sweep the street, clear a garden or spend quality time with the vulnerable.
- Hoover and clean up at your local mosque. Perhaps God will make a clean and expansive place for you in paradise.
- Serve the hungry and homeless at a soup kitchen. Nourish their body and their heart through your affection.
- In a workplace setting, sit with your people, do not hide away in your ivory tower office.
- Occasionally do the job of your most junior staff member. It will not diminish you, rather it will raise your standing in this life and the next.
- Make tea for your staff for a change. At a retreat, serve the food and eat last.
- Travel to a developing nation or refugee camp, if possible, and serve the vulnerable. Distribute food, clothes and medicine to them, and ask them to pray for you.
- Remember charity begins at home. Everyone wants to change the world, but no one wants to do the dishes. Be fair to your family and do more housework! This is the prophetic way.
- Develop your altruistic side. Give away something valuable without expecting something in return. Process the emotion associated and make this action a part of who you are.
- Recall an occasion when someone gave you a gift. How did you feel? Give that feeling to others.
- Remember everything you got in life altruistically and out of love, not utilitarianism. Give the same to those around you.
- Help a stranger this week, and experience the goodwill generated. Remember, such actions please God, and seeking God's pleasure is our ultimate goal.
- Read a biography of Mother Teresa.
- Read: *Leaders Eat Last* by Simon Sinek (2017)

CHAPTER 8

# PRACTICAL WISDOM

The quality of wisdom is truly fascinating. Many will use the word and claim to understand it, but will struggle to articulate it well. According to the Oxford Dictionary, wisdom is *'the quality of having experience, knowledge, and good judgement; the quality of being wise; the fact of being based on sensible or wise thinking'*.[1]

It is interesting that the word needed to be used to help define itself. It leaves one wanting to know more. What does it mean to be wise? What does wise thinking look like?

The ancient Greeks described wisdom as *phronesis*. In essence, it is the art of knowing the right thing to do, at the right time and in the right way. It is the ability to see ahead, anticipate how things might unfold, and the ability to foresee the consequences of a given course of actions.[2]

It hence becomes apparent why this is such an important leadership quality. The effectiveness of a wise leader will be determined by their ability to do the right thing at the right time in the right way. Leaders need to be able to see ahead, anticipate internal and external challenges, and understand the consequence and impact of their actions in order to be effective.

The word *hikmah* (wisdom) is used repeatedly in the Quran as a characteristic of great leaders and a praiseworthy quality (see Quran 2:129, 2:251, 4:54, 5:110, 31:12). We mentioned for example that in Surah Luqman, God says:

*'And We had certainly given Luqman wisdom' (31:12)*

The verse continues, explaining how Prophet Luqman counselled his son with wise advice. This included advising him to remember that nothing can be hidden from God, that he should promote good and prevent evil, that he should not turn his nose up at people, nor walk arrogantly. The surah also discusses God's wisdom in commanding people to be good to their parents, and how our mothers carried us through 'strain after strain', and that we should be grateful to them and to God.

It is noteworthy how God provides reasoning and invokes our emotions by talking of the suffering our mothers bore for us. Reflecting on this would surely incline anyone to be affectionate, caring and grateful to their mother. Wisdom hence can be cultivated through reflection and reasoning. It is something we should also actively seek out. The Prophet said:

*'Wisdom is the lost property of the believer.'* (Tirmidhi)

Hence, in the way we would eagerly grab something valuable that we find, having lost it before, we should treat wisdom the same, whether from a book or a person, and keenly seek it out and adopt it. He also said the following:

*'A Muslim never gives a fellow Muslim a better gift than wisdom through which God increases him in guidance or turns him away from harmful behaviour.'* (Baihaqi)

*'If you see a man who has been given zuhd (spiritual height of abstention) from the world, and has goodly speech, then draw close to him, for he has been taught wisdom.'*[3] (Ibn Majah)

We hence learn the critical importance of wisdom, what kind of person possesses it, and what difference it can make. It is noteworthy that abstention is associated with wisdom in the above narration, rather than something more expected such as knowledge. Other Eastern philosophies also recognised this. As the Zen proverb goes, *'knowledge is learning something every day. Wisdom is letting go of something every day'*.

## WISDOM IN THE SIRAH

When we look at the life, actions, choices and judgements of the Prophet, his great wisdom and acumen was apparent. Many of the examples from the Sirah discussed earlier represent examples of wisdom, and there are many more.

Once a Bedouin came to the mosque of the Prophet and when the call of nature came, he began urinating within the mosque and prayer area. Naturally, this infuriated the other worshippers and companions of the Prophet, who started marching towards him in anger. The Prophet intervened, not only by stopping the possibility of the Bedouin getting beaten up, but actually told the worshippers to let the Bedouin finish urinating!

This was not only very considerate of him but most wise. He recognised that this was not an act of aggression, but rather the simple Bedouin did not know about the etiquette of the mosque and needed to be taught. This was the wisdom of the great teacher – the Prophet, who proceeded to counsel the foolhardy Bedouin.

From this simple incident to the strategic, political and complex case of Hudaibiya, the Prophet applied his wise leadership across multiple levels effectively.

Returning to his astute handling of the Hudaibiya agreement, his sign-off approach to 'close' the deal was a particularly noteworthy act of wisdom. After leading the Muslims to Mecca on pilgrimage, he faced negotiations with the obstructive Quraysh who were not allowing Muslims to enter Mecca. The terms emerging appeared to favour the Quraysh at the expense of the Muslims. In exchange for peace, they wanted the Muslims to turn back and go home instead of making the pilgrimage for which they had come all the way from Medina; they required the document not to bear God's name *'al-Rahman'* and *'al-Rahim'*; they even demanded that the Prophet sign the document without identifying himself as the Prophet but just as 'Muhammad Ibn Abdullah', much to the anger of the companions.

However, to their surprise and dismay, the Prophet agreed to the terms and even the signature excluding his prophetic title. Clearly, he was applying his judgement, foresight and wisdom with the long term in mind, which may require short-term compromises. But his followers could not see it. In fact, such was the anger, that many of his closest companions directly questioned his actions. Others started making a scene over what had happened, and no one wanted to turn back and go home without completing the pilgrimage in Mecca.

The Prophet then tried to progress matters by instructing everyone to complete the pilgrimage rituals where they were, outside of the holy sanctuary, on the Western edge of Mecca, as the agreement meant that they could not enter Mecca that day. He essentially asked his followers to sacrifice their animals and shave their heads there and then outside the holy sanctuary, which was most unconventional. But no one moved. Perhaps for the first time, no one responded to the Prophet's call. This shocked and upset the Prophet, who then went to his tent and discussed what had happened with his wife, Umm Salamah. In her wisdom she advised him to go and implement the rituals himself and set the example in front of his people.[4] He agreed, and quietly went outside and began performing the rituals, including slaughtering his animal and shaving his head. The moment he invoked God's name as part of slaughtering the animal, his companions jolted into action in earnest, and began to follow the Prophet's example. Thus, with calmness, role modelling and wisdom he helped his people move on and move forward, despite their disappointment and misgivings.

What followed in the coming months and years was the steady strengthening of the Muslims and the decline of power and influence of the Quraysh, culminating in a peaceful victory (in Ramadan of 8AH) and the conquest of Mecca itself. Wisdom hence leads to better outcomes longer term.

After the Meccan conquest and during the Battle of Hunayn, the Muslims outnumbered the enemy for once and many among the ranks felt overconfident and complacent. The Prophet had been advising them to depend on God, rather than their strength and numbers. But some said: *'today we are invincible. Today we cannot lose, and no-one is a match for us.'* His advice proved wise and true, as the battle began with a shock ambush leaving the Muslims in disarray and retreat, before the Prophet with the help of God and His angels salvaged the situation.

Having navigated the Hudaibiya treaty, conquered Mecca, and seen off the Bani Hawazin threat, it is very interesting that he chose not to return to live in his city of birth. He returned to Medina and lived there until his death. Perhaps he wanted to avoid his grave becoming a shrine, distracting worshippers from the Ka'ba and from the worship of God. Perhaps it was to do with his promise to the Ansar during Hunayn, when he said: *'by God I will never leave you! If all the men were to go one way, and the men of Medina another, I would follow the men of Medina'.*[5] Whether for these reasons or others, there is no doubt great wisdom in his choice.

There are several other cases which are worth mentioning. For example, there is the well-known case where a group of companions were told to travel and pray Asr (the late afternoon prayer) in the location of Bani Qurayzah. This was believed to be a message of haste, so that the group travelled fast enough to make it within Asr time. Unfortunately, they were late and the time to pray Asr arrived while travelling. Some of the group decided to stop and pray in line with the general Prophetic direction of praying on time. But others felt that they had to act on the literal instruction of praying in Banu Qurayzah, and hence prayed late and only after reaching the destination.

When they returned to the Prophet and enquired about their actions to see who was right, the Prophet declared that they were both right! This was a curious and fascinating verdict. In an instance where one instruction appeared to clash with another general instruction, the fact remained that they both followed an instruction of the Prophet and not anything outside of it. In his wisdom, the Prophet realised that they were all sincere, and they all sought to follow his guidance and reasoned accordingly; hence, was accepting of both actions. This flexibility reflects the overall nature of the Prophet, who sought to make things easy for his people. The wise know that ease and nurture can achieve buy-in, while rigidity and rebuke will turn people away.

Sometimes a leader needs to turn someone away, but the manner in which this is done matters. When Abu Dhar sought a position of authority, the Prophet advised that *'leadership was not for the one who seeks it'*. While some interpret this as a general rule, others see this as a specific statement to the companion. Hence, he was indirectly telling Abu Dhar that the role was not for him, that the leadership role being sought was not suitable for the one who has just sought it, nor is he suitable for it. This decision on the appointment was a wise move. It is believed that his appointment and approach would have been problematic for the followers.

Another incident is the occasion when the Prophet became so engrossed in speaking to and persuading a delegation of leaders, that he overlooked a blind man who had also come to talk to him. Being divinely guided every step of the way, he received a revelation counselling him of a wiser approach:

> 'He frowned and turned away; because there came to him the blind man. And what would make you know that he might (spiritually) purify himself; or become reminded so that the reminder might profit him? As to one who regards himself self-sufficient, to him do you address yourself! Though it is no blame on you if he would not (spiritually) purify himself. But as to him who comes to you striving hard, and he fears (Allah in his heart), of him you were unmindful.'(80:1-10)

The wisdom and lesson here is that while it may be necessary to try to influence leaders and those with power and resources, one should not neglect the less powerful and those in junior positions in the process. The Prophet reflected on this divine wisdom, even honouring the blind man from time to time, pointing him out as the one who triggered a divine correction and taught him a lesson.

Another instance of divine wisdom was the way the Prophet weaned his people off alcohol. In light of a three-part series of revelations over the course of about a year, the Prophet advised first that 'there was more bad in it than good'. This was enough for some of the most committed companions to give up drinking. They were not just interested in what was halal (permissible), but what was tayyib (pure, and best practice).

Later, the followers were advised to refrain from prayer and the mosque when in a state of intoxication. For alcohol to be considered incompatible with one of the pillars of Islam was enough for many other companions to give up alcohol completely. But others continued with the addictive drink. Finally, a full prohibition was announced, compelling the last remaining followers to abandon alcohol altogether.

There is much wisdom to draw from here. One is that a leader should recognise how easy or difficult a change proposition might be for their followers, and seek ways to make it easier to buy in to the proposed change. Secondly, leaders should consider good arguments and 'business cases' for change which can help persuade their followers. Thirdly, even when people know what the right thing to do is, it can help to give people time to bring themselves to change their habits.

The Prophet was also careful about setting precedents. For example, he only did Hajj once in his life even though he had the chance to do it on more than one occasion, lest his *ummah* felt obliged and overburdened in trying to follow him.

Another case of managing and avoiding precedent was the way he handled the hypocrites. He knew who they were in his midst, feigning their belief and support and ever ready to undermine his mission and movement. It was common practice in those times for rulers to execute known traitors, and indeed this suggestion was made. But the Prophet was against such action. He did not want people to say 'Muhammad kills his own followers', nor encourage his sincere followers to do the same.

The end of the Prophet's life is also worth noting. Having established the great faith through great toil, loss and suffering, he would not have wanted the religion of Islam to die and the community of Muslims to be without leadership and direction. Yet he did not officially and formally appoint a successor, nor did God leave for him a living son to succeed him. Scholars speculate as to the reason for this. But what is clear is that the Prophet had already completed the difficult task of developing many capable and values-driven leaders, and hence could leave the Muslims to manage the formality of who should succeed, which they did.

Perhaps a further wisdom was to avoid giving out the message that leaders should always be appointed by a predecessor. And the lack of a male heir also suggests that dynastic leadership is unadvisable. Indeed, the 'rightly guided' four successors – Abu Bakr, Umar, Uthman and Ali were all selected based on their well-established merit and standing in the community, rather than for dynastic reasons.

## WISE COUNSEL

In addition to wise actions, the counsel and general teachings of the Prophet are replete with wise advice. Here are some examples:

*'A strong man is not the one who is strong in fighting, but one who controls himself in anger.'* (Bukhari)

*'Consider well, contentment, for it is a treasure without end.'* (Tabarani)

*'Fulfilment is not plenty of goods; rather it is self-fulfilment.'* (Bukhari)

He also once said, after returning from a battle:

*'We have returned from the lesser struggle, to the greater struggle.'* (Baihaqi)

This referred to the struggle with one's own self and one's ego, whims and base desires. This battle to reform our character is often the hardest thing to conquer, and can be viewed as a greater battle than the physical battles faced by the Muslims.

Wisdom was also the hallmark of the four great successors of the Prophet. In an incident mentioned earlier, once when Umar was given a tour of Jerusalem, including the Church of the Holy Sepulchre, the Patriarch Sophronius invited Umar to pray inside the Church, but Umar refused, lest Muslims use it as an excuse to convert it into a mosque – thereby depriving Christendom of one of its holiest sites. Instead, Umar prayed outside the Church, where a mosque (now called Masjid Umar – the Mosque of Umar) was later built, which can still be found to this day.

## BALANCE AND MODERATION

Being balanced is synonymous with being wise. Sadly, there are few wise and balanced leaders in the world today, whether Muslim or non-Muslim, and there is desperate need for a new generation of leaders to emerge who have developed their character and have gained wisdom. But one of the rare contemporary examples of wise leadership can be found in the great Nelson Mandela mentioned earlier.

When a fight broke out between some members of his ANC and rival party activists leading to a court case, Mandela was expected to step forward as a character witness for the ANC members involved. But he declined, much to the disappointment of many in his party. Explaining this he said:

> 'I regarded my role ... as not just the leader of the ANC, but a promoter of unity, an honest broker, a peacemaker, and I was reluctant to take a side in this dispute, even if it was the side of my own organisation. If I testified on behalf of the ANC, I would jeopardise my chances of bringing about reconciliation among the different groups.'

His wisdom and foresight led him to make a compromise that was uncomfortable in the short term, but that would lead to a long-term gain, and this is the hallmark of wise leadership, and indeed prophetic leadership.

In recent times, the challenge of extremism and violence has come to the fore, making the need for balance and moderation very important indeed. Muslims are often caught in the middle – between extreme political and military actions of certain powerful nations, and the extreme violence and reaction of some small but loud fringe groups, who abuse the honour of Islam and the name of our beloved Prophet. Allah says in the Quran:

> 'And We created you a nation justly balanced so that you may become witnesses unto mankind.' (2:143)

Hence, wise leaders must be *wasati* (balanced, moderate and on the middle way) as per the Quranic counsel, and must maintain balanced behaviour even during tough times. This is the path of wisdom.

There is much that needs to be addressed and changed in the world through wise leadership. The starting point in pursuing this is closer than we think. As the great spiritual master Rumi said:

'Yesterday I was clever, so I wanted to change the world. Today I am wise, so I am changing myself.'

## CASE STUDY

| | |
|---|---|
| **NAME** | SHEIKH RACHID GHANNOUCHI |
| **BRAND** | ENNAHDA PARTY AND TUNISIA |
| **LEADERSHIP QUALITY** | WISDOM |

**Sheikh Rachid Ghannouchi** is one of the Muslim world's leading Islamic thinkers and scholars, as well as the founder and president of the Ennahda Party, a Tunisian political party.

After the Arab Spring in 2011, Sheikh Rachid Ghannouchi returned to his home country from London, where he had been in exile for nearly two decades. His party, Ennahda, won the first ever general elections after the downfall of former President Ben Ali and his government. Since 2011, Sheikh Ghannouchi has provided wise leadership to not only his party, but also to his country, such that it is the only democratic Arab country standing. Were it not for the political and strategic wisdom of Sheikh Ghannouchi in steering his country to a peaceful transition from dictatorship to democracy, the story of Tunisia might have been different. All the other Arab countries which were part of the Arab Spring – Egypt, Syria, Libya, Yemen – are experiencing critical political, economic and security challenges. One could argue that what these countries lacked was wise leadership.

Ennahda under the leadership of Sheikh Rachid Ghannouchi, took several decisions which point to the wisdom of Sheikh Ghannouchi:

a) *Deciding not to nominate himself for presidency or any government post:* Sheikh Ghannouchi announced very soon after his return to Tunisia that he would not be nominating himself for the presidential elections or take up any government post. Despite the fact that he had every right to run for the post of president, given that he was the head of the largest political party in Tunisia, in the interests of Tunisia, he decided not to. Due to Ben Ali's three decades of vicious propaganda and demonization of Ennahda and Sheikh Rachid Ghannouchi, many Tunisians were fearful of their motives. To allay such concerns, Sheikh Ghannouchi not only announced that he would not nominate himself for presidency, but that should Ennahda win the elections, it would prefer to govern with coalition partners.

b) *Seeking coalition partners:* despite the fact that Ennahda won the first general election, it decided to enter into a coalition with Moncef Marzouki's party, and agreed to nominating and supporting him as the new President of Tunisia whilst the Secretary General of Ennahda Party became the Prime Minister of Tunisia.

c) *Supporting a controversial law granting amnesty to officials accused of corruption during the rule of Ben Ali* (à la the peace and reconciliation committee philosophy of Nelson Mandela): In the name of 'economic reconciliation', Ennahda supported legislation which was passed in the Tunisian parliament seeking not to prosecute or go after senior members of the former regime involved in corruption.

d) *Wise decision to step down from government and meet Beji Caid Essebsi in Paris:* immediately after President Morsi was deposed in Egypt by the Egyptian army, the Tunisian political situation was in crisis, with the opposition aiming to destabilise the country Sheikh Rachid Ghannouchi decided that his party should step down from power and hand it over to technocrats till new elections could be held to break the political deadlock. In order to make this happen, and despite the strong reservations of some in his own party, he flew to Paris to meet Essebsi, a former Interior Minister of in Bourguiba's regime, to carve out a peaceful strategy to maintain political stability. He later said that what concerned Ennahda was not partisan interests, but the interests of Tunisia and all Tunisians.

e) *Wise decision to separate preaching from politics at Ennahda's historic conference:* at a historic conference in May 2016, Ennahda announced its separation of political activity from its dawah (preaching), and essentially repositioned itself as a mainstream Tunisian political party. This was a courageous and wise decision, which also attracted criticism from several quarters. It no longer identified itself as an Islamist party, but as a Muslim Democratic party.

f) *Wisdom in carving out a secular-religious compromise and negotiating the public space:* for over five decades, Sheikh Ghannouchi, as a leading contemporary Muslim thinker, has been theorising and writing about shura, freedom, democracy, public liberties, human rights and equality, and negotiating secularism and religion in the public space. His role as a Muslim democrat in leading the most successful democratic Arab political party to power also provided him with practical insights. Searching for consensus is his wise philosophy and strategy in navigating the public and political spaces.

# TIPS  HOW TO GAIN WISDOM

- Recognise that acquiring wisdom takes time and maturity. However, there are ways to accelerate acquisition of some wisdom.
- Acquire as much life experience as possible to accelerate self-development. Challenging and difficult experiences, such as volunteering in prison or supporting a dying person in a hospice, can give one wisdom and perspective.
- Getting involved in mediation, arbitration and conflict resolution builds wise judgement.
- Spend time with elders and benefit from what life has taught them, so that you can acquire decades of wisdom without needing to have lived for decades. This is a smart way to accelerate your development.
- Regularly reflect and do *muhasaba* (self accountability); think about your mistakes and resolve to improve them. Learn also from the mistakes of others.
- Recognise that wisdom ennobles people, raises their standing, and nourishes the soul. It is hence an attractive quality to pursue, and is a key process in one's leadership development journey.
- Increase your knowledge as a pathway to wisdom. Read wise collections such as Al Ghazali's *Dear Beloved Son*, which distils decades of great scholarship into a few pages.
- Read the biography of the Prophet by Martin Lings, especially the chapter on the Hudaibiya Treaty.[6]

CHAPTER 9

# RESILIENCE

In any leadership role or position of responsibility, things will not always go to plan, and challenges will arise which require patience and resilience. As the former BBC Dragon James Caan OBE once said, *'if something can go wrong it usually will go wrong'*, and hence he advises, you need resilience and the ability to pick yourself up and continue on. Without this capacity, a leader will soon give up, and will fail to achieve anything. The Quran has many exhortations in this regard:

> *'And We appointed from among them leaders giving guidance under Our command so long as they had patience and continued to have faith in our signs.' (32:24)*

We also find many references in the Quran advising that *'God is with the patient ones...'* God also describes Himself with the attribute of forbearance (*al-Halim*) in many places in the Quran: 2:225, 3:155, 4:12, 22:59, 33:51.

The well-known short yet powerful Surah Al-Asr reads:

> *'By the fading day, surely mankind is in (deep) loss, except for those who have faith, do good deeds, urge one another*

*to truth, and urge another to patience.'(103:1-3)*

Hence one of the four things that can save one from being personally and spiritually lost is to have patience and encourage others to be patient. The importance of this quality is further emphasised by the Prophet, who said the following:

*'No one has been given anything more excellent and more comprehensive than patience.'* (Bukhari)

## DIFFERENCE BETWEEN PATIENCE AND RESILIENCE

Patience is, of course, a well-known exhortation in Islam, and we may use it interchangeably with resilience. However, resilience takes patience a step further, indeed many steps further forward, as the life and leadership of the Prophet demonstrate.

According to the HearthMath Institute,[1] resilience is one's ability to prepare for, adapt to, and recover from instances of stress or trauma. The ability to 'adapt to' is key, as it is about one's ability to cope well in real time.

The idea of patience can sometime manifest itself as apathy, as being a passive thing, about putting up with the status quo, about coping – just about.

Many may be prone to misinterpret Prophetic Patience as being a passive state of not coping well, but on closer examination of what the Prophet is actually doing (and as we begin to rename this – 'Prophetic Resilience'), readers should realise that Prophetic engagement with resilience is strongly linked to an effort towards, and is not a passive posture at all.

A resilient leader is a person who may face challenges but views this as a necessary step to growing, and views failure as a temporary setback that they can recover from quickly. Some even describe it as the art of bouncing back and in the process, they maintain a positive attitude and a strong sense of opportunity. When faced with ambiguity, a resilient leader finds ways to move forward and avoids getting stuck. Many studies have indicated the importance of resilience as a leadership trait.

American leadership firm Zenger Folkman created an assessment that measures resilience along with nine other leadership competencies. Data were collected on more than 500 leaders. The assessment used ratings from managers, peers, direct reports and others on 40 behaviours for the impact of leaders who rated highest on resilience (the top 10%) versus those rated at the bottom (the lowest 10%). When analysing the ratings of overall leadership effectiveness, it is obvious that the most resilient leaders are viewed as the most effective leaders as well. The graph below shows the different ratings for the two groups:

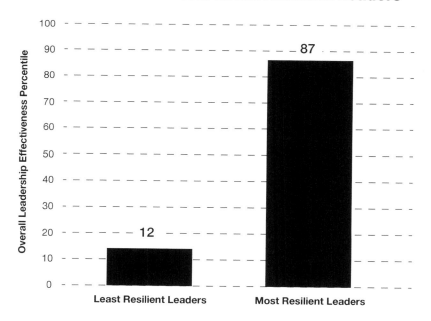

## Overall Leadership Effectiveness Ratings for the Most and Least Resilient Leaders

Building on this notion of resilience as an essential leadership quality, Rosabeth Moss Kanter, professor at Harvard Business School and chair of the Harvard Advanced Leadership Initiative writes: *'Resilience draws from strength of character, from a core set of values that motivate efforts to overcome the setback and resume walking the path to success. It involves self-control and willingness to acknowledge one's own role in defeat. Resilience also thrives on*

*a sense of community — the desire to pick oneself up because of an
obligation to others and because of support from others who want the
same thing. Resilience is manifested in actions — a new contribution,
a small win, a goal that takes attention off of the past and creates excitement about the future.'*[2]

## RESILIENCE IN THE SIRAH

The Prophet's life is actually is a story of resilience. In his early years,
he worked as a shepherd, which is something of a rite of passage
for the great Prophets through the ages. Shepherding is not easy
and take a lot of patience. From managing a fickle herd, and keeping
them together, to nursing their injuries and ensuring they get to new
pastures while staying safe from prey, there is a lot to deal with. And
once they are busy grazing and wandering on a suitable patch of
greenery, the shepherd should have the ability to wait, allowing space
and time for his flock. Shepherding teaches pace and patience which
can easily be transferred as a skill and quality to leadership situations.

For 13 years, he endured abuse and persecution at the hands of his
fellow Meccans, including times when his companions were beaten,
tortured and in some cases killed. Even the Prophet was not spared
having animal entrails thrown at him as he prayed. Yet he had to remain
patient and resilient while painfully seeing his beloved followers grossly
mistreated.

Bilal the slave was regularly beaten and tortured after his master
Umayya bin Khalaf found out he had embraced Islam and joined the
Prophet. He was routinely denied food and drink, and tortured in cyn-
ically creative ways. Once, a rope was fastened around his neck and
he was dragged through the streets of Mecca. Another time, he was
made to wear metal armour and forced to sit under the searing heat
of the sun so the overheated metal would burn him.

In an attempt to break his faith and spirits, he was pinned down
on burning sand with a large rock weighing on his back and told
he would die like this unless he renounced his faith. But they failed
to break his patient resolve as he replied and recited: *'One'*, *'One'*
– referring to the one God he believed in. There were many other
servants and slaves who had embraced Islam and faced torture,
and eventually some relief came when they were freed often by Abu
Bakr, who freed Bilal.[3]

Even the few noblemen who embraced Islam were not spared. Uthman Ibn Affan was tied up and beaten, and Abdullah Ibn Masud was attacked while reciting the Quran in the Ka'ba. And the case of Ammar Ibn Yasir was most tragic. As his family were not originally from Mecca, they could not secure protection from any tribe, and hence were exposed. Ammar was thrown into burning sand and badly beaten until he lost consciousness. His father was forced to lie on fiery glowing cinders causing severe burns. Even his dear mother Sumayya was not spared – she was tied up and stabbed to death by Abu Jahl. She gained the honour of being the first martyr in Islam.

It is one of the hardest things, for a leader to see their followers suffer on account of believing in and following them. How would our resolve be if we saw our beloved friends, supporters and followers die on our account? What would we say to them during their suffering? Was it time to respond with defensive measures, and fight back? Was it time to give up?

Many would respond in this way. The 'fight or flight' response has always been a part of human nature. Yet the Prophet asked his followers to stay put and stay strong. He told them not to retaliate but to be patient.

The Prophet would pass by the suffering family of Ammar and give words of hope, saying: *'be patient oh family of Yasir, Paradise is your promised abode'.*[4]

## ABYSSINIA

As the companions of the Prophet endured the persecution, the persecution also endured. The Prophet began considering options to ease the suffering of his companions, especially those who lacked tribal protection and were at greater risk to their lives. He then told these companions: *'it would be better for you to migrate to Abyssinia. There a king rules and in whose territory no one is wronged. Stay there until God makes circumstances favourable for you to return'.* Hence, five years into prophethood a small group of companions travelled to the land of King Negus, in what was the first emigration in Islam, and were welcomed and treated with justice.[5]

The great Negus of Abyssinia also had relations with the Quraysh, whose unrelenting pursuit of the Muslims led them to travel to see Negus and try to demand he return the Muslims to Mecca. As the king deliberated over his relational obligations to the Quraysh versus his obligation to a persecuted group he was hosting, the Muslims found themselves advocating for their safety which was at stake. Having patiently debated and presented their case, the King was able to weigh the truth, honesty and sincerity in the followers of the Prophet against the cunning of the Quraysh. *'You are safe in my land. Not for mountains of gold would I harm a single one of you'*, he declared, leaving the Quraysh representatives with no choice but to return home. This brief respite was much needed and welcome for the patient followers of the Prophet.[6]

Back in Mecca, the persecution only intensified as the Quraysh obsessed over ways to undermine and hurt the Prophet and his followers. The persecution reached its height when the Quraysh placed the infamous socio-economic boycott known as the *Shibh Abu Talib* on them. This was one of the harshest tests to face the Prophet and his early companions, and lasted some two to three years.[7] The boycott cut off essential supplies and all their ability to interact and function in society. It was complete and utter ostracization.

The boycott forced the Muslims and Banu Hashim to relocate somewhere away from the Quraysh, leading them to the narrow confines of a nearby valley on the outskirts of Mecca. There they scavenged for anything they could find to eat, resorting to leaves, the bark of trees and dried animal skin. Despite the hunger and the cries of children, the Prophet and his companions held on. They kept their trust in God and the Prophet, and found the inner resilience to make it through until the boycott was finally lifted. The respite came from Hashim Ibn Amr, who disagreed with the boycott and successfully lobbied for change despite continued opposition from the notorious Abu Jahl.[8]

This brief respite was short-lived, however. The Prophet was about to face one of his biggest tests. Perhaps the resilience built up from the boycott helped prepare him, but it was nevertheless painful and heart-breaking for him.

**THE YEAR OF SADNESS**

In about the tenth  year of prophethood, his dear uncle Abu Talib was on his deathbed. The one who gave him much needed protection died, and the Prophet was left with no powerful leader to protect his life. Although he was technically under the protection of Abu Lahab, who took over the reins of tribal leadership in the wake of Abu Talib's death, his protection was at best nominal and prone to violation.

That same year his first and most beloved wife Khadija also passed away. From the age of 25, when he married her, to the age of almost 50, she was his best friend, constant companion and affectionate counsellor. The Prophet later said of her: *'she believed in me when no one else did; she embraced Islam when people disbelieved me; and she helped and comforted me when there was no one to lend me a helping hand.'* [9]

The aftermath of such loss was characterised by the continued decline in treatment by the Quraysh. Although the Prophet was under the nominal protection of Abu Lahab, the Quraysh knew they had the license to harass and disturb as much as possible. They kept pushing the limits, constantly testing the patience of the Prophet, and at times causing him to lament and protest.

Once, a passer-by threw animal entrails into the Prophet's cooking pot. On another occasion, as he was worshipping and praying in his own courtyard, Uqbah, the disbelieving stepfather of Uthman, threw over him the blood-ridden and excrement-covered entrails of a sheep, causing him to call out to the Quraysh, *'what kind of protection is this?'* – referring to the nominal arrangement he had for protection which was surreptitiously being replaced by bad treatment.

This was difficult for the family of the Prophet to see and experience. Once, after visiting the Ka'ba, as he returned home he had dirt tossed on his face. Seeing him as such caused one of his daughters to burst into tears. But the patient and hopeful Prophet consoled her and said, *'Weep not, little daughter; God will protect your father.'*[10]

## TORMENT IN TAIF

The Meccan and the Quraysh seemed as stubborn and vitriolic as ever. It had been an exhausting experience dealing with their persecution and closed-mindedness. So, the Prophet decided the try and take his message to a new audience, and seek their support and protection, and this led him on a speculative trip to see the people of Taif, in the south east of Mecca.

He met with the three main leaders of Taif and shared his message with them. Rather than welcome and engage with him, they too rejected and ridiculed him, with one of them, Masud, rudely asking 'couldn't God find anybody else to send as His Prophet?!'[11] Such a disparaging remark can be very disheartening and upsetting for any human being. But the Prophet did not let it get to him or give up.

Seeing the he was not getting far with the leaders of Taif, he began to leave.  But the Taif chiefs would not let the Prophet leave peacefully. As he departed, they stirred up the crowd, unleashed their dogs and even got their children to attack the noble Prophet. The young of the city proceeded to hurl abuse and throw stones at the Prophet, causing him injury and bleeding. It is said that the blood flowed down to his sandals, causing them to stick. This continued for a few miles, until he was able to seek refuge in an orchard.

In desperation, the Prophet called on his creator:

*'Oh Lord, unto you do I complain of my weakness, of my helplessness, and of my lowliness before men. Oh Most Merciful of the merciful, you are Lord of the weak; and you are my Lord. Into whose hands will you entrust me? Unto some far-off stranger who will ill treat me?'*

*'Or an enemy who has dominance over my affairs? Your protection is a great shield for me. I seek your will and pleasure. No force or strength can come except from you.'[12]*

In reply, Allah sent angel Gabriel who came in his defence and offered to punish and destroy the people of Taif, but the Prophet did not act vengefully. Instead, he asked God to forgive them, and said he still held out hope that one day, perhaps the next generation among the people of Taif would be different. His patience gave him the foresight to realise that destroying the people of Taif would close the possibility of their future generations repenting and turning to God's way.[13]

## ESCAPING MECCA

While facing mistreatment in Mecca, the Prophet and his representatives had successfully been building relations with the people of Yathrib, who had welcomed his faith and message. Then the divine direction came to abandon Mecca to migrate to Yathrib. The Prophet had to secretly escape just as the Meccan's moved to finally kill him.

God had veiled him so he could escape without being seen.

Soon after realising the Prophet had escaped, the Quraysh sent trackers to pursue him. To throw them off, he set off in the opposite direction to Medina before rerouting back. But the trackers persisted in following his trail. En route, he hid in a cave patiently as his trackers closed in. Soon after entering the cave, a spider began swiftly weaving a web at the entrance. When the pursuers came and saw this, they concluded that the Prophet could not possibly have come this way, so they finally gave up and left. The Prophet's patient reliance on God had paid off.

## BATTLES AND SETBACKS

While the Medinan period had many better days than the day of Meccan persecution, the Prophet and his companions faced new state-level challenges. The initial and most famous battles from Badr to Uhud were great tests of endurance. Badr was, of course, a miraculous victory despite the odds, being outnumbered three to one. But the battle at mount Uhud was a setback and painful blow. The Prophet and his military deputies had arranged for fifty archers to guard a mountain pass as part of a tactical move to ensure they did not face a surprise ambush from behind as they focused on taking the fight to the main battleground.

As the effective Muslim army started to overcome the enemy and saw them starting to retreat, the archers started getting impatient. They began thinking about the booty and felt they might miss out, and hence began abandoning their positions, except for a small number of about ten who remained focused and steadfast. As soon as this happened, the experienced Meccan military commander, Khaled Ibn Walid (who had not yet embraced Islam), saw his opportunity and organised a counter-attack from behind. This shocked the Muslims, who found themselves in disarray, with some fleeing and others valiantly doing their best to fight the enemy until they perished. Among them, the Prophet's dear uncle and strong ally Hamza was killed, as were others. The Prophet was himself badly wounded in his face.

Hence, the lack of patience and the failure to follow the leadership of the Prophet led to heavy losses and a big military setback for the Muslims.

## ARMY OF HARDSHIP

The Muslims learnt their lesson at Uhud, and they went on to do better in subsequent battles. During the Battle of the Trench, the Muslims in Medina were under siege by the Quraysh, who mobilised multiple tribes against the Prophet. This was a major test, five years after migrating to Medina, as the Muslims faced some ten thousand enemies. While the creative use of the trench they had dug, stopped the enemy from advancing, the siege started to test everyone's patience as supplies ran dangerously short.

The hypocrites among the Muslims began questioning the help of God. To them, the state of difficulty was a reason to question. But the sincere followers remained patient and saw the challenges as a sign of God. They recalled that God had revealed, *'or do you figure that you will enter Paradise without such (trials) as came to those who passed away before you?'*

Then, after the Prophet prayed for divine help, God sent upon the Quraysh and their allies a severe storm lasting three days and three nights. This tore down their tents and damaged their belongings, and most of their steeds perished. The Quraysh had no choice but to gather what they could and retreat back to Mecca on foot. The Muslims were rewarded for their faith and patience.[14]

As God had revealed, *'Surely with hardship comes ease.'* (94:5)

While the Meccan period was replete with difficulty after difficulty, albeit with brief respites, the interchange between hard times and good times was a common experience of the Medinan Muslims. As the strength and size of the Muslim community steadily grew, they drew the attention of an empire beyond Arabia – that of the mighty Romans.

News came to the Prophet that the Romans had decided to launch an attack on the Muslims, so he set about preparing his defence. The 'army of hardship' was built to face the Romans, so-called due to the number of setbacks faced in forming such a large army, which eventually was formidably numbered at 30,000 troops.

The army, which was hard to form, faced hardships on its gruelling journey towards Tabuk, located somewhere between Medina and Damascus. This is where they would meet their Roman aggressors. The searing journey became unbearable, and some gave up and turned back home. But the Prophet endured and led on. Then, small mercies were granted by the Almighty to the resilient faithful in the form of rain such that all the followers were quenched. The journey culminated in a big moral victory, as the Romans opted not to turn up and face the Muslims in the end. They had hoped that the Muslims would not come, and were taken aback by their resolve and determination to take on the mighty Romans.[15]

Such patience and resilience is a key leadership quality, and while the Prophet displayed it to astounding levels, our challenge is to gain some basic levels of patience, in today's impatient world, where it only takes a late train or a slow WiFi connection to upset us!

Leaders today will need to be patient with their followers in order to be able to lead them long term. In a workplace context, this might mean allowing for mistakes as people learn and grow their skills, or tolerating occasional dissent, as the Prophet did with his people in Hudaibiyah. It may mean taking the time to consult people and get buy-in, even though one might prefer to force a decision down one's followers' throats.

Returning to the example of Mandela, few leaders in recent times demonstrated as much patience as him, having endured prison for some 27 years. Such a sentence would be enough to make anyone lose their mind and lose hope in life, but Mandela was able to find inner strength and resilience to survive, and eventually to thrive as the freed leader of a post-apartheid South Africa. Once, in prison he was playing chess with another prisoner. Even in chess he displayed such patience that he would take hours upon hours to decide his move. The game took several days, until his opponent voluntarily knocked over his king and gave up, saying he could not wait any longer for the game to conclude. Mandela hence won out of pure patience!

Leaders do not usually have the luxury of time for their tasks. However, there are times when patiently waiting out a difficult situation helps one to succeed. Prophetic leadership teaches us that resilience is a most critical quality to help one endure great challenges without breaking or giving up.

## CASE STUDY

**NAME**                          IMRAN KHAN

**BRAND**                         PAKISTAN TEHREEK-E-INSAF (PTI) AND
                                  PAKISTAN

**LEADERSHIP QUALITY**            RESILIENCE

**Imran Khan** is the current Prime Minister of Pakistan. His party, Pakistan Tehreek-e-Insaf (PTI), won a historic election victory in June 2018. His triumph offers resounding proof that there is a 'third way' in Pakistani politics — that a civilian leader not linked to family dynasties or older and established parties can rise to the very top.

Imran Khan's story is actually a story of life-long resilience. During his years as a world-class cricketer and sportsman, he dreamt of winning the world cup and was unable to achieve that dream, but he came back to captain the side in the 1992 Cricket World Cup and led them to unprecedented success. He played through a shoulder injury and never let the team give up, even though they had lost their first six games. He went on to become a national hero for Pakistan.

His efforts in building a cancer hospital in the name of his mother, the Shaukat Khanum Memorial Trust Cancer Hospital, is another story of inspiring resilience. To raise the required money was an impossible task. No one offered free cancer treatment across South Asia, let alone in Pakistan, and he was mocked in the press. Imran Khan mentioned in his various speeches that out of 20 doctors, 19 of them would tell him to discard the idea. It simply was not a feasible project. That did not deter him. He went from town to town, city to city, country to country, with people giving him rupees, pounds and dollars, and he achieved his goal despite all the odds.

His vision for establishing a university where 90% of its students get scholarship from the institution was also bold and challenging, especially given the site and location of the proposed university. Imran Khan once again displayed great determination and resilience, and in 2008 Namal University was inaugurated and secured affiliation status with the University of Bradford in the United Kingdom.

Imran Khan's political career was written off the moment he established his political party, Pakistan Tehreek-e-Insaf. His party lost its first election; it was humiliated and did not win a single seat. In the following general election, he was the only candidate from his party who won a seat, but he never gave up. He fought back, and was determined to be patient and resilient; in doing so, it cost him his marriage with Jemima Goldsmith. He was mocked, and to onlookers, his political career seemed to be on the brink of collapse. However, 22 years after founding PTI, Imran Khan was elected as the 22nd Prime Minister of the Islamic Republic of Pakistan and its citizens look forward to 'Naya (New) Pakistan'.

On resilience, Imran Khan states: *'It is not defeat that destroys you, it is being demoralised by that defeat which destroys you,'* and *'Never give up, no matter how hard life gets, no matter how much pain you feel. Pain will eventually subside, nothing remains forever, so keep going and don't give up.'*

## TIPS | HOW TO BE MORE RESILIENT

- Study the first 13 years of the Prophet's life in detail, and reflect on how much he endured with patience and resilience. Recognise that your issues are far easier, hence you should demand more patience from yourself.

- Spend time with parents and grandparent if you are still blessed to have them. Also visit a care home, help out and listen to the frail and elderly. Practice listening, just quietly listening. God gave us two ears and one mouth so our ratio of talking and listening should be the same. The Prophet said: *'An aspect of manliness and humanity is for a fellow to listen attentively to his brother when he addresses him'* (Al Khatib).

- Devote more time to your children (or your nephews/nieces if you do not have children) and share in childcare duties fairly. Men in particular need to recognise that spending time with your own child is not 'babysitting', it is their right and your duty. Fathers may not have the patience of mothers, but giving your children more (quality) time has the dual benefit of them being raised better and you developing your patience.

- Volunteer at a youth club and take a session with young people. Endure and work through it. It will forcibly build patience.

- Make the Hajj pilgrimage and fast a little throughout the year – these two pillars of Islam help build patience, as those rituals are not possible to complete without it.

- Use smart techniques to manage your expectations and configure your mind to be more patient. For example, when starting out with an initiative or new idea, do not expect everyone to love it. In fact, expect 100 people to dismiss the idea or even ridicule it. Then, when only 10 people dismiss it, you will not feel so bad, and if one – even one – person praises it, this becomes a pleasant surprise.

- Attend an anger management course or a resilience course to help understand your emotions and learn further techniques to stay patient.

- Play patience-testing games such as chess or even archery.

- Read: *Patience and Gratitude* by Ibn Qayyim.

# CHAPTER 10

# COMPASSION

Beyond great vision, and acts of courage, just leadership and impressive competence, there is another powerful dimension to leadership that often gets overlooked. It is to do with how much of a heart a leader has, and how much he or she cares about others. Many words can be brought forth to capture what it means to have a heart, of being heartfelt as a person. It is about gentleness, warmth, care and being appreciative of others. We have used compassion as the key description of this quality, but it includes all aspects of what it means to have heart as described.

The renowned leadership guru Professor John Adair uses the word 'warmth', and lists it as one of the seven most important 'generic' qualities all leaders should possess. Adair was impressed with the leadership of Muhammad, and noted these and other qualities in his own acclaimed book on the *Leadership of Muhammad*. He saw the Prophet as one *'who exemplifies such distinctively human qualities as goodness, kindness, humaneness and compassion'*.[1]

The Quran highlights this prophetic soft-heartedness when God says:

*'And by the mercy of God, you (oh Muhammad) dealt with*

*them gently; had you been severe or harsh-hearted, they would have run away from you.' (3:159)*[2]

We know that God is the ultimate in compassion, with almost every surah in the Quran starting *'In the name of God the most Compassionate'*. God similarly encourages compassionate leadership in His messenger as well, advising that without it, people would leave him.

No leader wants their followers to run away, but many followers find themselves lumbered with a leader who they wish they could run away from. A leader must hence recognise that they have to work hard to ensure that the followers around them are not mistreated or overwhelmed. Hadith literature contains numerous teachings on this. For example, Prophet Muhammad advised:

*'Facilitate things for people, and do not make it hard for them and give them good tidings (encouragement) and do not make them run away (discouragement).'*(Bukhari)

In recent research, Kouzes and Posner[4] make a similar exhortation, stating that it is important to plan small wins (i.e. 'good tidings') and help build confidence by not overburdening, such that the coached would feel discouraged (i.e. 'run away').

The Prophet was known for doing this, for giving his followers peace of mind, and showing them how deeply he cared about them. His good nature and heart were apparent from a young age, when he would help the needy. He was an active member of Hilf al-Fudul as a youth, whereby he contributed to social needs in Mecca.[3]

His life and eventual prophethood was characterised by a compassionate approach to leadership. He won hearts not arguments, would often be smiling and making light-hearted gestures and jokes. His compassionate words would heal any troubled companion.

He would make heartfelt gestures and show affection to those close to him. Once, Abu Bakr became upset when he learnt that the Prophet may not live long. The Prophet consoled him with these wonderful words:

*'I do not know of anyone whose companionship is dearer to me than yours. Of all the people in the world, I would choose*

*only Abu Bakr as a permanent friend and constant compan-
ion. His has been the friendship of true faith, and it will last
until God brings us together again (in the afterlife).'*

It is powerful when a leader can express affection, appreciation and warmth in this way with their followers. Such an approach builds deep relationships and commitment.

Keeping good relations with relatives, friends, neighbours and even acquaintances is a part of being compassionate and having a heart. When an old woman came to the Prophet who his wife Aisha did not know, she was curious why he spent considerable time asking about her welfare and how she was since the *hijra* (migration to Medina). Aisha asked the Prophet about her and he explained that when Khadijah was alive, this lady would regularly visit them, and that maintaining this relationship was a tacit obligation of the faith.

Similarly, there were other friends of Khadija that the Prophet kept in touch with and did not abandon after her death, even distributing gifts, such as a portion of the meat slaughtered in his house, to them.[4] Thus, the Prophet advised:

*'Exchange gifts, and mutual love arises; shake hands, and
enmity will fall away.'* (Ibn Asakir)

## THE POWER OF APPRECIATION

Related to compassion is approachability, gentleness and being appreciative. It is about being an open-hearted person that people warm to, and one who can warm other people's hearts. One of the ways to do that is to recognise and appreciate others.

This is also one of the most well-established insights in occupational psychology, human resources, and motivation theory. People are very motivated if they receive recognition and appreciation for their hard work and contribution. From Abraham Maslow and Frederick Herzberg to current leading thinkers such as Dan Pink and Daniel Goleman, all agree that showing appreciation and gratitude to people makes a difference.

It is hence no surprise that we find in the Quran and Hadith many references to gratefulness and appreciation. For example, in the Quran it says:

*'If you are grateful I will increase you (in blessings)...' (14:7)*

Similarly, many other verses speak about the importance of being grateful, especially to parents and ultimately to God, as outlined for example in Surah Luqman (31:14).

The Prophet also said:

*'Those who do not thank people cannot be grateful to Allah.'*
(Tirmidhi)

Hence, thanking people is linked and elevated to thanking God, such is its significance. According to Islamic teachings, a person should not themselves constantly seek praise, nor do actions just to get praise, as this risks compromising the sincerity of one's intentions and can make one vain. However, people are encouraged to praise others, hence engendering warm relations, which may inadvertently mean one may be in receipt of praise, which is not a problem.

## PROPHETIC GENTLENESS AND UMAR'S 'TOUGHNESS'

There are some Muslims who seek to justify rough and tough leadership, and a desire to rule by fear, by saying they take inspiration from Umar. Firstly, we must remind ourselves that the Prophet is our primary example superseding all other examples, and his softness and approachability is well established. On being gentle, he said:

*'Gentleness never accompanies anything without enhancing it, nor is it ever removed from anything without diminishing it.'* (Baihaqi)

Secondly, Islam allows for and accommodates people's innate nature, rather than trying to eliminate who you are, while seeking to temper and moderate one's weaknesses. As such, Islam allowed for some of Umar's tough nature to be tolerated, but this does not mean Islam is teaching roughness as a general rule or approach.

Thirdly, while Umar was indeed known for his tough and intimidating demeanour before Islam, this was challenged and moderated after he became a Muslim, and further moderated when he became leader of the Muslim world, however few appear to recognise or give credit to him for this.

In Umar's early time as a Muslim, the Prophet would advise him against being *zalaf*, tough and abrupt, and some companions often objected to and disapproved of this side of him. In fact, a group went to Abu Bakr when he was the Caliph and said that Umar must not take over after him, due to his *zalaf* nature. This makes it further apparent that such approaches to leadership were certainly not the general and default approach encouraged in Islam.

Abu Bakr, however, supported Umar as his successor, and advised that the leadership position would change Umar's tough nature. He was right. When Umar took over the reins of leadership as Caliph, he adjusted his style and became softer and more approachable, such that people did not fear to speak out and challenge him if they disagreed with him on something.

Indeed, Umar was tearful out of fear of wronging people as a leader. Once he felt he had wronged a companion, Hatim Ibn Abi Balta'a, and was tearful as he sought forgiveness from him, even though he was the great ruler of the Muslim world.

## COMPASSIONATE LEADERSHIP TODAY

When a leader is warm, approachable, appreciative and gentle, it is hard not to like them. Accordingly, in research by Deakin University,[5] likeability was found to be a significant factor for followers when deciding on their support for a leader or whether they consider them good leaders. And a compassionate leader is more likely to be liked. It is hence a quality not to be taken for granted.

In recent years, the UK Top 100 HR and leadership thinker Michael Jenkins has been working to promote compassionate leadership among major global companies and businesses, where it is often neglected. He demonstrates how it is the right thing to do and the smart thing to do for businesses. Whilst leading Roffey Park Institute, he developed a Compassion-at-work Index as a way to measure oneself, and this is also a useful tool for measuring one's warmth generally.[6]

The index provides an indicative view of your level of compassion at work across five attributes:

- Being alive to the suffering of others
- Being non-judgmental
- Tolerating personal distress
- Being empathic
- Taking appropriate action

However, these attributes may not come easily for everyone. Some leaders find it awkward and difficult to express compassion, warmth and a caring approach. However, one needs to find it in themselves and, as Mandela rightly noted, *'...deep down in every human heart there is mercy and generosity.'*

## CASE STUDY

| | |
|---|---|
| **NAME** | QUEEN RANIA AL-ABDULLAH |
| **BRAND** | QUEEN OF JORDAN |
| **LEADERSHIP QUALITY** | COMPASSION |

**Rania Al-Abdullah** is the Queen Consort of Jordan. Queen Rania is at the forefront of initiatives in Jordan and globally aimed at enhancing the well-being of children and families, and empowering women through microfinance.[7]

Listed by CNN as among the most inspirational leaders of 2008, her philanthropy is highlighted as her key attribute and contribution. Balancing a modern outlook with a deep concern for her people, Jordan's Queen Rania seems in many ways to represent the optimistic face of the Middle East's future.

Her appearances on the *Oprah Winfrey Show* underlined this optimistic face, speaking passionately about her faith and how she conducts ritual prayer five times a day. She went on to address misconceptions about Islam, and talked about her philanthropic passion.

Queen Rania reminds us that our world is interconnected, and when you realise that others are like you, you want for others what you want for yourself. That way, you start helping others – when there is a problem somewhere in the world, you cannot say it is their problem; it is our problem, and you have you help solve it.[8]

Born in Kuwait to a Palestinian family, she later moved to Jordan for work, where she met the then Prince Abdullah. Since marrying the now King of Jordan in 1993, she has become known for her advocacy work related to education, health, community empowerment, youth, cross-cultural dialogue and microfinance.

In November 2000, in recognition of her commitment to the cause of children and youth, the United Nations Children's Fund (UNICEF) invited Queen Rania to join its Global Leadership Initiative.[9]

The Queen worked alongside other world leaders, including former South African President Nelson Mandela, in a global movement seeking to improve the welfare of children. In January 2007, Queen Rania was named UNICEF's first Eminent Advocate for Children.

In August 2009, Queen Rania became Honorary Global Chair of the United Nations Girls' Education Initiative (UNGEI).[10]

She is also an avid user of social media, and she maintains pages on Facebook, YouTube, Instagram and Twitter, where she is followed by some 10.6 million people.

To coincide with the visit of Pope Benedict XVI to Jordan on Friday 8 May 2009, Queen Rania started using the microblogging website Twitter with the username @QueenRania.

On the occasion of the World Economic Forum held at the Dead Sea in Jordan in June 2009, Queen Rania conducted her first Twitter interview, answering five questions from the general public via her Twitter account.

When she joined Twitter, she also gave an interview with Tech-Crunch on 'how Twitter can help change the world', where she said *'It's about using social media for social change: creating a community of advocates who can use their voices on behalf of the voiceless, or leverage their talents, skills, knowledge, and resources to put more children into classrooms, or pressure their elected representatives to get global education top of the agenda.'*

## TIPS HOW TO DEVELOP COMPASSION AND AN APPRECIATIVE MINDSET

- Develop your warmth. Give gifts often, not only in Eid, but on other occasions too. When returning from a trip, do not come empty handed. When visiting a house do not go empty handed.
- Develop your hospitality. Invite people for a meal or host a social gathering with refreshments. Make people feel cared for.
- Practice saying 'thank you' and tell someone you value them once a week.
- Recall when someone recognised you or praised you for something you achieved. How did it feel? Give that joy to others in your family and your workplace.
- See people for their potential, not their mistakes. Remember all the good things they did, and feel grateful.
- Being warm, gentle and appreciative does not mean you cannot challenge poor behaviour or deal with chronic poor performance. You can be tough on an issue and still gentle on the person. Take the drama out of the process by not expressing anger or intense emotion, rather remain professional, and take the appropriate action even if difficult. You can even empathise, which is not the same as sympathising.
- Do not forget those who were there for you throughout your life. Foremost are your parents, but also remember and honour your elders, relatives, the friends who went out of their way for you, the teacher who was patient with you, the mentor who gave you time, the neighbour who put up with your noisy house, the colleague or team member who made your success possible. Thank them, send them gifts, and seek their prayers.
- Reading: Michael Jenkins' article on compassionate leadership

CHAPTER 11

# SPIRITUAL INTELLIGENCE

From the list of prophetic leadership qualities, perhaps the most curious and unknown one is spiritual intelligence. Yet this is arguably the most powerful quality for influencing people. This quality is not easily understood, and requires a multi-layered approach to unpick and unpack its immense nature.

For generations, society and its educational and workplace institutions have measured the value and talent of people in terms of their intelligence quotient (IQ). Indeed, in the early 20th century, psychologists discovered specific ways and methods to measure intelligence. Many believe that Aristotle's definition of a man as 'a rational animal' was a factor and that this developed into an obsession with IQ. The first mass use of IQ tools was during World War One, when some two million Americans were assessed for the army. The assessment was developed by Lewis Terman, a psychologist at Stanford University. Later, in the 1980s, Howard Gardner (a psychologist from Harvard University) refuted the view that IQ was the only real measure of a person's worth and chance of success. He laid some foundational ideas around emotional intelligence quotient (EQ), calling it *inter-* and *intra-personal intelligence*.

In the 1990s, Daniel Goleman developed and popularised research into emotional intelligence, pointing out that EQ was 80% important and IQ was 20% important for determining one's chances for success and prosperity in life. Soon, this bold claim caught on globally as more evidence emerged supporting this idea. Today in the 21st century, EQ is not only a well-established field in leadership science and business, there is enough collective evidence from psychology, neurology, anthropology and cognitive science to show us that there is a third 'Q' – SQ, or Spiritual Intelligence.

Let us first explore the well-known area of emotional intelligence. Goleman poses the apt question: *Why Do Smart People Do Stupid Things?* He further asked why some people with high IQ flounder in life, while many others with average IQ excel. Similarly, how was it that some of the most intelligent people we know fail in relationships, while others hold down fruitful long-term marriages and friendships? To take a more extreme example, why is it that some of the most qualified people in the world ended up working for people such as Hitler (many top PhD qualified experts worked for him), while there were many with few qualifications that stood against him?

The answer according to Goleman lies in the fact that IQ is not the only measure of intelligence, and recent research suggests that it is no longer the most important either. Beyond the cold logic of the rational mind, there are the emotions of the heart, and the spiritual dimension of the soul.

But as Martin Luther King Jr aptly noted, these dimensions have been neglected in recent times. He said, *'our scientific power has outrun our spiritual power. (Hence) we have guided missiles and misguided men'.* This reflection compels us to consider the spiritual domain more seriously.

Spirituality and intelligence make us different to other animals, and hence make us fully human. Harnessing both and building spiritual intelligence (SQ) is imperative to fulfil our humanity and what it means to be human.

From a faith perspective, the intellect (*aql*) and its preservation is one of the higher intents (*maqasid*) of Islamic law, while spirituality is at the core of our purpose of creation, a word often associated with Islamic notions such as spiritually driven (*ruhaniya*), Godly, (*rabbaniya*), servitude (*ubudiyah*), purification *(tazkiyah)* and God-consciousness (*taqwa*). We know that in the Quran (51:56) God tells us, *'And we have not created jinn or man except to worship (and serve) us'*, hence *'ubudiyya'*, or worship and servitude, is described as a spiritual purpose.

There is a difference between faith-based spirituality and spiritual intelligence, as it is technically possible for a person without religion to acquire some form of SQ. But faith-based spirituality and spiritual self-development can enrich and enhance one's spiritual intelligence capability in ways that those without religion cannot acquire.

Spiritual intelligence is a quality that connects and completes all the other prophetic leadership qualities. In addition to the linkage to the *maqasid* of preserving and nurturing the intellect, it can also help in serving the other higher intents, such as preservation of faith, life, wealth, posterity, dignity, freedom and justice. We have many leaders today, but far too few with spiritual intelligence or even emotional intelligence, and this perhaps partly explains why there is a lack of preservation of faith, life, wealth, posterity, dignity, freedom and justice in the world.

## ON MOTIVATION THEORY

Emotional and spiritual intelligence involves accessing higher levels of the mind, and connecting with the heart. The heart is, of course, associated with emotions and motivations. The psychologist Abraham Maslow developed arguably the best-known model for understanding human behaviour and motivation. His widely referenced 'hierarchy of needs' explains how people are motivated to meet basic needs such as food, shelter, clothing and security. Once these are present, new needs grow in the heart, such as love, belonging and appreciation. And once these are in place, further needs and desires emerge – the need for purpose, meaning and fulfilling one's potential. This eventually take you to a place of 'self actualisation', where the fullness of the human experience is realised.

The need for
self-actualisation

Experience purpose, meaning
and realising all inner potentials.

**Esteem Need**
The need to be a unique individual with self-respect
and to enjoy general esteem from others.

**Love and belonging needs**
The need for belonging, to receive and give love,
appreciation, friendship.

**Security Need**
The basic need for social security in a family and a society
that protects against hunger and violence.

**The Physiological Needs**
The need for food, water, shelter and clothing.

We consider the above in three levels – basic rational survival needs at the bottom, emotional and social needs in the middle, and visionary needs which inspire the human spirit at the top. This model can be transposed across the intelligence levels, hence IQ at the bottom, EQ in the middle and SQ at the top.

A leader will not be able to motivate a person to do much, if they only speak in the language of IQ, more motivation and engagement can be achieved through EQ-level interactions. The greatest potential and talent realisation can happen when one leads with spiritual intelligence.

Another well-known researcher, Fredrick Herzberg, found similar results in his study of what motivates employees. He outlined how certain things were not real motivators but 'hygiene factors' – things which should be a given, the presence of which is not necessarily motivating but the absence of which can be very demotivating, such as health and safety conditions, work environment, and even salary (dispelling the notion that money is the main motivator). Instead, the real motivators were gaining a sense of achievement, being recognised and appreciated, and professional growth. The chart below outlines the findings.

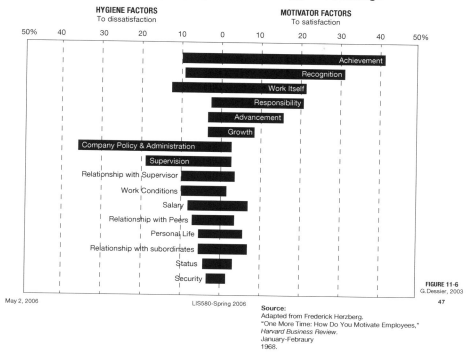

**Summary of Herzberg's Motivator-Hygiene Findings**

Source:
Adapted from Frederick Herzberg.
"One More Time: How Do You Motivate Employees,"
*Harvard Business Review.*
January-Febraury
1968.

May 2, 2006     LIS580-Spring 2006

FIGURE 11-6
G.Dessier, 2003

47

It is apparent from this list that deeper emotionally and spiritually relevant matters are more powerful motivators than is often suggested. Hence, having a sense of achievement and seeking growth is indicative of the desire to find meaningfulness and fulfilment in life.

## GOLEMAN'S FIVE DOMAINS OF EMOTIONAL INTELLIGENCE

Emotional intelligence can be defined as the skill or ability to identify, assess and control the emotions of oneself, of others and of groups. It provides a new way to understand and assess people's behaviours, management styles, attitudes, interpersonal skills and potential.

To break this down, Goleman identified the five 'domains' of EQ as:

1. Knowing your emotions
2. Managing your own emotions
3. Motivating yourself
4. Recognising and understanding other people's emotions
5. Managing relationships, i.e. managing the emotions of others

Those who can develop the ability to do the above will discover new-found influence upon others.

The diagram below offers another way to think about the domains of emotional intelligence by thinking about how the self and the social dimension interact with the awareness (recognition) and the managing (regulation) levels.

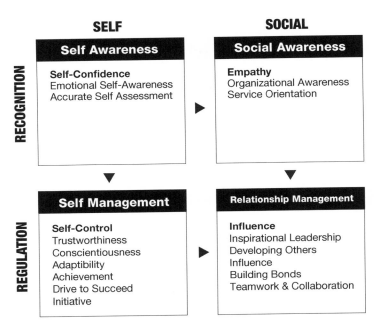

One hence has to begin with self-awareness and work one's way to building relational management skills by extending their scope from self to others, and by extending skills from awareness to management of collective emotions. When you achieve this, you have shown real leadership capability.

**WIDER BENEFITS OF EQ**

Goleman and other psychologists note the many important benefits of EQ. These include preserving and strengthening our relationships; improving our mental (and physical) health (toxic emotions impact lives like smoking!); avoiding horrors generated by emotional deficiencies (e.g. depression, violence, drugs, eating disorders etc); and raising children better (we cannot just give them IQ-based education and leave emotional development to chance). EQ brings (balanced) emotions into our intellect, and intelligence into our emotions, cultivating much-needed altruism, which ultimately can bring civility into our lives, our streets and our societies.

The above is even truer for spiritual intelligence. Let us consider some ideas in this regard.

## RESEARCHERS ON SQ

It is fair to say that research on spiritual intelligence is still in its early days and not many researchers have produced extensive, original or new contributions that significantly build on emotional intelligence research, which is far more extensive. However, among the few noted researchers and authors on spiritual intelligence are Danah Zohar, Cindy Wigglesworth and Ary Ginanjar.

Ginanjar attempted to transpose ideas about spiritual intelligence on to basic Islamic frameworks, such as the idea of one God, six pillars of Iman and five pillars of Islam, calling it the 1-6-5 principle. While it did not break new ground, it was an interesting exploration of how Muslims might engage with spiritual intelligence, leveraging off their existing belief system.

Wigglesworth defined spiritual intelligence as the ability to behave with wisdom and compassion, while maintaining inner and outer peace, regardless of the situation. While this is a useful definition, it does not go far enough in distinguishing it from emotional intelligence. Wisdom and compassion are also expected in emotionally intelligent people, but Wigglesworth's emphasis on being in a state of peace is valuable, and her SQ21 skills framework of measuring one's spiritual intelligence points to useful stages, such as the idea of the higher self and living one's values.[1]

Zohar is one of the first to write on spiritual intelligence, and as a pioneer has arguably made the most significant contribution. She argued that unlike IQ, which computers have, and EQ, which exists in higher mammals, SQ is uniquely human and the most fundamental of the three.

It is linked to humanity's need for purpose, and our longing and capacity for meaning. It relates to our ability to have powerful visions and values, and our desire to dream and to strive. It underlies the things we believe in, and the role our beliefs and values play in the actions that we take and the shape that we give to our lives. With these points, Zohar does well to highlight a real distinction about emotional intelligence.

Recent motivational thinkers such as Dan Pink outlined similar findings from extensive research, noting that once money issues have been taken off the table, the three real motivators are *mastery, autonomy* and, most importantly, *purpose*.[2]

Hence, SQ is the next level of intelligence, used to solve problems of meaning and purpose, value, goals and vision. A good way to distinguish the three levels of intelligence is outlined as follows:

- IQ – solves logical problems
- EQ – allows us to judge situations and behave appropriately
- SQ – allows us to ask if we want to be in that situation in the first place, and gives us power to change direction and transform our future.

## SCIENTIFIC STUDIES AND DISCOVERING THE 'GOD SPOT'

In today's world, there is an obsession with measurability and empirical evidence as the only valid way to make an assessment or conclusion about anything. But even Einstein recognised that this had its limits. He once said, '*not everything that can be counted counts; not everything that counts can be counted*'. Hence, not all things that we measure matter, and not everything that matters can be measured. Love is a case in point!

Spiritual intelligence reminds us of this reality, and hence does not require empirical evidence to prove its existence or usefulness. However, as a scientist and physicist who went into philosophy, Danah Zohar was keen to show empirical and 'physical' evidence for the metaphysical inclination of human beings, and compiled some very interesting discoveries.

She highlighted four significant studies by Micheal Persinger (Canadian neuropsychologist), V.S. Ramachandran (neurologist at the University of California), Wolf Singer (Austrian neurologist) and Terrance Deacon (Harvard neurologist and anthropologist). These studies included brain scans that were taken via positron emission topography, which were designed to show how neural areas light up in one's brain depending on what kind of subject is being discussed.

The scans found that when discussing matters requiring logic, analysis and calculation (IQ related), a particular part of the brain would light up. When discussing one's family, friends, community and people one loves or belongs to, another part of the brain would light up. But when talking about one's values, dreams, aspirations, vision and purpose, a completely different part of the brain exclusively lit up. In what was described aptly as the 'God spot', the scans revealed that whether you were religious or not, we all had a spiritual centre in our brain. We are hardwired to be spiritual creatures that seek meaning and purpose in our lives, and those that deny this, deny what it means to be human.

## UNIQUE DIMENSIONS OF SQ

There are clearly some overlaps between emotional and spiritual intelligence. Indeed, while in conversation with Goleman,[3] we learnt that he viewed spiritual intelligence as being part of a broader notion of emotional intelligence. But there are some important differences worth outlining:

Emotional intelligence can be applied through empathy, positive psychology and affection. It does not require or involve harnessing the language of purpose and meaning, which we believe can access the highest levels of motivational power.

SQ requires sincerity and integrity, and not manipulation (which EQ can sometimes be used and abused for). Some politicians, media outlets and sales people are prone to applying EQ unethically to influence, seduce or manipulate people and their emotions. In such instances, even if they try to cosmetically use the language of purpose, we do not recognise it as genuine SQ.

SQ appeals to our higher/visionary intellect and the mature level of our brain,[4] leading to IQ–SQ harmony. IQ and EQ do not quite achieve this.

SQ can be strengthened and cultivated through faith and spiritual exercises, giving people of faith a unique opportunity to develop this quality.

## A NEW DEFINITION

Let us now offer our own definition for spiritual intelligence. It is one's ability to effectively *direct oneself* and *inspire others* towards a (shared) *purpose*. It involves leveraging the power of purpose and values to create *meaningfulness*, and making a difference. It is one's ability to tap into people at the level of purpose and meaning, and subsequently being able to leverage that to propel people to act, change behaviour or commit to a cause.

Possessing SQ in its entirety implies one already has emotional intelligence and has built on it,[5] and in the process, one has acquired a deeper insight into human nature.

## THE DIFFERENCE BETWEEN SPIRITUAL INTELLIGENCE AND SPIRITUALITY

One can be forgiven for confusing these two important concepts, but it is important to recognise that they are not the same. In fact, a religious person may not be spiritually intelligent, and a spiritually intelligent person may not be religious or even have a religion at all.

Spirituality is a deep state of connection with the creator, and, as mentioned earlier, relates to Islamic concepts such as *ruhaniyya*, *rabaniyyah*, and *taqwa*. Spiritual intelligence, however, is one's sense of deep purpose (which can be non-religious), and one's ability to access a particular part of the brain which exists to give us meaning and direction. One can think of many people who are not committed adherents to their faith, or indeed have no faith, but who have a deep sense of purpose and mission, and the ability to inspire others to follow them. As such spiritual intelligence is faith neutral yet faith friendly.

However, I believe faith and spirituality, when applied correctly, can access our spiritual intelligence and leverage its power in unrivalled ways. Because a sense of purpose comes naturally to religious people (particularly those who are religiously learned), they simply have to translate that into their personal and professional lives. Finding purpose does not come quite as easily to those outside the religious world.

## SQ, CHRONO-BIOLOGY AND ETHICAL BEHAVIOUR

Our behaviour can be affected by many factors, even something such as our sleeping patterns and body clock (chrono-biology), which we might not normally think about. According to a *Harvard Business Review*[6] article, people's body clock can affect their ethical judgement. They found that morning people are less ethical at night, and night people are less ethical in the morning. The implications of this for leaders and major decision makers are huge. (Just imagine if you were at the mercy of a court judgement or downsizing decision when the decision maker is at their weaker time of day!)

An antidote to this is the morning and evening invocations (*adhkar*) encouraged in Islam. This develops ethical stamina and ensures that you are always spiritually alert and ethical in character. This practice, introduced by the Prophet over 1,400 years ago, is a huge developmental intervention to build ethical people, and insulate them from their own weaknesses. This process complements one's spiritual intelligence quality.

## USING SQ LANGUAGE

The difference between IQ, EQ and SQ conversations can easily be noted from language and the words people use. Hence, when a leader or manager says, *'Your performance is inadequate and effort lacking. I have evidence. What am I paying you for?'*, or *'It is legally possible for us to sack 30 staff within 6 weeks, so let's start'*, you know this is an uninspired IQ-level statement bereft of empathy and emotional awareness. But when a leader or manager says, *'I'd like to share my appreciation for all your hard work'*, or *'You are a great asset to the organisation'*, this is an example of an EQ statement, which will help engagement and motivation of staff.

But when a leader or manager says something such as *'The work you are doing is making a real difference to those less fortunate, this is surely why we are here'*, it touches a deeper part of people. If they were to say, *'I believe each of you don't have strengths and weaknesses, you have strengths and potential. Don't count the days, make your days count and leave a legacy'*, it accesses the highest level of Maslow's hierarchy and gives people meaning and purpose. This is what SQ language looks like, and lifts people from a monetary relationship to a human and spiritual relationship with one another.

It is no wonder that HR and leadership gurus such as Ulrich (who pioneered the business partnering model) wrote about 'the why of work', urging leaders to give their people a reason, a purpose and a

mission to pursue, if they wanted to see the greatest levels of produc-
tivity, engagement and performance.

## PROPHETIC APPROACH: SQ IN ACTION

It is quite apparent that SQ has a connection with good character.
The Prophet said:

*'The best among you are the best in character.'*(Bukhari)

Good character builds ethical behaviour, and this coupled with a
sense of higher purpose allows one to go beyond the useful world of
EQ to the powerful world of SQ. A famous narration of the Prophet is
that '...*even smiling is an act of charity'*. This teaches us that showing good emotions and the cultivation of the human spirit should be
encouraged, and can indeed be done through something as simple
as smiling. This includes being empathetic to those in distress, hence
he also said:

*'If a Muslim consoles his brother during a crisis, God will
adorn him in garments of grace on the day of judgement.'*
(Ibn Majah)

The Prophet's life is indeed a treasure chest of stories exemplify-
ing good character, empathy and SQ. His playfulness with children,
his sense of polite humour with companions, his good judgement of
people's emotions and aspirations in the Battle of Hunayn, and his
tolerance of the misbehaving neighbour who used to throw rubbish
in the Prophet's pathway... all show his immense and unparalleled
character and spiritual intelligence. It teaches us that a spiritually
intelligence leader is consultative, light-hearted, aware of people's
emotional states, nurturing and authentic.

The Prophet was also known for adapting his leadership to varying
situations and for varying emotions with spiritual power. We mentioned in the first chapter how he applied what we now know as Hersey and Blanchard's 'situational leadership model', Thus he was:

- *Directive* at the important battle of Uhud,
- *Coaching* with the companion Abu Dhar,
- *Supportive* with the mature Salman Farsi and
- *Delegating* with the reliable Abu Bakr.[7]

It takes a lot of EQ and SQ to change and adapt one's style of leadership to one that the situation demands. This quality is particularly indispensable for leaders in today's fast-changing world. An emotionally and spiritually intelligence leader is one who thinks like a man of action and acts like a man of thought. This was the prophetic way.

## THE STORY OF THUMAMA IBN UTHAL

This a story mentioned many times in this book due to the profound insights it contains. Let us narrate the story in full here:

In the sixth year after the migration to Medina, the Prophet sent eight letters to rulers in the Arabian peninsula, inviting them to Islam. One of these rulers was Thumama ibn Uthal, one of the most powerful Arab rulers in pre-Quranic times. He was consumed by anger and rejected the invitation, instead deciding to kill the Prophet and bury his mission.

In the pursuit of his murderous plan, Thumama killed a group of the Prophet's companions. The Prophet thereupon declared him a wanted man, deserving of execution.

Not long afterwards, Thumama decided to perform pilgrimage to the idols in Mecca. He left al-Yamamah for Mecca and, as he passed near Medina, some patrols intercepted him and took him to the Prophet's mosque, without realising who they had in custody.

When the Prophet arrived, he immediately knew it was Thumama and thanked those who had captured him. Then, to everyone's surprise, he returned home to his family and said, '*Get what food you can and send it to Thumama.*' He then ordered his camel to be milked for him. This hospitality to a wanted man perplexed the companions, and Thumama himself.

The Prophet then approached Thumama and simply asked, '*What do you have to say for yourself?*'

Thumama replied, '*If you want to kill in reprisal, you can have someone of noble blood to kill. If, out of your mercy, you want to forgive, I shall be grateful. If you want money in compensation, I shall give you whatever amount you ask.*'

The Prophet then left him for two days, but still personally sent him food and drink, and milk from his camel. He went back to him and asked the same question, *'What do you have to say for yourself?'* Thumama repeated what he had said before.

The Prophet then left, and came back to him the following day to ask, *'What do you have to say for yourself?'* Thumama repeated what he had said once more. Then the Prophet turned to his companions and to their astonishment said, *'Set him free.'*

Thumama could not quite believe what had happened. He proceeded to leave the mosque of the Prophet and rode away, until he came to a palm grove on the outskirts of Medina near al-Baqi (a place of luxuriant vegetation which later became a cemetery for many of the Prophet's companions). Then something made him stop. He proceeded no further. Instead, he curiously turned and began making his way back to the Prophet's mosque.

He arrived and stood before the Prophet and his companions, and said the famous words:

*'I bear witness that there is no god but Allah and I bear witness that Muhammad is His servant and messenger.'*

He then went to the Prophet and said: *'O Muhammad, by God, there was never on this earth a face more detestable than yours. Now, yours is the dearest face of all to me.' 'I have killed some of your men'*, he continued, *'I am at your mercy. What will you have done to me?'*

*'There is now no blame on you, Thumama'*, replied the Prophet. *'Becoming a Muslim cleanses one of all past actions and marks a new beginning.'* Thumama was greatly relieved. His face showed his surprise and joy and he vowed, *'By God, I shall place my whole self, my sword, and whoever is with me at your service and at the service of your faith.'*[8]

An amazing transformation hence took place, where the Prophet's spiritual intelligence and goodness permeated into Thumama's consciousness with few words and a lot of heart. The power of SQ is such that it is one's ability to touch hearts and change lives without the need for excessive discussion, debate and argumentation. For when one talks from the mouth, it reaches people's ears and goes out the other ear. But when you communicate from the heart, it reaches other hearts.

## MANDELA'S SPIRITUALLY
## INTELLIGENT PERSPECTIVE

Spiritual intelligence has the ability to enhance the other prophetic leadership qualities. It can make you more visionary, it can make you a warm and approachable person, it can give you patience and foresight.

This was true for Mandela who was able to move beyond the crisis before him and find solutions by seeing things differently. He said: *'I wanted South Africa to see that I loved even my enemies while I hated the system that turned us against one another'*. He believed that deep down in every human heart one can find mercy and goodness. He would speak of the African principle of *Ubuntu* which means, *'we are people through other people'*. Hence, *'we only realise our humanity by ensuring the humanity of others, regardless of who the victim or the perpetrator is.'* Such heart and foresight is only possible for a spiritually intelligent person; one who has spiritual capital, a deep sense of values, and can inspire a noble purpose for an entire nation to move forward to a better place.

By reflecting on these classical and contemporary examples, we hope to see the emergence of a new generation of spiritually intelligent leaders and citizens, who can provide the ethical, effective and inspired leadership desperately needed everywhere in the world. Unless this is pursued, and demanded of those in authority, little will change in our world for the better.

## CASE STUDY

| | |
|---|---|
| **NAME** | MR D.E. (VICE PRESIDENT OF STRATEGY AT MAJOR GLOBAL BANK AND HOUSEHOLD BRAND) |
| **BRAND** | MURABBI CONSULTANTS WORKING WITH MAJOR GLOBAL BANK |
| **LEADERSHIP QUALITY** | SPIRITUAL INTELLIGENCE |

**Mr D.E.** is the head of a Europe-wide division at a major financial and banking firm. He has been actively looking to take his annual employee 'pulse' report from good to great, as his scores have been among the very highest in the whole company.

Ranging from 70s to 80s in percentage terms, his employee survey indicates a leader who is not only very emotionally intelligence, but also one who wants to go from good to great.

Staff views around engagement, alignment, leadership and career development were all in the 80s percentage wise, while the 'agility' of the division was in the 70s, which is still a noteworthy score.[9]

In terms of Mr D.E.'s leadership in particular, staff cite his collaborative and open approach, which inspires high performance and commitment to the firm.

However, Mr D.E. was keen to explore ways to score even higher, and invited Murabbi Consultants[10] to deliver interventions that might help. He noted how his managers were emotionally intelligent, hence there are good workplace relationships and interactions, and no grievances or major workplace conflicts; however, he felt something was missing – that deeper sense of purpose, and ability to inspire.

Murabbi Consultants outlined how shifting from an *emotional* to a *spiritually* intelligent mindset can offer the necessary shift that Mr D.E. needed.

A series of practical and experiential workshops were then commissioned to work with the division's staff and managers, outlining ways to develop one's capacity to help create a working culture where values and a sense of purpose are harnessed to create meaningfulness in the work that everyone does.

Murabbi helped the team, especially the managers, develop their ability to tap into people at the level of purpose and meaning by building alignment between the company's values and the employees' personal values.

This process allowed managers to begin leveraging their *spiritual* intelligence (which involved a shift in their own choice of words, use of language and type of behaviour) to propel staff to act differently, change their behaviour as well, and commit to a cause – whether specific to their role, or the broader cause and objectives of the division generally.

Mr D.E. continues to apply the above interventions to build the kind of workplace environment that remains the envy of other divisions in his global organisation.

## TIPS | HOW TO DEVELOP YOUR EMOTIONAL AND SPIRITUAL INTELLIGENCE

- Get a basic sense of your current emotional intelligence. Score yourself (out of 10) against Goleman's five domains, then ask someone who knows you well to score you separately. Then put the results together in the table below and consider the variations and low scores. The scores may surprise or even worry you, but knowing where you are at is good news, as you can now focus on what aspects to work on, and develop yourself in ways most people fail to do.

- Attend educational courses on EQ and SQ, and read on the subject, such as the works of Daniel Goleman, Danah Zohar and Ary Ginanjar. Also read from the scholars of the heart such as Imam Ghazali and Khurram Murad. Through this study you can begin to understand your mind, your heart and your nature.

- Watch speeches by noted leaders such as Martin Luther King, Nelson Mandela, Steve Jobs, King Faisal, Recep Tayyip Erdogan, Bernie Sanders, Rachid Ghannouchi and even Barack and Michelle Obama, who are both known for oratory talent and using purposeful language. Also, Ingrid Mattson, Ebrahim Rasool, Hamza Yusuf, Nouman Ali Khan, T. J. Winters, Omar Sulaiman, Jamal Badawi and Sharif H. Banna are noteworthy leaders and scholars whose language indicates spiritual intelligence.

- Take up people management roles and observe how you lead people. Invite feedback and survey engagement levels, and take the feedback on board.

- Study the Johari's Window model for self-awareness, which advises how self-reflection and getting feedback helps one reduce one's blind-spots and helps one discover new capabilities.

- Practice expressing yourself and expressing affection, and take interest in people. This awakens your emotional intelligence.

- When emotions run high, pause, think, and let your gears move to the higher levels of your mind. Sometimes it helps to step away from the situation and gather your thoughts. Act on long-term implications, not short-term emotions.

- Practice observing without judgement. Cultivate it in you. As EQ consultant Donal O'Reardon advised, when you observe something which tends to trigger a reaction and switch off judging it, this frees up energy to come up with alternative ways to deal with the situation.

- Try to coach, counsel and mentor someone and develop this skill, as it can help build EQ and SQ. Taking an interest in another's future and their development cultivates one's EQ/SQ.

- Make an effort to attend funerals and console the bereaved. This was recommended by the Prophet and not only helps to develop our EQ by supporting others emotionally, but reminds us about our mortality, and triggers us to reflect on our life and its purpose (which in turn awakens our SQ).

- Use the language of purpose to give people meaning. Tap into people's dreams. Speak from the heart and connect with their deeper mind. Give hope, give affection, give warmth and give meaning – empower people to succeed.

- Great leaders work on their character. Indeed Mandela *'learned to overcome prejudice, control anger, discipline his soul, and embrace the counter instinctive'.*

- Engage in regular prayer and meditation. If you find that you are too busy, remember the advice of Gandhi. He used to meditate and reflect for one hour a day. When he was asked how he managed to maintain this during busy times or during crises he said, on those days he meditated for two hours!

- Reading – Danah Zohar, Ary Ginanjar and Cindy Wigglesworth.

# CRISIS: THE FINAL FRONTIER IN LEADERSHIP DEVELOPMENT

The American leadership guru James McGregor Burns oversaw a gathering of leading figures in leadership science, including the noted ethical leadership authority Professor Joanne Cuilla.

They attempted to discover a general theory on leadership, and realised that leadership science (like human nature) was too complex and sophisticated to get boiled down to one general theory, model or idea; as such, it was something deep and profound, rather than simple and unworthy of being an entire field or science.[1]

Indeed, leadership has truly become a central issue globally, and is worthy of more than one field or subject matter. From politics to sociology, psychology to human resources and people management, leadership is at the heart.

It can be argued that almost all major problems worldwide, even many natural disasters, boil down to a lack of good leaders. However, Harvard's Barbara Kellerman, in her book *The End of Leadership*, raises an important question about why the world appears to see a rise in leadership programmes and simultaneously a rise in bad leaders worldwide.

This is a poignant question and challenge to us all who are leadership development practitioners, running training programmes all over the world. Our initial response would be that this may be happening in spite of our efforts, not because of them. However, one then has to accept that somehow it does appear that we are not winning this war of producing enough ethical leaders that the world needs, while the vacuum is becoming occupied by an abundance of unethical leaders.

Why might this be happening? Part of the problem is that there remains a lack of education on integrity and ethical leadership, and if there is some education, it lacks quality and depth. As Katalin Il-les, the Head of Leadership Development at Westminster Business School, noted, the business schools have to bear some responsibility for focusing too much on being an effective leader but not enough on being an ethical leader.

Clearly, we need both, as the Wise Owl combination of ethics and effectiveness framework outlines. But when we find a whole gener-ation of professionals in the workplace – whether public, private or third sector, educated to be effective and competent, having been measured  by the company's 'assessment centres' and measured against the company's 'competency framework', how many firms tried to measure people based on the company's values and ethics? And if they did, have they found a way to assess the candidate's values in a high-quality, in-depth and meaningful way? The answer is unfortunately not promising.

What organisations are also forgetting is that when we have com-petent professionals who do not have values or a moral compass, they can be dangerous and a big risk to the organisation, as they can use their competence to harm the organisation and its people in countless ways. Whereas, when you have values-driven professionals who have integrity and a moral compass, any gaps in competence can usually be addressed through training and development interventions.

Our framework of 11 Prophetic Leadership Qualities mapped four qualities which fall within a skills and competency domain as per the 'al-Qawi and al-Amin' dual framing we presented at the very begin-ning – namely Competence itself, Vision, Pragmatic Decisiveness and Holistic Justice. The rest of the seven qualities in the Integrity/Ethics box can be understood within a deeper character-oriented domain.

However, we would argue that the other four qualities, while hav-ing a skills and technical know-how nature about them, are also qual-ities which can be adopted and embraced in a deep and meaningful way. Hence, we can view Competence (with a Big 'C') and the other qualities as being part of the Prophetic Leadership model, where values, ethics and one's character are the heart of every one of the 11 leadership qualities, even the 'al-Qawi' box of four skills-oriented qualities.

All this leads us to the following questions: How can you truly measure values and ethics? How can you assess a person's true character? What can one ask to gain insight into a person's life experience and inner personality?

The novel answer is to ask how one dealt with a *crisis* personally or professionally. Nothing reveals a person's true character like a crisis. This is why experiential learning is key to self-development and character development, because a crisis offers us this experience, and the world can finally discover who you are. When this discovery happens, you might inadvertently be the most surprised person in the world!

## THE TEA BAG MOMENT

As the saying goes, *'Leadership is like a tea bag, you don't know how good it is until it's in hot water'*. Being in hot water, and hence a crisis, is the only way to reveal who you are and what you are made of. The tea bag moment is that moment of truth.

If we study Johari's window (as suggested in the tips section in the Spiritual Intelligence section), there are four windows to each of us. There are some things we know and others know about us, such as our name, height or skin colour. This is window 1. Then there are things we know about ourselves that others do not know, such as private matters, or what we had for lunch. This is window 2. This can be expanded through appropriate self disclosure and becoming a more transparent person, which in turn can make people trust you more, as they feel they know you well.

Then there are things that you had not realised about yourself, but others noticed about you, such as how you laugh, or how you look when you get angry. This is window 3, and can be an awkward place to be in. This can be addressed through seeking honest feedback.

The fourth  window are the things about oneself that we do not know and others do not know, but this is something that is real – one's potential. Here one can land safely through 'shared discovery', where one explores a new experience in a planned and anticipated way with the help of mentors and coaches. Hence, asking for a new responsibility in a job role, or applying for a new role or challenge, can be a way in which one can explore one's potential in a planned way.

But if you land unplanned in a new task that you have been asked to do due to unexpected circumstances, such as a colleague becoming unwell, this may feel like a crisis.[2] And how you handle and approach it reveals your true leadership potential.

Consider the following:

**E + R = O**
**EVENT + RESPONSE = OUTCOME**

The event is the crisis you are facing. Then you have your chosen response to that crisis. And then you have the outcome. One can face an event or crisis in a negative way, complain 'why me?' and waste a lot of time complaining about something that one cannot control. This will lead to a poor 'outcome'.

One can blame the economy, the weather, lack of money, lack of education, racism, the current government, our other half, our boss's attitude, the lack of support and so on.

Or, one can accept the event or crisis, and choose to respond positively and constructively.

The choice is ours. The control is in our hands. And our response will literally shape the outcome. From a faith perspective, this is metaphysically true as well, as God can change your fate and destiny if your response is positive.[3] In fact, God has ordained that our choices and actions also shape our own destinies!

## MASTERING VUCA

The well-known *Harvard Business Review* article on VUCA by Bennett and Lemione[4] helped us to recognise VUCA as our new reality – that we live in a Volatile, Uncertain, Complex and Ambiguous world. It is not just a reality in the West. It is in the East, in the North and in the South as well. Hence, Adrian Lock of Roffey Park Institute[5] notes our world as a 'VUCA-G' world, that we are VUCA-globally, because it really has permeated all corners of the globe.

In Dr Spencer Johnson's famous work *Who Moved My Cheese?*,

we discover how we must embrace the changing world and consider the future auspicious. We must be agile and master the wave of change. We must anticipate volatility and uncertainty, have our 'running shoes' handy, and learn to 'let go of the old cheese, get our shoes on and follow the scent of the new cheese, and learn to enjoy the new cheese'[6]

This means no rigid 5–10-year plans and strategies, when the world is not affording us the luxury of such predictability. We should get comfortable with ambiguity, and good at handling and breaking down complexity. We cannot be slow to embrace changes such as Artificial Intelligence (AI). We must be among those who embrace 'disruptors', when we have companies that were born only five years ago that have greater global impact than many other firms that have been around for 50 years but are struggling to survive. This compels us to think and behave completely differently.

The late Stephen Hawking suggested that AI spelled the end of the human race. That is only true if we remain analogue beings in the digital age. If we embrace reality, we use it to our advantage. But not naively. We must address ethical issues emerging from AI and ensure that we do not lose our EQ and SQ capacities which uniquely make us human, as discussed by Danah Zohar in the chapter on Spiritual Intelligence. We must build our character and ethics, and our Prophetic Leadership Qualities; we can then be the ethical conscience for the beast that is AI and allay Hawking's concerns.

We must become 'VUCA-G' Masters!

## SUSTAINABILITY AND THE VITAL THINGS WE NEGLECT

How do we sustainably become ethical and effective leaders who are VUCA-G Masters? It is by ensuring that we do not neglect three important things in life: our health, our faith and our family.

Your health is arguably the most important thing. You might say that it is your faith or your family that is most important, but without good health you cannot enjoy your faith or your family. The Prophet taught us that our body has a right over us. And the richest person in the world will tell you that if health goes, having all the money in the world means very little. Hence, let us not ruin our health in pursuit of wealth, only to then spend all our wealth trying to recover our health.

Our faith is also critically important. However, without our health we cannot enjoy our faith either, as we are forced to become exempt from many ritual duties.

However, beyond some bare minimum engagement with our faith (e.g. carrying out the *faraid* – compulsory duties and rituals or earning a halal income), we must recognise that our faith has a *halal* dimension and a *tayyib* dimension as the Prophet taught. This is the idea that some things might be permissible but not entirely ethical. And just as we must personally challenge ourselves to move beyond legal minimums, professionally, we must stop boardrooms only asking if it is legal, but also consider if it is ethical and morally appropriate.

As Sharif H. Banna outlines,[7] something may be *halal* but can still be un-Islamic. He argues that the ethical core of Islam be restored and the 'legal hegemony' of contemporary Muslim thought and practice be reconsidered. Becoming an ethical leader in a sustainable manner requires us to apply *tayyib*, i.e. best practice standards and interventions, not halal bare minimums.

And finally, family. Many will argue that this is the most important. Let us ask, do we truly appreciate our family when we are away from home? Are we able to move beyond earning a halal income to giving those regular moments each day to express our affection for one another, have quality conversations and one-to-ones rather than getting buried in devices or wasting time surfing the net or watching TV? Even here, if we value our family as we should, poor health can hinder one's ability to give the quality time to enjoy this fully.

Interestingly, research consistently shows that people who face a serious health condition or are at the end of their lives, were triggered by their health to cite their sources of happiness – this being their faith, their family and quality relationships. In whichever order we decide, if we embrace and prioritise these three things, we will have the kind of foundation from which sustainable leadership can grow.

This process of building sustainable leaders and human beings must start with our children. This means we must plant values in our children. Then, when they face crisis, the values will guide them and grow their soul, and they will handle their 'tea bag moment' better.

When children are not given values, they will not know how to handle crises, and then we end up producing a world of broken human beings who may find themselves carrying out unimaginable horrors – whether that is flying a plane into a tower, shooting innocent people in a mosque or church, or even a school, generating an ocean of suffering and life-long trauma for countless innocent people whose lives would have been destroyed by this vicious cycle of violence.

Building a sustainable foundation for ethical and effective leaders who are VUCA-G Masters can help change the world for the better.

## STEPPING UP

So, what are we waiting for? If we know what to do, and can turn a crisis to our advantage, should we sit back and let others make a mess of it? Should we bury ourselves in more studies as we are 'not ready yet'?

Bertolt Brecht aptly said in Galileo, 'unhappy is the land that needs a hero!' But let us declare, the land is unhappy, and a hero is called for.

Hence, the need to step up is nigh. In a land of good men, no-one wants to be a leader.[8] But the punishment of this approach is that we give permission for unethical or ineffective people to fill the post. In that sense, we are to blame for the world we find ourselves in.

Maybe we are afraid of power after what Abraham Lincoln said, and after what we have seen it do to other people. There are no doubt risks to power. But the solution is not to run away from power, but to mitigate its side effects. For believers, this not only means committing to ethical excellence but being God-conscious (taqwa) and realising that God is all aware of what we do as human beings. We will all individually be held accountable in another life for decisions we take in this life.

In the end, the world is left with three kinds of people. And only one of them involves a choice to embrace leadership to make a difference in the world. There are those who make things happen, those who watch things happen and those who wonder, 'what happened?'

Which will you choose to be?

# SELF ASSESEMENT

We have now had a detailed look at each of the 11 Prophetic Leadership Qualities (PLQ). Having understood them, we can now consider our own strengths and challenges with respect to these qualities. By using the 'wheel of leadership' tool we can create a map of our leadership nature.

**RATING YOURSELF**

Based on the 11 PLQs the wheel of leadership is as follows:

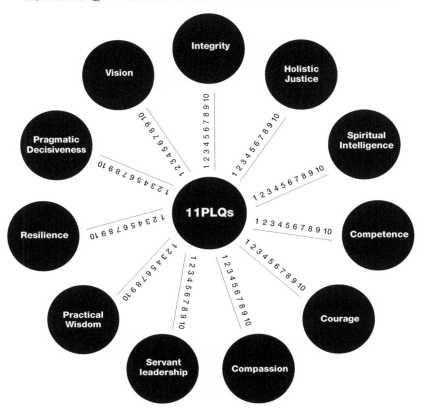

This outlines the 11 PLQs with lines against each quality for you to score yourself out of 10 in terms of the extent to which you believe you exhibit the quality concerned. When considering your score, you should not be too harsh or too generous, but balanced. You should consider, the kind of feedback, appraisal assessment and comments you have received over the years, and any other evidence that might point to the quality concerned.

For example, when considering whether you are a visionary person, consider if you have had any feedback about your ideas, whether you are requested to support the development of an organisational vision, whether you have ever set any project or initiative up because of your drive to see change. Similarly, on spiritual intelligence, consider if you are in tune with your feelings and your motivations. Are you cognisant of people, and their feelings and aspirations? Do you use the language of purpose in conversation? Do you ask deep questions or steer conversations towards that which is meaningful? Have you chosen your career or company based on its vision and values? These considerations may give you some clues.

If you proceed to draw the wheel on a sheet of paper and mark off your scores, you should then join the dots from one quality to the other and go around the entire wheel. Your wheel should then look something like the ones below:

You will find the next steps rather revelatory!

## THE BICYCLE ANALOGY

You should now have your leadership wheel shape. You can then draw this shape again, twice, adjacent to each other. Then draw yourself a simple bicycle diagram using the wheels. This might look something like this:

You should now have your leadership bicycle. So, the big question you should ask yourself looking at your bike is: how smooth is your journey right now as a leader?

Perhaps you are having a rather bumpy ride! If that is the case, you can be reassured that you are not alone. Have a look over your wheel again; see if there is any particular score that is striking or a bit concerning. Which qualities did you score lowest on? You may consider these your leadership 'punctures' that require some attention.

Then ask yourself: *What ideas do you have to improve on your area of focus? How will you implement your plan? What are the likely*

*obstacles you may face? How will you deal with those obstacles? Who can help you in this journey?*

By thinking through these steps, making some immediate plans for change and starting to implement them, you can begin to repair the punctures, and strengthen your leadership wheel. This, in turn, will lead to improved effectiveness and impact in whatever work, project or endeavour you are engaged in.

It is worth remembering that big and smooth wheels take you far. Too many punctures and you will struggle. And if the wheel is very small (for example, if you scored only 1 out of 10 for everything), that might seem like a smooth wheel, but even after much exertion and cycling, you cannot go very far in your journey on tiny wheels!

## MEASURING LEADERSHIP CALIBRE

The wheel offers a helpful way to identify areas to focus your development on. But where are you on the overall spectrum of leadership calibre? Are you currently an emerging leader, a high-calibre leader, or even of world leader calibre?

To help answer this, the following is a very simple and imperfect assessment which is nevertheless useful and indicative of where you might be on the spectrum. Simply populate your scores from the wheel, and tally up the total in the table below.

## CALIBRE SELF ASSESSMENT TABLE

| LEADERSHIP QUALITY | SELF ASSESSMENT SCORE X/10 |
| --- | --- |
| INTEGRITY | |
| COMPETENCE | |
| VISION | |
| COURAGE | |
| HOLISTIC JUSTICE | |
| PRAGMATIC DECISIVENESS | |
| SERVANT LEADERSHIP | |
| PRACTICAL WISDOM | |
| RESILIENCE | |
| COMPASSION | |
| SPIRITUAL INTELLIGENCE | |
| | __/110 |

Once you have your total, you can consider yourself against four grouped ranges from 'not leadership calibre yet' to 'world leader' level. The following score key has been designed based on mapping score ranges against a wide selection of leaders in business, politics, education, charity and community contexts. These leadership reference points are contemporary and not limited to one geographical region, given our belief in the universality of the PLQs. The score ranges are as follows:

| Score Key | |
| --- | --- |
| **95–110** | World leader/transformational leader |
| **80–95** | High-calibre leader/emergent leader |
| **50–80** | Manager/transactional leader/Leadership potential |
| **0–50** | Not leadership calibre yet |

If you find yourself scoring from 0–50, do not despair. Many great leaders started from humble beginnings and went on to become unexpected leaders. We mentioned earlier in the section on competence that personal development was 80% nurture and 20% nature; hence, anyone can develop their leadership calibre.

If you scored 50–80, this may reflect a transition point that many people face between followership and leadership. You may be content where you are, as not everyone has to become a world leader, however it is advisable to reflect on your punctures and gradually work on strengthening those, even if you plan to 'stay where you are' in your personal and professional life. If, however, you are determined to accelerate your growth as a leader, then a concerted effort to grow your wheel and repair your punctures is essential. You may want to attend leadership development programmes, and seek to enrich your professional role and build your experience through promotion or seeking new responsibilities within your existing role. You may also benefit from regular mentoring with an experienced leader.

If you have made it to the 80–95 range, this is a great achievement. Clearly you have a good-size wheel, and even if some worrying punctures exist you have compensated for this by having a good score in other leadership qualities. Those qualities will have carried you to succeed in many personal and professional endeavours. You are likely to have a sense of direction, life experience and confidence, and will have projected this on to others who are influenced by you. As an emergent leader, you are only a short step away from becoming a transformational leader; however, those additional steps are not easily made. And reading the odd book or attending the odd course will not be enough, if you wish to make a further developmental leap. You may hence like to consider executive coaching. Unlike a mentor or teacher who answers your questions, a skilled coach questions your answers. They will help you think through your ideas and plans, and facilitate your growth. They will expand your self-awareness, ask searching questions and help you to tap into your inner power and capabilities.

If, however, you have actually made it to the 95–110 range (and that this is a fair reflection of your true level), firstly, I am honoured that you are reading my book! You are clearly a transformational leader, likely to have global influence and impact. You lead other leaders, and shape the agenda that others respond to. You have built a track record of achievement, perhaps won awards in recognition of your contributions, and are called upon by others to share your insights in various platforms and major conferences. You will have averaged above 8.6 in your scores; hence, you will have many 8s and 9s, and perhaps some 10 out of 10s, against the PLQs, which is a rare accomplishment.

At such a level, there are not many ways to develop further leadership calibre beyond the challenging role you are already carrying out, and learning from it. However, it is still advisable to have a senior coach of some kind. Indeed, Bill Clinton and Oprah Winfrey famously had coaches, such as the well-known Tony Robbins. Even if a professional coach is not engaged, finding the right special advisor as we find around prime ministers and presidents is worth considering. An able sounding board is invaluable to any leader.

# THE 360° COMPARTOR

Having mapped your wheel and scored your calibre table in Appendix I, this self-assessment approach will naturally have some limitations to bear in mind. Clearly, the accuracy of such an assessment is heavily dependent on your self-awareness and objectivity with your own self (we can understandably be very subjective about number 1!). To verify your accuracy, you should apply a 360° feedback approach. Hence, find someone who knows you well, knows how you work, and is willing to provide honest feedback. This might be a colleague, a friend or even a family member. Within a workplace, you should consider your superiors, peers, and subordinates to get a rounded (360°) view.

The chosen individual can then score the wheel based on a fair view they have about you and your leadership qualities. It is important that you make it clear to them that you welcome honest feedback, and they should feel at liberty to express that. Ideally, you may want to make this process anonymous for those giving feedback. Note: it is not necessary for them to do the table as well, nor should they see the leadership calibre ranges, they should simply score the wheel.

Then comes the key part; once the feedback is in, compare it with your self-assessment. You will likely find that not all your scores are matching. On some qualities you may be scored higher by others than you assessed for yourself. This might suggest you have not given yourself enough credit in regard to that that quality. But you may well find that some have scored you lower on certain qualities (if they were being honest enough!). And this may (or may not) have some bearing on the total score, which in turn could affect where they see you on the leadership calibre spectrum.

When you discover a low score, you may well find it uncomfortable, perhaps a little painful to swallow. This is understandable, but you must persevere and take it on board by at least reflecting on it. Great leaders are more interested in criticism than praise. Praise teaches you nothing, and does not develop you. Criticism and constructive feedback can help you grow to a higher calibre and excel.

Those who have done this have gone on to achieve great things, as we have seen in the case studies outlined in the chapters.

# ACTION-CENTRED LEADERSHIP AND THE SIRAH

*The following maps out further details of the official content of the Adair ACL™ model, which was highlighted in the chapter on the leadership quality of 'competence'. These can be downloaded from the official Adair International website.*

*In light of this universal 3-circle model, some reflections are offered here on the life of the Prophet Muhammad, where the ACL framework and its three levels are mapped across key moments in the Sirah.*

*To attend the training of trainers and gain a formal licence as an accredited ACL trainer visit http://www.adair-international.com/*

The world's first leadership professor outlined his own list of generic and universal qualities that he believed all leaders should possess. John Adair thus outlined that a leader should have the following qualities:

- Enthusiasm
- Integrity
- Toughness and Fairness
- Warmth
- Moral Courage
- Resilience
- Humility

As one can see, most of these overlap with our own prophetic leadership framework, even though the two frameworks were derived from different means and created at different times. It is noteworthy that the great professor felt compelled to write a book on 'The Leadership of Muhammad', making him the only major global leadership authority in the West to have done so in recent times. He noted how the Prophet displayed all the above qualities and considered him one of the greatest leaders in history.

## ACTION-CENTRED LEADERSHIP

Adair has written some 50 books and developed some of the most noteworthy leadership ideas and frameworks of the past half century. His most renowned contribution is his discovery of the 3-circle 'action-centred leadership' model.

Where the Prophetic leadership qualities provide a framework for building the character of great and authentic leaders (what a leader must be), the Action-Centred Leadership (ACL) model provides the function and role of leadership; in other words, what a leader must do. We will explore this framework and then look at how the model played out in the life and leadership of the Prophet.

The framework is as follows:[1]

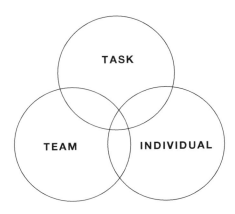

The three interconnected circles show that a leader has to take responsibility for the achievement of the task, build and maintain an effective team, and manage and develop each individual. It is a simple model. But not simplistic.

We mentioned in the opening chapter that there had been over 200 varying definitions of leadership between the 1920s and early 2000s, and an effort to integrate these yielded the following simple definition:

> *'leadership is about a person ... somehow moving other people to do something'*

Again, simple but not simplistic. This was the sum total of nearly a century of leadership thought, revealing in simple terms the deep philosophy of what leadership is about. And it is most striking that this definition also has the three main elements – a 'person' (individual), other people (team), who need to do something (task). Although developed separately, this study essentially confirmed the truth of Adair's 3-circle model, a model that incidentally reflects nearly a hundred years of research.

Leadership hence boils down to this. One may then ask who this 'person' should be, why should 'other people' follow him or her, and what is that 'something' they are moving people towards. This is where the qualities can come in – that some may follow the leader due to their integrity, their fairness, perhaps the power of their vision, or being impressed with their competence. There may be many other reasons beyond the qualities, and these things embellish our discussion on leadership. However, all things said and done, leadership comes back to the three fundamental functional elements – task, team and individual.

It is not difficult to identify how the Prophet paid attention to these three areas in his leadership. We will explore these three areas further before sharing their prophetic application.

## EXPLORING THE TASK ELEMENT

The 'task' element is about providing a vision, defining aims, setting SMART[2] objectives and specifying targets. It is about devising a plan with milestones, describing outcomes and agreeing measures of success. More broadly, it is about creating purpose and clarity around the task.

It is also about establishing competencies, and the standards of behaviour which relate to and affect the output of the task. A leader then has to allocate responsibilities and leads for each task, ensure adequate resources are made available, and check that the required systems, policies and processes are in place to support the effective and appropriate delivery of the task.

To ensure performance and delivery, reporting mechanisms need to be created, and the effective management of information is necessary (note: this can be done efficiently using technology and performance management software systems). Strong communication and feedback channels are required, and need to be used and leveraged. Plans should regularly be reviewed, adjusted and fine-tuned in light of results and impact.

In summary, a leader should be asking the following in relation to the task:
- Are the targets clearly set out?
- Are there clear standards of performance?
- Are available resources defined?
- Are responsibilities clear?
- Are resources fully utilised?
- Are targets/standards being defined?
- Is a systematic approach being used?
- Are there appropriate measurement methods?

## EXPLORING THE TEAM ELEMENT
The 'team' element is about building cooperation, collaboration and synergy. It is about cultivating a common sense of purpose, and motiving the group. Leaders must also work to build in collective discipline, with routines, rituals and team working standards which in turn will aid performance, quality and expected behaviour.

Leaders should be careful not to micromanage, and allow any given team space to work. However, support is important, to help when necessary to coach and steer. In addition, teams can be developed as a collective through training events, learning activities, away days and team challenges.

Part of human nature is for disagreements to arise between people, whether at the level of ideas or even personalities. Leaders must help their teams to be able to deal with conflict – both internally within a given team and with other teams and departments. Creating a transparent culture of courtesy and feedback is part of building an effective team that can cope with conflict and accommodate healthy disagreements.

In summary a leader should be asking the following in relation to the team:

- Is there a common identity?
- Is there a common sense of purpose?
- Is there a supportive climate?
- Is the team or unit growing and developing?
- Does the team know about their role?
- Does the team respond to the leader's engagement?
- Is there a sense of collective endeavour and achievement?

## EXPLORING THE INDIVIDUAL ELEMENT

The 'individual' element is about supporting and empowering each person to thrive and succeed. It is about making the effort to understand each person as a unique individual with specific needs, wants and drivers.

Leaders must make time to understand, support and develop the individuals who make up the team and organisation under their stewardship. This involves regular one-to-ones where the leader does as much listening as talking, if not more. One should get to know their team members – their personalities, their preferences, their strengths, their areas for development, their concerns and aspirations.

Leaders should also engage in the performance management and appraisal process, and while this has many forms and approaches, what is key is to have regular communication, feedback and support. Each individual should also have a personal and professional development plan. This may involve arranging for training and coaching, shadowing and secondments.

The individual element additionally involves delegating important responsibilities (not just things a leader does not feel like doing!) in order to enrich the followers' skills and experience. This includes being supportive when they occasionally get things wrong in the process of learning and growing.

One of the most powerful ways to motivate people is to give recognition, praise and constructive feedback after a good piece of work or display of good behaviour. It matters to people when their hard work and effort is noticed, especially by their leader, and when it is forthcoming, their commitment and motivation further increases. It signals to them that this kind of work or behaviour should be repeated.

The individual element is not just about supporting people in the present, but also about looking for their potential in the future. Hence, leaders need to look for the talents of tomorrow and provide the necessary support to help individuals fulfil their long-term potential.

In summary, a leader should be asking the following in relation to individuals:

Does each individual feel accepted?

Does each individual know what is expected of them?

Is each individual involved in the organisation?

Has every individual been able to contribute?

Does each individual feel valued by the organisation?

Is there provision for individual growth and development of each individual's potential?

## INTERDEPENDENCY OF ACL

When it comes to the 3 circles, many, perhaps most leaders are pre-occupied with the 'task', the job at hand, the objectives and the deliverables of the organisation concerned. It is commonplace to hear professionals complain of workload and pressure from their bosses to deliver and perform. This obsession with work and performance is often accompanied with a neglect of the team and the individual's needs. People hence come second, and in today's digital age, people are increasingly being taken out of the equation.

Some spend a good amount of time building a harmonious team, and ensuring inter- and intra-departmental engagement is taking place. But while everyone might be getting on well, they may lose sight of the task at hand, miss deadlines or fail to perform generally.

Perhaps the most neglected area is that of the individual. A harmonious team does not necessarily mean that each individual's needs have been met. It is hence essential to allocate time for this oft-forgotten element.

Indeed, as the ACL model shows, it is essential to pay attention to all three elements at all times, and the neglect of one affects the other. This interdependency is illustrated here:

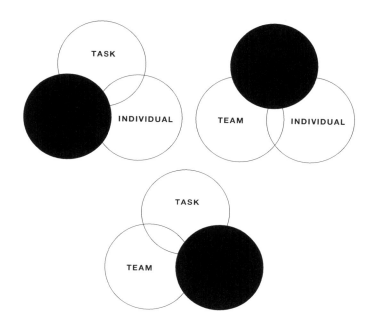

When the task is neglected, then rather like a coin covering the task circle, the other two circles are encroached. The team cannot thrive and starts to become redundant if they are not delivering anything. The individual will not feel utilised or fulfilled if they are not doing anything.

Similarly, if the team is neglected, the quality and timely delivery of the task will eventually get affected. And a neglected team is one where individuals within the team are either sidelined, disengaged, distracted or unfulfilled in some other way.

And finally, if the individual is neglected, as is often the case, not only will their tasks get affected, but the organisation's potential to achieve its overall vision can be harmed as well. And no team can fully thrive if some of its individuals and their needs have been relegated in importance.

It hence becomes clear that the task, team and individual elements are truly interdependent and require simultaneous time and attention by leaders.

## COMMON NEEDS

Within each of the three elements of the Action-Centred Leadership model, there are eight things which need to be done. These 'common needs', as Adair calls them, are as follows:

1. Defining
2. Planning
3. Briefing
4. Controlling
5. Supporting
6. Motivating
7. Evaluating
8. Setting an Example

Whether at a task level, team level or individual level, the leader has to define the task, the group's role, the individuals' responsibilities and essentially define their purpose. The leader has to facilitate the planning process for effective management and delivery. They have to brief and communicate, and encourage others to do the same. They need appropriate control mechanisms, especially where financial and legal risks are at stake.

Leaders also need to build a climate of support for the task, for the team and for each individual. They need to motivate people to take ownership of the task, to work as a cohesive team, and to give each individual a sense of drive and purpose. After the appropriate passage of time and as work output emerges, there is need for evaluation and quality feedback in relation to the task, the effectiveness of the team and the performance of the individual.

And finally, none of the above can really achieve its full potential unless the leader sets the example, acts as a role model, and shows the way. The impact of leadership example setting should not be underestimated. Indeed, as research by HayMcber shows, the example of leaders influences some 50–60% of the whole organisation's climate, which in turn shapes culture. Hence, these eight needs are common to all the three elements of the ACL model, and they need to be carried out in the context of the task, the team and the individual.

## THE HELICOPTER VIEW

Once a leader has an effective routine, system and culture of caring for, and giving time to, the task, team and individual, there is a need to step back, take stock and take an overview posture. Adair describes this as the 'helicopter view', where the leader hovers above the three circles, providing autonomy, and avoiding micromanagement.

This does not mean that they are disconnected or detached. Nor should they go out of the loop of what is going on. Rather, they should keep an eye on all three circles from a distance, rather like the helicopter, but if something starts to go wrong, the leader can fly down to the circle of concern and help remedy the situation, then fly back up.

Perhaps a task is not getting done or output is not what was required. The leader can fly in to clarify the task and offer the necessary support and resources. Or perhaps a team is stuck in disagreement over a project, or are not communicating well between themselves or with other departments. The leader can fly in to mediate the matter, and get the team moving again, then step away and fly back up. Or it could be that an individual does not look happy, or their performance has started to dip. The leader can fly down and enquire as to what the problem is, and facilitate a solution to help the individual or address the issue.

In this way, a leader should balance the need to manage in person with giving their people space to work and succeed.

## THE OPERATION AND STRATEGIC LEVELS

The above overview of the ACL model represents the foundational level which can be applied in any team context, however small. Hence, team leaders running a small unit or department can draw on this. Once a leader has a larger remit of responsibility, perhaps a medium to large team or the leadership of more than one team, further responsibilities need to be considered.

Adair outlines the following things that leaders need to do at the 'operational level' of leadership:

1.  Influencing
2.  Informing
3.  Interpreting
4.  Initiating

5. Implementing
6. Networking
7. Succession planning

An operational leader, in addition to the foundational unit and team level responsibilities, needs to develop greater depth in their work and engagement, from influencing skills and the ability to interpreting complex information, to initiating projects that will help implement the organisation's deliverables, and networking within and beyond the organisation to build collaboration, and managing recruitment and succession – all are key operational responsibilities.

At the most senior level, Adair outlines the following things that leaders need to do. Hence, the 'strategic level' of leadership includes the following functions:

1. Providing direction for the organisation as a whole
2. Strategic thinking and planning
3. Making it happen
4. Relating the whole to the parts
5. Releasing the corporate spirit
6. Building partnerships
7. Developing today's and tomorrow's leaders

Hence, a strategic leader from an ACL perspective has to take a macro view and bring the organisation together. This involves setting the overall direction, then facilitating the detailed thinking and planning involved. It goes beyond basic implementation efforts to making thing happen, one way or another.

It involves sense-making, to help others understand how their part of the organisation relates to other parts as building blocks that make the organisation possible. It is about building a culture and positive spirit – an energy that helps and motivates everyone.

The leader must build inter-divisional relations to ensure other leaders are collaborating and cooperating with one another, and forge key partnerships externally, particularly at an institutional level, which can be leveraged to further the goals of the organisation.

And finally, any leader wanting to build a sustainable future must work to develop other high-calibre leaders who can share in the current responsibilities and be ready to step up when the times comes.

## PROPHETIC LEADERSHIP QUALITIES AND ACL

The 11 Prophetic Leadership Qualities are necessary while applying the Action-Centred Leadership approach. While they are relevant in each of the three elements, from task to team to individual, some qualities have a closer association with certain ACL circles.

Hence, the qualities of being visionary and strategic, pragmatic in decision making, competent and having a servant leader approach become particularly relevant in relation to tasks. A vision or strategy is intrinsically about the task to be pursued. Decisions typically relate to work matters and tasks – such as the decision to prioritise one task over another. One's ability to apply a servant leader approach manifests itself when a leader shares in the tasks of their followers. And one's competence and capability are usually measured in light of one's ability to perform a task well.

When considering the team circle, a leader needs to demonstrate just leadership and fairness in his or her dealings with team members, and failure to do so will quickly get noticed by the team. A leader has to have courage to deal with teams and groups of people, which for many can be an intimidating experience, even if they are the leader. They need to have patience while managing many personalities, recognising that the patience will pay off long term and is better than the alternative. And they need practical wisdom to help the team move forward, especially during times of conflict that need mediation and fair resolution.

At the individual, one-to-one level, the fundamental quality of integrity is a must, which then cascades to the other circles of the ACL model. Having trust between one another is the starting point, as followers will rarely engage with leaders that they do not trust. Leaders will need to have compassion and be warm, gentle and appreciative of individuals. This will make them feel that the leader cares, and this can engender an incredible amount of commitment and loyalty. This also relates to the quality of emotional intelligence, but the next level, that of spiritual intelligence, can take this individual commitment to the highest level, when the leader is able to give a sense of purpose and meaning to their followers.

In short, when we combine leadership *being* with leadership *doing*, we can achieve our goals, as is illustrated below:

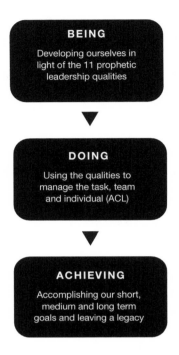

## ACL IN THE SIRAH

The life of the Prophet was in no doubt action centred and dynamic. At the task level, he was always active and driven from a young age. Since the age of 12 he would join trade caravans to Syria. At 16, he ran the 'Hilf al-Fudul', an organisation whose task and goal was to help the needy.[3] Soon after Prophethood, where he was given a divine task, he set out on the path to promote the belief in one God. He was very clear about his mission, having endured 13 years of persecution and mistreatment from those opposed to change.

He was good at delegating tasks, ensuring the right person was given the right role. He would assign the highly respected Abu Bakr to lead prayers in his place, give the great commander Khaled bin Walid challenging military responsibilities and empower the learned Muadh ibn Jabal to go to new lands to deliver the spiritual message of Islam.

Achieving great tasks requires great ambition, and the Prophet showed immense ambition during the battle of the trench.[4] In the midst of a siege, as he helped to dislodge a rock blocking the trench-digging process, he spoke of a vision of spreading the message of God to faraway places such as Persia. It is not easy to speak of success when you appear to be on the verge of possible defeat, but a leader must be able to articulate a vision and task which can inspire.

At the team level, the Prophet was very keen on collectivism and community. Prayers would be in congregation – something that is repeatedly emphasised as important. He would hold regular team meetings, classes and circles for learning and development.

Major journeys took place in groups. He sent a group of persecuted Muslims to Abyssinia (now Ethiopia) for safety. He sent a small team to Yathrib (later renamed Medina) to lay the foundations ahead of the mass migration (*hijra*) of the Muslim community in 622AD.[5] From defence and war, to the construction of his mosque, it was always a team effort.

He was also eager to promote good relations between colleagues, facilitated mediation and encouraged forgiveness. Hence, as we noted before, the Prophet advised: *'Exchange gifts, and mutual love arises; shake hands, and enmity will fall away'* (Ibn Asakir).

This positive team culture led to amazing instances where companions would go out of their way to be accommodating and forgiving. On one occasion, two companions had an argument and then walked off. Later they both went to the Prophet at different times, but not to complain or press their arguments upon him, but in a state of anxiousness at how they could get the other person to forgive them!

Sometimes teams may not be ready to follow their leader's instructions. Earlier we mentioned that during the treaty of Hubaibiyah, the Prophet had given the unconventional instruction to his large team to complete the pilgrimage rituals outside of the holy sanctuary, in light of the treaty which did not allow entrance to the Ka'ba that year. His team, struggling to process his instructions, sat in their places and did not move. He eventually proceeded to set the example and carry out the instructions and rituals himself. In seeing him act, his team soon overcame their misgivings and followed.

At the individual level, the Prophet projected a great presence in the way that he carried himself and the dignified way he treated people. It is said that he had the ability to make every individual feel like they were the most special to him.

He would frequently have one-to-ones with his companions, from the top talents such as Abu Bakr and Umar, to the lesser known, the poor and the weak. He kept his future successors close to him, always training and developing them. While some were clearly suitable for major leadership roles, others such as Abu Dhar were not. How does a line manager tell an eager employee they are not ready for a promotion? The Prophet had to have that conversation with Abu Dhar, gently and sensitively counselling him that he was not going to get the governorship he sought.

When the great Abu Bakr became stressed as he and the Prophet hid from the Meccans in Cave Thawr, he was able to calm and counsel Abu Bakr against fear, reminding him that God was with them and would protect them.

At both an individual and team level, it is worth mentioning the famous pact of sharing that the Prophet established between the Medinan Muslims (the Ansar or 'helpers') and the Meccan Muslims (the Muhajirin or 'migrators'). This was a special team arrangement to help the individual needs of the Muhajirin who lost everything as they were forced to leave Mecca. The Ansar shared open-heartedly, arranging food, accommodation and even a marriage partner.

It is hence abundantly apparent that the Prophet paid a lot of attention to all three circles of the ACL model, and as such role modelled the very truth of leadership. He would keep an eye on the task, team and individual, take a helicopter view, and intervene as and when needed.

In light of the above examples, his leadership at an operational and strategic level is not difficult to see. He was an *influencer* who, even in a position of weakness in Mecca, was able to place incredible pressure on the Quraysh who were unable to ignore his influence and impact. He *initiated* a manoeuvre, turning up to *implement* the pilgrimage, forcing the Quraysh into negotiations which eventually lead to the conquest and takeover of Mecca.

He was *providing direction* to his organisation of followers every day, *strategically thinking* and *planning* the achievement of his divine task by identifying tribes and cities to engage and reach out to. His leadership provided an energy and impetus for action, and hence he was able to turn talk into action and *make things happen*.

He would relate the whole to the parts, making each individual think of the wider community of Muslims, symbolised by his famous statement: *'the believer in their affection, mercy and compassion, is like one body; if one part suffers, the whole body responds in sleeplessness and fever'.* He forged alliances and *built partnerships* where possible, even during his challenging time in Mecca, from the King of Abyssinia, who sheltered the besieged Meccan Muslims, to his uncle Abu Talib, who provided protection even though he did not believe in the faith.

Perhaps the strategic level which is most distinctive is the fact that he was one of the few leaders in history who successfully *developed today's and tomorrow's leaders.* Aside from the astonishing leadership talent he built around him leading to the unlikely establishment of Islam across Arabia, despite their humble beginnings, he developed a series of able and worthy successors who led and hugely expanded the Muslim world after him, and few great leaders in history were able to do the same. As the renowned French poet and politician Alphonse de Lamartine once said: *'if greatness of purpose, smallness of means and astounding results are the three criteria of human genius, who could dare to compare any great man ... with Muhammad.'*

# THREE PATHWAYS TO PERSONAL AND LEADERSHIP DEVELOPMENT

Self-development and behaviour change is a deep science. And people have diverse learning styles and ways in which they grow. I believe that learning has not really occurred until there is a change in behaviour. But to achieve this level of learning and change, one has to take a comprehensive approach in the leadership development journey.

Among the array of ways to frame the learning and development process, the following may be helpful. There are three levels of self-development to bear in mind – the intellectual level, the experiential level and the spiritual level; in a sense, the mind, body and soul. To truly develop yourself in any of the 11 Prophetic Leadership Qualities (and beyond), one must pursue interventions at all three levels. Some suggestions have been shared earlier in the 'tips' accompanying each PLQ, and these generally cut across all three levels of self-development.

The *intellectual pathway* involves academic and conceptual engagement with the subject in question. Hence, reading books, listening to topical and self-help audios, watching educational videos, attending courses, and even gaining a qualifications, all fall under the intellectual pathway.

This is very helpful in building one's knowledge base. However, in most cases it is not enough, without gaining practical experience. One can read about cars and driving theory, but until one gets behind the wheel, you have not actually learnt how to drive a car.

The *experiential pathway* is, hence, a critical follow-on accompaniment to the intellectual pathway. Life experience, work experience and having experience in any subject counts for a lot, and reflects ability and credibility in that area. Hence, with any of the 11 PLQs (and indeed anything else), you should embark on gaining experience of the area in question.

Some of the suggestions in the competence section are experiential in nature, and practical suggestions have also been provided in the other 'tips' sections. In leadership development generally, there is no substitute for the actual experience of managing and leading other people. You should pursue and take up people management roles, and observe how you lead people. By drawing on regular feedback and modifying your behaviour and approach, you will accelerate your leadership capability.

Within a secular and a religious context, the intellectual and experiential pathways would usually be as far as the scope of development discussions would go. However, those with an appreciation of the innate spiritual nature of human beings will recognise that a holistic approach to personal development requires engagement with the spiritual level as well.

We noted earlier how the like of Danah Zohar and others attempted to explore the spiritual dimension of people without proper recourse to religion. However, these efforts are limited in depth, and lack the rootedness that a religious tradition such as Islam offers.

In pursuing the *spiritual pathway,* one unlocks a metaphysical dimension that is not achievable purely through intellectual or experiential means. Prophetic rituals and practices relating to '*tarbiyatul iman'* (nurturing one's faith) and '*tazkiyatun nafs'* (purifying oneself), can opens one's heart, reveal insights, invite blessings, and build one's cosmic disposition destined for leadership and enlightenment.

This is often the difference between the proverbial wise owl and the cunning fox, described earlier,[1] where the cunning fox can reach leadership and influence through intellectual and experiential development, but the wise owl ethical leader draws on the spiritual dimension as well.[2]

In the case of the former, their hearts are closed and their legacy as a moral leader diminished. In the Quran, Allah speaks of such hypocritical people, saying:

> *'Their example is that of one who kindled a fire, but when it illuminated what was around him, Allah took away their light and left them in darkness [so] they could not see. Deaf, dumb and blind – so they will not return [to the right path].'* (2:17–18)

By the same token, those who devote time in spiritual development and obedience to the divine, they will hear, speak and see in alignment with their creator. They will access deeper domains of the human experience which others fail to do. This three-level comprehensive approach, if engaged with properly, has the potential to give one an edge and an advantage in leadership.

In addition, one needs *'suhba'* (good companionship), and learned mentors (a *murabbi* or *shaykh*) who can cultivate one's character, give feedback and impart wisdom. The Prophet said:

> *'A person's spiritual practice is only as good as that of his close friends; so consider well whom you befriend.'* (Tirmidhi)

He also said:

> *'A person who teaches goodness to other while neglecting his own soul is like an oil lamp, which illuminates other while burning itself out.'* (Tabarani)

Hence, even a mentor should have a mentor, and leaders at all levels should have advisors and wise counsel.

Ultimately, the spiritual pathway is a journey to build *taqwa* (God consciousness), and developing closeness to our creator. It is to want more than just spiritual experiences, or even paradise, but to seek the highest aspiration and the purest intention – that of seeking God's pleasure.

And in that journey, we must never forget to raise our hand, shed some tears and maintain the divine dialogue (*dua*). The greatest leaders in Islamic history were the greatest weepers in their prayers. To understand this, we must recount the wise words of Ali Ibn Abi Talib, who said:

> 'The shortest distance between a problem and its solution is the distance between your knees and the floor. The one who kneels to God can stand up to anything.'

# ENDNOTES

## INTRODUCTION

1    Philip Green bought BHS for £200m in 2000, but the firm performed poorly, so he sold it for just £1 in 2015. By April 2016, BHS had debts of £1.3bn, including a pensions deficit of £571m. Despite the deficit of £571m, Green and his family collected £586m in dividends, rental payments and interest on loans during their 15-year ownership of the retailer. Simon Walker, the Director General of the Institute of Directors, described Green's 'lamentable failure of behaviour', which was deeply damaging to the reputation of business.

2    Habil and Qabil were the good and bad sons of Adam. Hence, we indicate the subsequent inclinations drawn from the earliest examples of mankind

3    See Adair, John (2010) The Leadership of Muhammad, London, UK: Kogan Page

4    John Adair is the world's first leadership professor, based in the UK, having written some 50 books. The ACL model is his most famous and widely used theory. For more information on the ACL model visit http://www.adair-interna-tional.com/ and http://www.johnadair.co.uk/

5    Leadership ideas are countless, and we have only highlighted a handful from recent years. All these are easily found from open sources online. Many of these are discussed in the works of Keith Grint (Grint, K (2010), Leadership: A Very Short Introduction, OUP Oxford).

6    Davis, K. (1967). *Human Relations at Work: The Dynamics of Organisational Behavior.* New York, McGraw-Hill, p.96

7    Drucker, Peter F. *The Practice of Management*. Oxford: Elsevier Ltd., (1955)

8    In 1999, when I joined Manchester Business School, our opening lecture was with Professor Jeff Henderson, who I am quoting directly.

9    Dr Illes is a rare Western academic who values faith and spiritual perspectives

in leadership, and believes it can add value in solving many of today's leadership problems.

10 See Adair, John (2010) The Leadership of Muhammad, London, UK: Kogan Page

11 We hence find countries in the geographic East such as Australia, Singapore, Japan and South Korea that adopt Western values, while countries in the geographic West often align more to Eastern faith-based values, such as Bosnia, Turkey, Italy (especially the Vatican) and Brazil – the world's largest Catholic country.

12 By 'religionism', I mean those who believe religion represents a primary source of governance in life and society including politics, in a way that secularism does not always appear to allow in many countries.

13 Ref: http://ilmfeed.com/a-non-muslim-poets-testimony-of-prophet-muhammad-peace-be-upon-him/

14 These refer to the five regular prayers, spiritual invocations, Quranic recitation and night prayer.

15 From Al-Ghazali's work titled al-Tibr al-Masbuk fi Nasihat al-Muluk or Ingots of Gold for the Advice of Kings. See also http://www.dinarstandard.com/imam-ghazali-on-leadership-ethics/

16 One observes vested interests leading people to engage in controversial activities, which they then retrospectively try to embellish with values, although in reality they were not values-driven activities. And even where the ends are moral, the means are not always so.

## CHAPTER 1: INTEGRITY

1 The Quranic references in relation to describing Prophet Muhammad also leads with integrity.

2 See Kouzes, J. and Posner, B. (1995) The Leadership Challenge, John Wiley & Sonsp.17. See also 2002 edition which covered over 70,000 responses across six continents which broadly confirmed similar results.

3 Taken from Adair, J (2010) p.61. Also stated in his speech at Imperial on 2 March 2011 (see http://murabbi.com/events.php?id=1&art=8)

4 For details see https://www.transparency.org/news/feature/corruption_perceptions_index_2016. Results in year end 2018 worsened in many ways, which underlines the urgency of the situation.

5 For surveys and statistics on this see http://www.ibe.org.uk/

6 Read Owen Jones acclaimed book Jones, O, (2015) The Establishment: And How They Get Away With It, Penguin, UK (2015) for a deeper insight into the powerful in business, the media and politics.

7 Taken from Ciulla, J. B.Å(2003), Ethics and Leadership Effectiveness, Edward Elgar (Cheltenham, UK & MA, USA).

8 See Ihya Ulum al Din by Abu Hamid Al Ghazali for a deep psycho-ethical study on character development

9 Based on Nadwi, S (1999)Nadwi, S (1999) Ethics in Islam, Darul-Ishaat (Karachi). Note the pyramid has been designed by us, drawing on the sequence explained in prose by Nadwi.

10 A word on terminology: the definitions of virtues and values are closely related, and while they vary in the way they are used, we will use them interchangeably for our purposes.

11　Compiled from Nadwi, S (1999)Nadwi, S (1999) *Ethics in Islam*, Darul-Ishaat (Karachi) .

12　Note: These are broad philosophical concepts, and there are variant scholarly perspectives on how best to categorise and understand the nature of Islamic law and of ethics. We offer one plausible way to view these subjects but note this is by no means the only view or understanding.

13　See Nadwi, S (1999)Nadwi, S (1999) *Ethics in Islam,* Darul-Ishaat (Karachi) p.81.

14　See Al-Banna (2013) article 'Halal but Un-Islamic'.- https://www.cilecenter. org/resources/articles-essays/halal-un-islamic-restoring-ethical-core-islam [Accessed in 2019]

15　Based on Al-Banna, S.M.H. (2002)Al-Banna, S.M.H. (2002), *Seerah of the Final Prophet*, Awakening (UK) p.159.

16　See Quran: Surah At-Tawba 9:25-27.

17　This is one of the many meanings of Ihsan. Other meanings include excellence, doing good, best practice and forgiveness.

18　See James, K. and Baddeley, S (1987), *Owl, Fox, Donkey or Sheep: Political Skills for Managers.* (Management Education and Development. Vol. 18. Pt. 1. 1987. pp. 3-19) James, S. and Baddeley, K. (1987) p3-19.

19　See James, K. and Baddeley, S (1987), *Owl, Fox, Donkey or Sheep: Political Skills for Managers.* (Management Education and Development. Vol. 18. Pt. 1. 1987. pp. 3-19) James, S. and Baddeley, K. (1987) p3-19.

20　Ali, Muhammad; Ali, Hana Yasmeen (2013) *The Soul of a Butterfly*, Simon & Schuster. p. 85.

21　"Muhammed Ali's Pilgrimage to Makkah". Emel. No. 17. February 2006. Retrieved September 4, 2016.

22　Bryan, Chloe (June 4, 2016). "Muhammad Ali had a thought-provoking response when asked about his retirement plans". Mashable. Retrieved September 4, 2016.

23　"Muhammad Ali: The Face of 'Real Islam'". Al Jazeera. June 6, 2016. Retrieved September 4, 2016.

## CHAPTER 2: COMPETENCE

1　Based on Al-Banna, S.M.H. (2002)Al-Banna, S.M.H. (2002), *Seerah of the Final Prophet*, Awakening (UK) p.22-23.

2　Based on Adair, John (2010) The Leadership of Muhammad, London, UK: Kogan Page Adair, John (2010) p.60.

3　See www.constitution.org/cons/medina/macharter.htm

4　Reproduced with copright permission from John Adair.

5　See Coffey, B (2011), *The Four Companies That Own 147 Companies That Own Everything* – see https://www.forbes.com/sites/brendancof-fey/2011/10/26/the-four-companies-that-control-the-147-companies-that-own-everything/#f08d30b685bc [Accessed 2017] (The four are: Barclays, McGraw-Hill, CME Group, Northwestern Mutual.)

6　See https://en.wikipedia.org/wiki/Omar_Al_Olama

## CHAPTER 3: VISION

1    See Pink, D (2018), Drive: *The Surprising Truth About What Motivate Us*, Canongate Books  (2018).

2    Fitra refers to our divinely created natural state

3    Based on Al-Banna, S.M.H. (2002), *Seerah of the Final Prophet*, Awakening (UK) p.32-33

4    See Lings, M (1988), *Muhammad: His Life Based on the Earliest Sources*, ITS (Cambridge).

5    Based on Adair, John (2010) *The Leadership of Muhammad*, London, UK: Kogan Page p.70

6    Taken from Lings, M (1988), *Muhammad: His Life Based on the Earliest Sources*, ITS (Cambridge) , p.216

7    This is at the Western edge of Makkah. See http://www.arabnews.com/hudaibiyah-turning-point-history-islam for more information on Hudaibiyah.

8    A small short-lived skirmish on one flank aside, there was no significant battle.

9    See Wain, Barry (2010). *Malaysian Maverick: Mahathir Mohamad in Turbulent Times*. Palgrave Macmillan; p.208-14.

## CHAPTER 4: COURAGE

1    Based on Al-Banna, S.M.H. (2002), *Seerah of the Final Prophet*, Awakening (UK) p.32-33.

2    Mandela, N (1995*, Long Walk to Freedom, Abacus*

3    See http://awakening.org/ for all the statistics [Accessed in 2019]

4    See https://www.globalpeoplesummit.org/speaker/sharif-banna [Accessed in 2019]

5    See Isaacson, Walter (2011), *Steve Jobs – The Exclusive Biography*, Little Brown (US)

## CHAPTER 5: HOLISTIC JUSTICE

1    Martin Luther King Jr., Letter from the Birmingham Jail [see https://www.goodreads.com/quotes/631479-injustice-anywhere-is-a-threat-to-justice-everywhere-we-are]

2    Read more at: https://www.brainyquote.com/quotes/desmond_tutu_106145

3    See also references and verses listed in *Nadwi, S (1999) Ethics in Islam, Karachi, Darul-Ishaat* (p.280)

4    God has 99 names and attributes which can be found across the Quran and in Prophetic traditions.

5    Based on Lings, M (1988), *Muhammad: His Life Based on the Earliest Sources*, ITS (Cambridge)

6    Based on Lings, M (1988), *Muhammad: His Life Based on the Earliest Sources*, ITS (Cambridge)  p.123-124.

7    This gender justice section is largely drawn from Dr Jamal Badawi's well-known paper on Gender in Islam. See http://www.islamswomen.com/articles/status_of_women_in_islam.php /

8    See https://www.ted.com/talks/lesley_hazelton_on_reading_the_koran#t-84344

9    The period leading up to the emergence of the Prophet was known as the 'days of ignorance' which he came to challenge through education and counsel. At their worst, these days of ignorance were symbolised by this incredibly brutal practice of female infanticide.

10   See Nadwi, M. A. *Al Muhaddithat: The Women Scholars in Islam* (Interface

Publications, UK (2013)

11   See Shuruq Naguib, Ingrid Mattson, Jasser Auda, Naima Roberts and others for more on this.

12   Under UK Government Gender Pay Gap Data 2019-20, Analysed by CIPD on 5 April 2019

13   Taken from Nadwi, S (1999) *Ethics in Islam*, Darul-Ishaat (Karachi) p.137-8.

14   13. Quoted from Nadwi, S (1999) *Ethics in Islam*, Darul-Ishaat (Karachi) p.137.

15   Taken from Adair, John (2010) *The Leadership of Muhammad*, London, UK: Kogan Page (p.71)

16   Note: this is why we placed fairness under the competence box earlier when talking about the overarching qualities of *Qawi* (competent) and *Amin* (trustworthy), as we view this to mainly be a skill, although the desire to be fair come from being Amin and having values.

17   See Wintour, Patrick (5 August 2014). "Lady Warsi resigns over UK's 'morally reprehensible' stance on Gaza". The Guardian. London, UK. Retrieved 5 August 2014.

18   See "Baroness Warsi: Conservatives must act on Islamophobia". BBC News. 31 May 2018. Retrieved 9 June 2018.

19   Bienkov, Adam (11 June 2018). "The Islamophobia scandal in the Conservative party goes 'right up to the top'". Business Insider. Retrieved 9 June 2018.

## CHAPTER 6: PRAGMATIC DECISIVENESS

1   More details about the Black Stone's history can be found on http://www.islam-iclandmarks.com/makkah-haram-sharief/hajar-al-aswad

2   See Ronald Heifetz and Marty Linsky and their book here: https://www.amazon.com/exec/obidos/ASIN/1578514371/ittakesachurc-20

3   See Tafsir Ibn Kathir on http://www.recitequran.com/tafsir/en.ibn-kathir/3:159

4   Raysuni, A (2011), *Al-Shura: The Quranic Principle of Consultation*, IIIT (UK) p.166

5   Raysuni, A (2011), *Al-Shura: The Quranic Principle of Consultation*, IIIT (UK) p.168

6   We have personally facilitated this exercise multiple times with hundreds of participants across the UK, the Middle East and Asia. The 90% result is based on our direct observations.

7   More than one prophetic leadership quality will usually be on display at any given time or incident, hence we note how this decision was also courageous and visionary, bold and strategic.

8   See https://historiafactory.wordpress.com/2016/06/22/al-fatih-the-liberator/

## CHAPTER 7: SERVANT LEADERSHIP

1   See Greenleaf, R. K. (1970), *The Servant as Leader, The Greenleaf Center for Servant Leadership* (US); See also rev Edition (2015)

2   See Lings (1988), Al-Banna (2002) and other Sirah books for further details of examples

3   Based on Adair, John (2010) *The Leadership of Muhammad*, London, UK: Kogan Page p.69-70

4   Based on Adair, John (2010) *The Leadership of Muhammad*, London, UK: Kogan Page p.69

5   Based on Adair, John (2010) *The Leadership of Muhammad*, London, UK:

Kogan Page p.77

6    Taken from Adair, John (2010) *The Leadership of Muhammad*, London, UK: Kogan Page p.77

7    A psychological contract is a concept known in the social sciences and used in the human resources profession to describe the nature of a relationship as perceived in the minds of those concerned.

8    Referring to the famous four companions and successors of the Prophet, namely Abu Bakr, Umar, Uthman and Ali – may God be pleased with them all.

9    Ahmed, Munir (8 July 2016). "Pakistan's legendary 'Angel of Mercy' Abdul Edhi dies at age 88". Toronto Star. Retrieved 8 July 2016.

10    The World's Greatest Living Humanitarian May Be From Pakistan, The Huffington Post. Retrieved 24 March 2016

11    "Abdul Sattar Edhi, Pakistan's 'Father Teresa' who 'adopted' 20,000 children". The Telegraph. Retrieved 26 June 2017.

## CHAPTER 8: PRACTICAL WISDOM

1    See https://en.oxforddictionaries.com/definition/wisdom

2    Based on Adair, John (2010) *The Leadership of Muhammad*, London, UK: Kogan Page p.37

3    See Tim Winter's introduction in Al-Ghazali A.H. (2009), P.xxii

4    Based on Lings, M (1988), *Muhammad: His Life Based on the Earliest Sources*, ITS (Cambridge) p.252

5    Based on Al-Banna, S.M.H. (2002), *Seerah of the Final Prophet*, Awakening (UK), p.163

6    Lings, M (1988), *Muhammad: His Life Based on the Earliest Sources*, ITS (Cambridge)

## CHAPTER 9: RESILIENCE

1    Visit https://www.heartmath.com/ for more information about resilience

2    See article on Resilience is the New Skill in https://hbr.org/2013/07/surprises-are-the-new-normal-r

3    Based on Al-Banna, S.M.H. (2002), *Seerah of the Final Prophet*, Awakening (UK), p.42

4    Based on Al-Banna, S.M.H. (2002), *Seerah of the Final Prophet*, Awakening (UK), p.43

5    Based on Al-Banna, S.M.H. (2002), *Seerah of the Final Prophet*, Awakening (UK), p.46

6    Based on Lings, M (1988), *Muhammad: His Life Based on the Earliest Sources*, ITS (Cambridge) p.84

7    Lings (1988) p.90 suggests two or more years while Al-Banna (2002) p.52 suggest three full years.

8    Based on Al-Banna, S.M.H. (2002), *Seerah of the Final Prophet*, Awakening (UK), p.52

9    Based on Al-Banna, S.M.H. (2002), *Seerah of the Final Prophet*, Awakening (UK), p.54

10    10. Taken from Lings, M (1988), *Muhammad: His Life Based on the Earliest Sources*, ITS (Cambridge) , p.96-98

11    Based on Al-Banna, S.M.H. (2002), *Seerah of the Final Prophet*, Awakening (UK), p.57
12    Based in part on Lings (1988) p.98, and Al-Banna (2002) p.57
13    Based in part on Lings (1988) p.98-99, among other sources
14    Based on Al-Banna, S.M.H. (2002), *Seerah of the Final Prophet*, Awakening (UK), p.127
15    Based on Al-Banna, S.M.H. (2002), *Seerah of the Final Prophet*, Awakening (UK), p.168-169

## CHAPTER 10: COMPASSION

1    Taken from Adair, John (2010) *The Leadership of Muhammad*, London, UK: Kogan Page p.15
2    Drawing on Abdel Haleem, M.A.S. (201) p.46 and Ibn Kathir http://www.recite-quran.com/tafsir/en.ibn-kathir/3:159
3    Based on Al-Banna, S.M.H. (2002), *Seerah of the Final Prophet*, Awakening (UK), p.186-187
4    Further discussion of this can be found in Nadwi, S (1999) *Ethics in Islam*, Darul-Ishaat (Karachi)  p.292
5    See Sophie Perreaud work here: http://centreforhumanitarianleadership.org/wp-content/uploads/sites/17/2017/02/CHL-Report-Leading-the-Way.pdf
6    See www.roffeypark.com/compassion-at-work-index/
7    See http://edition.cnn.com/services/opk/heroes/blue_ribbon_panel.html
8    See Interview with Oprah on https://www.youtube.com/watch?v=ilKl8WX8Btw
9    See Queen Rania Joins UNICEF Leadership Initiative, U.N. Wire, 15 November 2000.
10   See Queen Rania designated as Honorary Global Chair of the United Nations Girls' Education Initiative (UNGEI) Archived 3 March 2016 at the Wayback Machine, UNGEI, 15 July 2009.

## CHAPTER 11: SPIRITUAL INTELLIGENCE

1    See Wigglesworth, C (2012), *SQ21:The Twenty One Skills of Spiritual Intelligence*, Select Books Inc (USA) for more information
2    See Pink, D (2018), *Drive: The Surprising Truth About What Motivate Us*, Canongate Books
3    Based on a personal meeting with Daniel Goleman at an event in London in September 2015, where he mentioned he was planning to write on spiritual intelligence too, which is an exciting prospect as his profile would help mainstream this, and put SQ on the map in a significant way.
4    See Goleman, D (1996) and Zohar, D (2000), who discuss the anatomy of the brain, the limbic system, the amigdala etc.
5    We make this point as it is technically possible for someone with weak emotional intelligence to have a sense of purpose, thereby partially accessing SQ, but in our view not in its entirety.
6    See Barnes, C., Gunia, B., and Sah, S. (2014) article on 'Morning People Are Less Ethical at Night', see https://hbr.org/2014/06/morning-people-are-less-ethical-at-night
7    Taken from Beekun, R. and Badawi, J (2005), Leadership: An Islamic Perspective, Amana Publications (USA)
8    See Murad, K. (2007), *In The Early Hours: Reflections on Spiritual and Self*

Development, Revival Publications, Leicester (UK) and "Companions of The Prophet", Vol.1, By: Abdul Wahid Hamid.

9    Data drawn from internal staff survey report which is retained due to confidentiality obligations.

10   See www.murabbi.com for more about Murabbi's interventions on Spiritual Intelligence.

## EPILOGUE

1    See proceedings of Pulitzer prize-winning leadership Guru James McGregor Burns, captured in the book: Goethals, G and Sorenson, G (2006), *Towards a General Theory in Leadership* Edward Elgar (Chelt, UK & MA, US)

2    According to the well-known personality assessment tool, the Myers–Briggs Type Indicator (MBTI), if you are a 'J' (structured/planner typology and preference), then an unplanned and unstructured change can feel like a crisis. In such a situation, how you respond can reveal your true leadership potential.

3    Hadith Qudsi – 'Allah's responds to his servant as per his opinion of him'

4    See https://hbr.org/2014/01/what-vuca-really-means-for-you (Accessed in 2019)

5    See https://www.roffeypark.com/author/adrianlock/page/3/ (Accessed in 2019)

6    See Johnson, Spencer (1999), *Who Moved My Cheese?*, Vermilion, London

7    See https://www.cilecenter.org/resources/articles-essays/halal-un-islamic-restoring-ethical-core-islam

8    Plato

## APPENDIX III

1    As an Adair ACL licensed trainer I am sharing the following overview, further details of which can be found on http://www.adair-international.com/acl.html

2    SMART is the well-known acronym for smart, measurable, achievable, relevant and time-bound objectives.

3    Banna p.199.

4    See p218 of Lings for details on the Trench, and Lings generally for the sirah incidents mentioned.

5    Banna p.200-201.

## APPENDIX IV

1    See James, K. and Baddeley, S (1987), *Owl, Fox, Donkey or Sheep: Political Skills for Managers*. (Management Education and Development. Vol. 18. Pt. 1. 1987. pp. 3-19)

2    For clarity, I do not suggest that all those who neglect the spiritual dimension end up as cunning foxes, but that all cunning foxes have neglected the spiritual dimension

Made in the USA
Middletown, DE
24 January 2025

69951788R00161